“雅思 9 分真题库”丛书

雅思 9 分真题库
——阅读密题及解析

启德考培产品中心　编著

電子工業出版社
Publishing House of Electronics Industry
北京 · BEIJING

图书在版编目(CIP)数据

雅思9分真题库. 阅读密题及解析 / 启德考培产品中心编著. —北京：电子工业出版社，2023.10
ISBN 978-7-121-46604-5

Ⅰ.①雅⋯ Ⅱ.①启⋯ Ⅲ.①IELTS－阅读教学－自学参考资料 Ⅳ.①H310.41

中国国家版本馆CIP数据核字（2023）第214157号

雅思9分真题库——阅读密题及解析
启德考培产品中心 编著

责任编辑： 王昭松
印　　刷： 三河市良远印务有限公司
装　　订： 三河市良远印务有限公司
出版发行： 电子工业出版社
北京市海淀区万寿路173信箱　　邮编：100036
开　　本： 787×1 092　1/16　　**印张：** 17.75　　**字数：** 590.72千字
版　　次： 2023 年 10 月第 1 版
印　　次： 2023 年 10 月第 1 次印刷
印　　数： 3 000 册　　**定价：** 69.00 元

凡所购买电子工业出版社图书有缺损问题，请向购买书店调换。若书店售缺，请与本社发行部联系，联系及邮购电话：（010）88254888，88258888。
质量投诉请发邮件至zlts@phei.com.cn，盗版侵权举报请发邮件至dbqq@phei.com.cn。
本书咨询联系方式：（010）88254015， wangzs@phei.com.cn。

《雅思9分真题库——阅读密题及解析》

编委会

主　编：郑庆利

编　委：（按姓氏笔画排序）

牛　佳　乐　乐　石金娥　刘　苏

杨　帆　张　萌　其格乐军　俞　丹

郭星彤　高璨然　曹　彧　Michael Tai

前言 PREFACE

随着全球新冠疫情的逐渐缓解，我们迎来了一个新的时代，一个恢复和振兴的时代。国际教育与留学行业不断回暖，留学申请人数不断回升，对雅思考试的需求也随之反弹。顺应这一趋势，我们精心打造了“雅思9分真题库”这套备考丛书，旨在帮助各位考生顺利通过雅思考试，被心仪的学校录取。

雅思考试是每一位想要出国留学的学生需要闯过的语言关。无论是计划攻读学士、硕士还是博士学位，雅思成绩都是迈向梦想之门的第一步。“雅思9分真题库”丛书包含听、说、读、写四本书，以还原真题为主，提供大量切实可用的表达素材和解题思路，帮助考生全面提升各项技能，使备考更加系统和有针对性。我们深入了解备考的压力和难点，在书中总结了诸多备考攻略和技巧，帮助考生合理规划备考时间、提高答题速度、增强口语和写作表达能力。

听力和阅读部分各包含六套历年雅思考试还原真题。这些题目都是经过精心挑选的最具代表性的题目，还原度非常高。每一篇文章或听力材料后面都非常详细地总结了相关的核心词汇，更重要的是，我们对每一道题都进行了非常详尽的解析，包括各类题型的解题技巧、如何定位、如何分析选项等，帮助考生更好地理解题目要求和掌握解题思路。我们深知，掌握好解题技巧是备考的关键，因此我们特别注重解析部分的详细性和清晰度。阅读部分还精选了一些长难句进行讲解，这些句子中的词汇、句式结构和语法点不但能帮助考生更好地理解阅读文章，也可以助力写作。

写作和口语部分以话题为基础，为考生准备了大量高扩展性、高实用性、地道的表达和素材及通用的答题结构，让考生高效备考。口语部分为相关素材提供了图片，便于联想和记忆。写作部分独创“雅思写作母题方法论”，揭露雅思写作“套路”。书中讨论的话题均经过精心整理，覆盖绝大多数的雅思口语和写作题目。从词汇到句子，从逻辑结构到题库母题解析，解决雅思口语和写作备考中无话可说、不会组织语言的问题。

然而，“雅思9分真题库”丛书并非仅是书中的内容。我们深知在备考过程中刷题的重要性，通过大量的练习，考生可以熟悉考试形式、掌握解题技巧，储备有用的素材，从而更好地应对考试。为此，我们在启德考培在线网站（https://online.eickaopei.com）特别推出了6套真题。这些真题均模拟了真实的考试场景，通过这些真题，考生将有机会进行更多的练习，巩固和扩展知识，全面提高备考水平。我们自主研发的“启德 i 备考”小程序不但有最新的雅思口语和写作题目，还有由母语为英语的外教撰写的范文。此外，我们还特别推出了口语音频，考生可以在这一平台上直接进行口语练习，解决口语不知道怎么练和练了无从知道效果的问题，这将大大提高考生的口语表达能力，为考生在口语考试中取得优异成绩提供有力支持。

鸣谢

首先，我们要由衷地感谢所有的学生。正是因为你们的坚持和不断地突破自我，我们才有了足够的动力来编写这套丛书。

其次，感谢产品中心每一位成员的辛苦付出。他们的专业素养和无私奉献是本套丛书成功出版的重要保证。他们在题目挑选和内容组织等方面投入了大量心血，力求将最优质的内容呈现给广大考生。我们衷心希望“雅思9分真题库”丛书能够成为考生攻克雅思考试的一把利剑，实现自己的留学梦想。

祝愿各位考生都能在雅思考试中取得优异成绩，开启崭新的留学之旅！

启德考培产品中心

★ 本书使用指南

雅思阅读技能的提高是一个系统学习和持续练习的过程，以下是本书的一些使用建议。

1. 计时答题

每篇文章计时20分钟进行答题，之后核对答案。

记录用时和错误题数，以便监测和追踪学习效果。

2. 答案分析

使用本书中的解析，精准标注每道题的答案句。

对照题干和答案句进行深度分析，理解每道题的解题过程，尤其注意对错题的分析。

3. 同义替换词总结

总结每道题中的同义替换词，并牢记。

4. 全篇精读

参照文章参考译文，精读每篇文章，确保理解每一句话。

对每篇文章的长难句进行重点学习。

想考取高分的考生还需总结段落主旨，可参考每篇解析前的“文章结构”，明确是否把握了文章重点。

5. 模拟考试环境

保留两套试卷进行模拟考试，按照正式考试的时间和流程，计时一小时完成答题，然后评估得分情况。

通过反复练习和不断改进，相信本书可以帮助各位考生更好地应对雅思阅读考试，提高阅读技能，取得理想的分数。

目录 CONTENTS

Section 1 真题还原

Section 2　逐题精讲

Section 3　参考答案

READING

01

Section 1

真题还原

READING

TEST 1

READING PASSAGE 1

Undersea Movement

A The underwater world holds many challenges. The most basic of these is movement. The density of water makes it difficult for animals to move. Forward movement is a complex interaction of underwater forces. Additionally, water itself has movement. Strong currents carry incredible power that can easily sweep creatures away. The challenges to aquatic movement result in a variety of swimming methods, used by a wide range of animals. The result is a dazzling underwater ballet.

B Fish rely on their skeleton, fins, and muscles to move. The primary function of the skeleton is to aid movement of other parts. Their skull acts as a fulcrum and their vertebrae act as levers. The vertebral column consists of a series of vertebrae held together by ligaments, but not so tightly as to prevent slight sideways movement between each pair of vertebrae. The whole spine is, therefore, flexible. The skull is the only truly fixed part of a fish. It does not move in and off itself but acts as a point of stability for other bones. These other bones act as levers that cause movement of the fish's body.

C While the bones provide the movement, the muscles supply the power. A typical fish has hundreds of muscles running in all directions around its body. This is why a fish can turn and twist and change directions quickly. The muscles on each side of the spine contract in a series from head to tail and down each side alternately, causing a wave-like movement to pass down the body. Such a movement may be very pronounced in fish such as eels, but hardly perceptible in others, e.g. mackerel. The frequency of the waves varies from about 50/min in the dogfish to 170/min in the mackerel. The sideways and backward thrust of the head and body against the water results in the resistance of the water pushing the fish sideways and forwards in a direction opposed to the thrust. When the corresponding set of muscles on the other side contracts, the fish experiences a similar force from the water on that side. The two sideways forces are equal and opposite, unless the fish is making a turn, so they cancel out, leaving the sum of the two forward forces.

D The muscles involved in swimming are of two main types. The bulk of a fish's body is composed of the so-called white muscle, while the much smaller areas at the roots of the fins and in a strip along the centre of each flank comprise red muscle. The red muscle receives a good supply of blood and contains ampler quantities of fat and glycogen, the storage form of glucose, which is used for most day-to-day swimming movements. In contrast, the white muscle has a poor blood supply and few energy stores, and it is used largely for short-term, fast swimming. It might seem odd that the body of an animal which adapts so efficiently to its environment should be composed almost entirely of a type of muscle it rarely uses. However, this huge auxiliary power pack carried by a fish is of crucial significance if the life of the fish is threatened by a predator, for instance, because it enables the fish to swim rapidly away from danger.

E The fins are the most distinctive features of a fish, composed of bony spines protruding from the body with skin covering them and joining them together, either in a webbed fashion, as seen in most bony fish, or more similar to a flipper, as seen in sharks. These usually serve as a means for the fish to swim. But it must be emphasized that the swimming movements are produced by the whole of the muscular body, and in only a few fish do the fins contribute any propulsive force! Their main function is to control the stability and direction of the fish: as water passes over its body, a fish uses its fins to thrust in the direction it wishes to go.

F Fins located in different places on a fish serve different purposes, such as moving forward, turning, and keeping an upright position. The tail fin, in its final lash, may contribute as much as 40 percent of the forward thrust. The median fins, that is, the dorsal, anal and ventral fins, control the rolling and yawing movements of the fish by increasing the vertical surface area presented to the water. The paired fins, pectoral and pelvic, act as hydroplanes and control the pitch of the fish, causing it to swim downwards or upwards according to the angle to the water at which they are held by their muscles. The pectoral fins lie in front of the centre of gravity and, being readily mobile, are chiefly responsible for sending the fish up or down. The paired fins are also the means by which the fish slows down and stops.

G The swimming speed of fish is not so fast as one would expect from watching their rapid movements in aquaria or ponds. Tuna seem to be the fastest at 44 mph, trout are recorded as doing 23 mph, pike 20 mph for short bursts and roach about 10 mph, while the majority of small fish probably do not exceed 2 or 3 mph. Many people have attempted to make accurate measurements of the speed at which various fish swim, either by timing them over known distances in their natural environment or by determining their performance in man-made swimming channels. From these studies, we can broadly categorise fish into four groups: "sneakers", such as eels that are only capable of slow speeds but possess some staying power; "stayers", that can swim quite fast over long periods; "sprinters" that can generate fast bursts of speed (e.g. pike); and "crawlers" that are sluggish swimmers, although they can accelerate slightly (bream, for example).

H One type of sailfish is considered to be the fastest species of fish over short distances, achieving 68 mph over a three-second period, and anglers have recorded speeds in excess of 40 mph over longer periods for several species of tuna. One is likely to consider a fish's swimming capabilities in relation to its size. However, it is generally true that a small fish is a more able swimmer than a much larger one. On the other hand in terms of speed in miles per hour a big fish will, all other things being equal, be able to swim faster than a smaller fish.

Questions 1-6

Reading Passage 1 has eight paragraphs, A-H.

Which paragraph contains the following information?

Write the appropriate letter, A-H, in boxes 1-6 on your answer sheet.

1. categorizations of fish by swimming speed
2. an example of fish capable of maintaining fast swimming for a long time
3. how fish control stability
4. frequency of the muscle movement of fish
5. a mechanical model of fish skeleton
6. energy storage devices in a fish

Questions 7-10

The diagram below gives information about fish fins and their purposes.

Complete the diagram with ***NO MORE THAN THREE WORDS*** *from the passage for each blank.*

Write your answers in boxes ***7-10*** *on your answer sheet.*

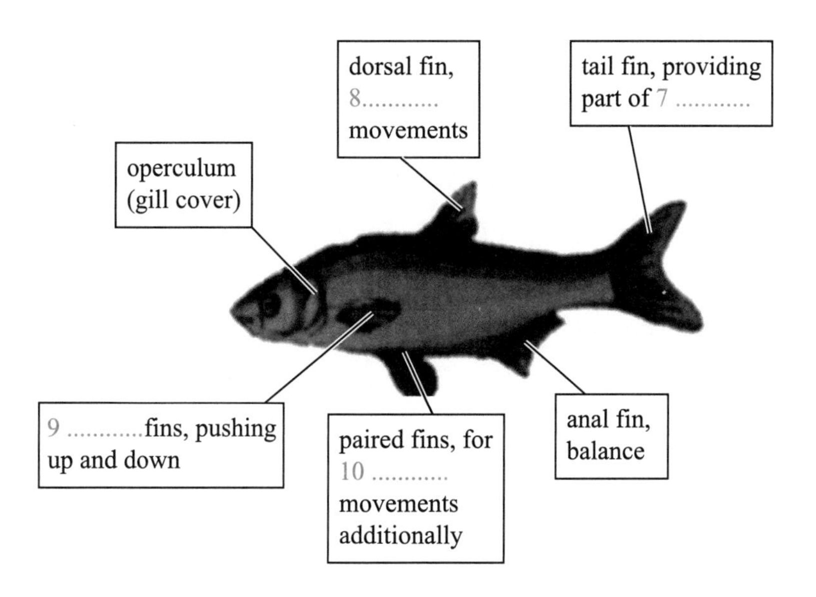

Questions 11-13

Complete the summary below using ***NO MORE THAN THREE WORDS*** *from the passage for each blank.*

Write your answers in boxes ***11-13*** *on your answer sheet.*

Two types of muscles are involved in fish swimming. The majority of a fish's body comprises the **11**............, and the red muscle is found only at the roots of the fins and in a strip along the centre of each flank. For most of its routine movements, the fish uses lot of its **12**...........saved in body, and white muscle is mostly used for short-term, fast swimming, such as escaping from **13**..........

READING PASSAGE 2

Coral Reefs

Coral reefs are underwater structures made from calcium carbonate secreted by corals. Coral reefs are colonies of tiny living animals found in marine waters that contain few nutrients. Most coral reefs are built from stony corals, which in turn consist of polyps that cluster in groups.

A Coral reefs are estimated to cover 284,300 km^2 just under 0.1% of the oceans' surface area, about half the area of France. The Indo-Pacific region accounts for 91.9% of this total area. Southeast Asia accounts for 32.3% of that figure, while the Pacific including Australia accounts for 40.8%. Atlantic and Caribbean coral reefs account for 7.6%. Yet often called "rainforests of the sea", coral reefs form some of the most diverse ecosystems on Earth. They provide a home for 25% of all marine species, including fish, mollusks, worms, crustaceans, echinoderms, sponges, tunicates and other cnidarians. Paradoxically, coral reefs flourish even though they are surrounded by ocean waters that provide few nutrients. They are most commonly found at shallow depths in tropical waters, but deep water and cold water corals also exist on smaller scales in other areas. Although corals exist both in temperate and tropical waters, shallow-water reefs form only in a zone extending from 30°N to 30°S of the equator. Deep water coral can exist at greater depths and colder temperatures at much higher latitudes, as far north as Norway. Coral reefs are rare along the American and African west coasts. This is due primarily to upwelling and strong cold coastal currents that reduce water temperatures in these areas (respectively the Peru, Benguela and Canary streams). Corals are seldom found along the coastline of South Asia from the eastern tip of India (Madras) to the Bangladesh and Myanmar borders. They are also rare along the coast around northeastern South America and Bangladesh due to the freshwater release from the Amazon and Ganges Rivers, respectively.

B Coral reefs deliver ecosystem services to tourism, fisheries and coastline protection. The global economic value of coral reefs has been estimated at as much as $US375 billion per year. Coral reefs protect shorelines by absorbing wave energy, and many small islands would not exist without their reef to protect them.

C The value of reefs in biodiverse regions can be even higher. In parts of Indonesia and the Caribbean where tourism is the main use, reefs are estimated to be worth US$1 million per square kilometer, based on the cost of maintaining sandy beaches and the value of attracting snorkelers and scuba divers. Meanwhile, a recent study of the Great Barrier Reef in Australia found that the reef is worth more to the country as an intact ecosystem than an extractive reserve for fishing. Each year more than 1.8 million tourists visit the reef, spending an estimated AU$4.3 billion (Australian dollars) on reef-related industries from diving to boat rental to posh island resort stays. In the Caribbean, says UNEP, the net annual benefits from diver tourism was US$2 billion in 2000 with US$625 million spent directly on diving on reefs. Further, reef tourism is an important source of employment, especially for some of the world's poorest people. UNEP says that of the estimated 30 million small-scale fishers in the developing world, most are dependent to a greater or lesser extent on coral reefs. In the Philippines, for example, more than one million small-scale fishers depend directly on coral reefs for their livelihoods. The report estimates that reef fisheries were worth between $15,000 and $150,000 per square kilometer a year, while fish caught for aquariums were worth $500 a kilogram against $6 for fish caught as food. The aquarium fish export industry supports around 50,000 people and generates some US$5.5 million a year in Sri Lanka along.

D Unfortunately, coral reefs are dying around the world. In particular, coral mining, agricultural and urban runoff, pollution (organic and inorganic), disease, and the digging of canals and access into islands and bays are localized threats to coral ecosystems. Broader threats are sea temperature rise, sea level rise and pH changes from ocean acidification, all associated with greenhouse gas emissions. Some current fishing practices are destructive and unsustainable. These include cyanide fishing, overfishing and blast fishing. Although cyanide fishing supplies live reef fish for the tropical aquarium market, most fish caught using this method are sold in restaurants, primarily in Asia, where live fish are prized for their freshness. To catch fish with cyanide, fishers dive down to the reef and squirt cyanide in coral crevices and on the fast-moving fish, to stun the fish, making them easy to catch. Overfishing is another leading cause for coral reef degradation. Often, too many fish are taken from one reef to sustain a population in that area. Poor fishing practices, such as banging on the reef with sticks (muro-ami), destroy coral formations that normally function as fish habitat. In some instances, people fish with explosives (blast fishing), which blast apart the surrounding coral.

E Tourist resorts that empty their sewage directly into the water surrounding coral reefs contribute to coral reef degradation. Wastes kept in poorly maintained septic tanks can also leak into surrounding ground water, eventually seeping out to the reefs. Careless boating, diving, snorkeling and fishing can also damage coral reefs. Whenever people grab, kick, and walk on, or stir up sediment in the reefs, they contribute to coral reef destruction. Corals are also harmed or killed when people drop anchors on them or when people collect coral.

F To find answers for these problems, scientists and researchers study the various factors that impact reefs. The list includes the ocean's role as a carbon dioxide sink, atmospheric changes, ultraviolet light, ocean acidification, viruses, impacts of dust storms carrying agents to far flung reefs, pollutants, algal blooms and others. Reefs are threatened well beyond coastal areas. General estimates show approximately 10% of the world's coral reefs are dead. About 60% of the world's reefs are at risk due to destructive, human-related activities. The threat to the health of reefs is particularly strong in Southeast Asia, where 80% of reefs are endangered.

G In Australia, the Great Barrier Reef is protected by the Great Barrier Reef Marine Park Authority, and is the subject of much legislation, including a biodiversity action plan. Inhabitants of Ahus Island, Manus Province, Papua New Guinea, have followed a generations-old practice of restricting fishing in six areas of their reef lagoon. Their cultural traditions allow line fishing, but not net or spear fishing. The result is both the biomass and individual fish sizes are significantly larger than in places where fishing is unrestricted.

Questions 14-19

Reading Passage 2 has seven paragraphs, **A-G.**

Which paragraph contains the following information?

Write the correct letter, ***A-G****, in boxes* ***14-19*** *on your answer sheet.*

NB *You may use any letter more than once.*

14. geographical location of world's coral reef

15. how does coral reef benefit economy locally

16. the statistics of coral reefs' economic significance

17. the dangerous situation faced by coral reefs

18. physical approach to coral reef by tourists

19. unsustainable fishing methods are applied in regions of the world

Questions 20-25

Do the following statements agree with the information given in Reading Passage 2?

TRUE	*if the statement agrees with the information*
FALSE	*if the statement contradicts the information*
NOT GIVEN	*if the information is not given in the passage*

20. Coral reefs provide habitat to a variety of marine life.

21. Coral reefs distribute around the ocean disproportionally.

22. Coral reefs are increasingly important for scientific purpose.

23. Coral reefs are greatly exchanged among and exported to other countries.

24. Reef tourism is of economic essence generally for some poor people.

25. As with other fishing business, coral fishery is not suitable for women and children.

Question 26

Choose the correct letter, ***A, B, C*** *or* ***D****.*

Write your answer in box ***26*** *on your answer sheet.*

What is the main purpose of this passage?

A. to demonstrate how coral reefs grow in the ocean

B. to tell that coral reefs are widely used as a scientific project

C. to present the general benefits and an alarming situation of coral reefs

D. to show the vital efforts made to protect coral reefs in Australia

READING PASSAGE 3

Sand Dunes

A One of the main problems posed by sand dunes is their encroachment on human habitats. Sand dunes move by different means, all of them aided by the wind. Sand dunes threaten buildings and crops in Africa, the Middle East, and China. Preventing sand dunes from overwhelming cities and agricultural areas has become a priority for the United Nations Environment Program. On the other hand, dune habitats provide niches for highly specialized plants and animals including numerous rare and endangered species.

B Sand is usually composed of hard minerals such as quartz that cannot be broken down into silt or clay. Yellow, brown and reddish shades of sand indicate their presence of iron compounds. Red sand is composed of quartz coated by a layer of iron oxide. White sands are nearly pure gypsum. Sand with a high percentage of silicate can be used in glassmaking. Sandstone is created by sand, mixed with lime, chalk or some other material that acts as a binding agent, that is deposited in layers at the bottom of a sea or other area and pressed together into rock by the great pressure of sediments that are deposited on top if it over thousands or millions of years.

C The most common dune form on Earth and on Mars is the crescentic. Crescent-shaped mounds are generally wider than they are long. The slipfaces are on the concave sides of the dunes. These dunes form under winds that blow consistently from one direction, and they also are known as barchans, or transverse dunes. Some types of crescentic dunes move more quickly over desert surfaces than any other type of dune. A group of dunes moved more than 100 metres per year between 1954 and 1959 in China's Ningxia Province, and similar speeds have been recorded in the Western Desert of Egypt. The largest crescentic dunes on Earth, with mean crest-to-crest widths of more than 3 kilometres, are in China's Taklamakan Desert.

D Radially symmetrical, star dunes are pyramidal sand mounds with slipfaces on three or more arms that radiate from the high centre of the mound. They tend to accumulate in areas with multidirectional wind regimes. Star dunes grow upward rather than laterally. They dominate the Grand Erg Oriental of the Sahara. In other deserts, they occur around the margins of the sand seas, particularly near topographic barriers. In the southeast Badain Jaran Desert of China, the star dunes are up to 500 metres tall and may be the tallest dunes on Earth. Straight or slightly sinuous sand ridges typically much longer than they are wide are known as linear dunes. They may be more than 160 kilometres (99 mi) long. Some linear dunes merge to form Y-shaped compound dunes. Many form in bidirectional wind regimes. The long axes of these dunes extend in the resultant direction of sand movement. Linear loess hills known as pahas are superficially similar.

E Once sand begins to pile up, ripples and dunes can form. Wind continues to move sand up to the top of the pile until the pile is so steep that it collapses under its own weight. The collapsing sand comes to rest when it reaches just the right steepness to keep the dune stable. This angle, usually about 30 ° - 34 ° , is called the angle of repose. Every pile of loose particles has a unique angle of repose, depending upon the properties of the material it's made of, such as the grain size and roundness. Ripples grow into dunes with the increase of wind and sand input.

F The repeating cycle of sand inching up the windward side to the dune crest, then slipping down the dune's slip face allows the dune to inch forward, migrating in the direction the wind blows. As you might guess, all of this climbing then slipping leaves its mark on the internal structure of the dune. The image (not provided) shows fossil sand dune structure preserved in the Merced Formation at Fort Funston, Golden Gate National Recreation Area. The sloping lines or laminations you see are the preserved slip faces of a migrating sand dune. This structure is called cross-bedding, and can be the result of either wind or water currents. The larger the cross-bedded structure, however, the more likely it is to be formed by wind, rather than water.

G Sand dunes can "sing" at a level up to 115 decibels and generate sounds in different notes. The dunes at Sand Mountain in Nevada usually sing in a low C but can also sing in B and C sharp. The La Mar de Dunas in Chile hum in F while those at the Ghord Lahmar in Morocco howl in G sharp. The sounds are produced by avalanches of sand generated by blowing winds. For a while it was thought that the avalanches caused the entire dune to resonate like a flute or violin but if that were true then different size dunes would produce different notes. In the mid 2000s, American,

French and Moroccan scientists visiting sand dunes in Morocco, Chile, China and Oman published a paper in the *Physical Review Letters* that determined the sounds were produced by collisions between grains of sand that caused the motions of the grains to become synchronized, causing the outer layer of a dune to vibrate like the cone of a loudspeaker, producing sound. The tone of the sounds depended primarily on the size of the grains.

H Scientists performed a computer simulation on patterns and dynamics of desert dunes in laboratory. Dune patterns observed in deserts were reproduced. From the initial random state, star and linear dunes are produced, depending on the variability of the wind direction. The efficiency in sand transport is calculated through the course of development. Scientists found that the sand transport is the most efficient in the linear transverse dune. The efficiency in sand transport always increased through the evolution, and the way it increases was stepwise. They also found that the shadow zone, the region where the sand wastes the chance to move, shrinks through the course of evolution, which greatly helps them build a model to simulate sand move.

Questions 27-34

*Choose the correct heading for paragraphs **A-H** from the list below.*

*Write the correct number, **i-x**, in boxes **27-34** on your answer sheet.*

List of Headings

i. Potential threat to buildings and crops despite of benefit
ii. The cycle of sand moving forward with wind
iii. Protection method in various countries
iv. Scientists simulate sand move and build model in lab
v. Sand composition explanation
vi. Singing sand dunes
vii. Other types of sand dunes
viii. The personal opinion on related issues
ix. Reasons why sand dunes form
x. The most common sand type

27. Paragraph A
28. Paragraph B
29. Paragraph C
30. Paragraph D
31. Paragraph E
32. Paragraph F
33. Paragraph G
34. Paragraph H

Questions 35-36

Answer the questions 35-36 and choose the correct letter, A, B, C or D.

35. What is the main composition of white sand according to the passage?

A. quartz

B. gypsum

C. lime

D. iron

36. Which one is not mentioned as a sand dunes type in this passage?

A. linear

B. crescentic

C. overlap

D. star

Questions 37-40

Complete the summary using the list of words, A-J, below.

Write the correct letter, A-J, in boxes 37-40 on your answer sheet.

Crescentic is an ordinary **37**....... on both Earth and Mars, apart from which, there are also other types of sand dunes. Different color of the sand reflects different components, some of them are rich in **38**....... that can not be easily broken into clay. Sand dunes can "sing" at a level up to 115 decibels and generate sounds in different notes. Sand dunes can be able to **39**....... at a certain level of sound intensity, and the different size of grains creates different **40**....... of the sounds.

A. quartz	**B**. shape	**C**. pressure	**D**. tone
E. protection	**F**. category	**G**. minerals	**H**. sing
I. lab	**J**. direction		

TEST 2

READING PASSAGE 1

Bondi Beach

A Bondi Beach, Australia's most famous beach, is located in the suburb of Bondi, in the Local Government Area of Waverley, seven kilometers from the centre of Sydney. "Bondiu" or "Boondi" is an Aboriginal word meaning water breaking over rocks or the sound of breaking waves. The Australian Museum records that Bondi means a place where a flight of nullas took place. There are Aboriginal rock carvings on the northern end of the beach at Ben Buckler and south of Bondi Beach near McKenzies Beach on the coastal walk.

B The indigenous people of the area at the time of European settlement have generally been welcomed to as the Sydney people or the Eora (Eora means "the people"). One theory describes the Eora as a sub-group of the Darug language group which occupied the Cumberland Plain west to the Blue Mountains. However, another theory suggests that they were a distinct language group of their own. There is no clear evidence for the name or names of the particular band(s) of the Eora that roamed what is now the Waverley area. A number of place names within Waverley, most famously Bondi, have been based on words derived from Aboriginal languages of the Sydney region.

C From the mid-1800s Bondi Beach was a favourite location for family outings and picnics. The beginnings of the suburb go back to 1809, when the early road builder, William Roberts, received from Governor Bligh a grant of 81 hectares of what is now most of the business and residential area of Bondi Beach. In 1851, Edward Smith Hall and Francis O'Brien purchased 200 acres of the Bondi area that embraced almost the whole frontage of Bondi Beach, and it was named the "The Bondi Estate." Between 1855 and 1877 O'Brien purchased Hall's share of the land, renamed the land the "O'Brien Estate" and made the beach and the surrounding land available to the public as a picnic ground and amusement resort. As the beach became increasingly popular, O'Brien threatened to stop public beach access. However, the Municipal Council believed that the Government needed to intervene to make the beach a public reserve.

D During the 1900s beach became associated with health, leisure and democracy - a playground everyone could enjoy equally. Bondi Beach was a working class suburb throughout most of the twentieth century with migrant people from New Zealand comprising the majority of the local population. The first tramway reached the beach in 1884. Following this, tram became the first public transportation in Bondi. As an alternative, this action changed the rule that only rich people can enjoy the beach. By the 1930s Bondi was drawing not only local visitors but also people from elsewhere in Australia and overseas. Advertising at the time referred to Bondi Beach as the "Playground of the Pacific".

E There is a growing trend that people prefer relaxing near seaside instead of living unhealthily in cities. The increasing popularity of sea bathing during the late 1800s and early 1900s raised concerns about public safety and how to prevent people form drowning. In response, the world's first formally documented surf lifesaving club, the Bondi Surf Bathers' Life Saving Club, was formed in 1907. This was powerfully reinforced by the dramatic event of "Black Sunday" at Bondi in 1938. Some 35,000 people were on the beach and a large group of lifesavers were about to start a surf race when three freak waves hit the beach, sweeping hundreds of people out to sea. Lifesavers rescued 300 people. The largest mass rescue in the history of surf bathing, it confirmed the place of the lifesaver in the national imagination.

F Bondi Beach is the end point of the City to Surf Fun Run which is held each year in August. Australian surf carnivals further instilled this image. A royal Surf Carnival was held at Bondi Beach for Queen Elizabeth II during her first visit in Australia in 1954. Since 1867, there have been over fifty visits by a member of the British Royal Family to Australia. In addition to many activities, the Bondi Beach Markets is open every Sunday. Many wealthy people spend Christmas Day at the beach. However, the shortage of houses occurs when lots of people crush to seaside. Manly is the seashore town which solved this problem. However, people still choose Bondi as the satisfied destination rather than Manly.

G Bondi Beach has a commercial area along Campbell Parade and adjacent side streets, featuring many popular cafes, restaurants, and hotels, with views of the contemporary beach. It is depicted as wholly modern and European. In the last decade, Bondi Beach's unique position has seen a dramatic rise in svelte houses and apartments to take advantage of the views and scent of the sea. The valley running down to the beach is famous world over for its view of distinctive red tiled roofs. Those architectures are deeply influenced by British costal town.

H Bondi Beach hosted the beach volleyball competition at the 2000 Summer Olympics. A temporary 10,000-seat stadium, a much smaller stadium, 2 warm-up courts, and 3 training courts were set up to host the tournament. The Bondi Beach Volleyball Stadium was constructed for it and stood for just six weeks. Campaigners oppose both the social and environmental consequences of the development. The stadium will divide the beach in two and seriously restrict public access for swimming, walking, and other forms of outdoor recreation. People protest for their human rights of having a pure seaside and argue for healthy life in Bondi.

I "They're prepared to risk lives and risk the Bondi Beach environment for the sake of eight days of volleyball", said Stephen Unicake, a construction lawyer involved in the campaign. Other environmental concerns include the possibility that soil dredged up from below the sand will acidify when brought to the surface.

Questions 1-5

Do the following statements agree with the information given in Reading Passage 1?

*In boxes **1-5** on your answer sheet, write*

TRUE *if the statement agrees with the information*

FALSE *if the statement contradicts the information*

NOT GIVEN *if there is no information on this*

1. The name of Bondi Beach is first called by the British settlers.
2. The Aboriginal culture in Australia is different when compared with European culture.
3. Bondi Beach area holds many contemporary hotels.
4. The seaside town in Bondi is affected by British culture for its characteristic red color.
5. Living near Bondi seashore is not beneficial for health.

Questions 6-9

*Answer the questions below using **NO MORE THAN TWO WORDS AND/OR NUMBERS** from the passage for each answer.*

*Write your answers in boxes **6-9** on your answer sheet.*

6. At the end of 19th century, which public transport did people use to go to Bondi?
7. When did the British Royalty first visit Bondi?
8. Which Olympic event did Bondi hold in 2000 Sydney Olympic games?
9. What would be damaged if the stadium was built for that Olympic event?

Questions 10-13

*Complete the following summary of the paragraphs of Reading Passage 1, using **NO MORE THAN TWO WORDS** from the passage for each answer.*

*Write your answers in boxes **10-13** on your answer sheet.*

Bondi Beach holds the feature sport activities every year, which attracts lot of **10**............ choosing to live at this place during holidays. But local accommodation cannot meet with the expanding population. A nearby town of **11**............ is the first suburb site to support the solution, yet people prefer **12**......... as their best choice. Its seaside buildings are well-known in the world for the special scenic colored **13**............. on buildings and the joyful smell from the sea.

READING PASSAGE 2

When the Tulip Bubble Burst

Tulips are spring-blooming perennials that grow from bulbs. Depending on the species, tulip plants can grow as short as 4 inches (10 cm) or as high as 28 inches (71 cm). The tulip's large flowers usually bloom on scapes or sub-scapose stems that lack bracts. Most tulips produce only one flower per stem, but a few species bear multiple flowers on their scapes (e.g. Tulipa turkestanica). The showy, generally cup or star-shaped tulip flower has three petals and three sepals, which are often termed tepals because they are nearly identical. These six tepals are often marked on the interior surface near the bases with darker colorings. Tulip flowers come in a wide variety of colors, except pure blue (several tulips with "blue" in the name have a faint violet hue).

A Long before anyone ever heard of Qualcomm, CMGI, Cisco Systems, or the other high-tech stocks that have soared during the current bull market, there was Semper Augustus. Both more prosaic and more sublime than any stock or bond, it was a tulip of extraordinary beauty, its midnight-blue petals topped by a band of pure white and accented with crimson flares. To denizens of 17th century Holland, little was as desirable.

B Around 1624, the Amsterdam man who owned the only dozen specimens was offered 3,000 guilders for one bulb. While there's no accurate way to render that in today's greenbacks, the sum was roughly equal to the annual income of a wealthy merchant. (A few years later, Rembrandt received about half that amount for painting The Night Watch.) Yet the bulb's owner, whose name is now lost to history, nixed the offer.

C Who was crazier, the tulip lover who refused to sell for a small fortune or the one who was willing to splurge. That's a question that springs to mind after reading *Tulipomania: The Story of the World's Most Coveted Flower & the Extraordinary Passions It Aroused* by British journalist Mike Dash. In recent years, as investors have intentionally forgotten everything they learned in *Investing 101* in order to load up on unproved, unprofitable dot-com issues, tulip mania has been invoked frequently. In this concise, artfully written account, Dash tells the real history behind the buzzword and in doing so, offers a cautionary tale for our times.

D The Dutch were not the first to go gaga over the tulip. Long before the first tulip bloomed in Europe—in Bavaria, it turns out, in 1559—the flower had enchanted the Persians and bewitched the rulers of the Ottoman Empire. It was in Holland, however, that the passion for tulips found its most fertile ground, for reasons that had little to do with horticulture.

E Holland in the early 17th century was embarking on its Golden Age. Resources that had just a few years earlier gone toward fighting for independence from Spain now flowed into commerce. Amsterdam merchants were at the center of the lucrative East Indies trade, where a single voyage could yield profits of 400%. They displayed their success by erecting grand estates surrounded by flower gardens. The Dutch population seemed torn by two contradictory impulses: a horror of living beyond one's means and the love of a long shot.

F Enter the tulip. "It is impossible to comprehend the tulip mania without understanding just how different tulips were from every other flower known to horticulturists in the 17th century," says Dash. "The colors they exhibited were more intense and more concentrated than those of ordinary plants." Despite the outlandish prices commanded by rare bulbs, ordinary tulips were sold by the pound. Around 1630, however, a new type of tulip fancier appeared, lured by tales of fat profits. These "florists," or professional tulip traders, sought out flower lovers and speculators alike. But if the supply of tulip buyers grew quickly, the supply of bulbs did not. The tulip was a conspirator in the supply squeeze: It takes seven years to grow one from seed. And while bulbs can produce two or three clones, or "offsets", annually, the mother bulb only lasts a few years.

G Bulb prices rose steadily throughout the 1630s, as ever more speculators wedged into the market. Weavers and farmers mortgaged whatever they could to raise cash to begin trading. In 1633, a farmhouse in Hoorn changed hands for three rare bulbs. By 1636 any tulip—even bulbs recently considered garbage—could be sold off, often for hundreds of guilders. A futures market for bulbs existed, and tulip traders could be found conducting their business in hundreds of Dutch taverns. Tulip mania reached its peak during the winter of 1636-1637, when some bulbs were changing hands ten times in a day. The zenith came early that winter, at an auction to benefit seven orphans whose only asset was 70 fine tulips left by their father. One, a rare Violetten Admirael van Enkhuizen bulb that was about to split in two, sold for 5,200 guilders, the all-time record. All told, the flowers brought in nearly 53,000 guilders.

H Soon after, the tulip market crashed utterly, spectacularly. It began in Haarlem, at a routine bulb auction when, for the first time, the greater fool refused to show up and pay. Within days, the panic had spread across the country. Despite the efforts of traders to prop up demand, the market for tulips evaporated. Flowers that had commanded 5,000 guilders a few weeks before now fetched one-hundredth that amount. Tulip mania is not without flaws. Dash dwells too long on the tulip's migration from Asia to Holland. But he does a service with this illuminating, accessible account of incredible financial folly.

I Tulip mania differed in one crucial aspect from the dot-com craze that grips our attention today: even at its height, the Amsterdam Stock Exchange, well-established in 1630, wouldn't touch tulips. "The speculation in tulip bulbs always existed at the margins of Dutch economic life," Dash writes. After the market crashed, a compromise was brokered that let most traders settle their debts for a fraction of their liability. The overall fallout on the Dutch economy was negligible. Will we say the same when Wall Street's current obsession finally runs its course?

Questions 14-18

Reading Passage 2 has nine paragraphs, A-I.

Which paragraph contains the following information?

Write the correct letter, A-I, in boxes 14-18 on your answer sheet.

14. difference between bubble burst impacts by tulip and by high-tech shares
15. spread of tulip before 17th century
16. indication of money offered for rare bulbs in 17th century
17. Tulip was treated as money in Holland.
18. comparison made between tulip and other plants

Questions 19-23

Do the following statements agree with the information given in Reading Passage 2?

*In boxes **19-23** on your answer sheet, write*

TRUE *if the statement is true*

FALSE *if the statement is false*

NOT GIVEN *if the information is not given in the passage*

19. In 1624, all the tulip collection belonged to a man in Amsterdam.
20. Tulip was first planted in Holland according to this passage.
21. Popularity of tulip in Holland was much higher than any other countries in 17th century.
22. Holland was the wealthiest country in the world in 17th century.
23. From 1630, Amsterdam Stock Exchange started to regulate tulips exchange market.

Questions 24-26

*Complete the following summary of the paragraphs of Reading Passage 2, using **NO MORE THAN TWO WORDS** from the passage for each answer.*

*Write your answers in boxes **24-26** on your answer sheet.*

Dutch concentrated on gaining independence by **24** .... against Spain in the early 17th century; consequently, spare resources entered the area of **25** .... Prosperous traders demonstrated their status by building great grand estates and with gardens in surroundings. Attracted by the success of profit on tulip, traders kept looking for **26** .... and speculators for sale.

READING PASSAGE 3

Termite Mounds

Could the vast towers of mud constructed by insects in sub-Saharan Africa hold the key to our energy-efficient building of the future?

A To most of us, termites are destructive insects which can cause damage on a devastating scale. But according to Dr. Rupert Soar of Loughborough University's School of Mechanical and Manufacturing Engineering, these pests may serve a useful purpose for us after all. His multi-disciplinary team of British and American engineers and biologists have set out to investigate the giant mounds built by termites in Namibia, in sub-Saharan Africa, as part of the most extensive study of these structures ever taken.

B Termite mounds are impressive for their size alone; typically they are three metres high, and some as tall as eight metres by found. They also reach far into the earth, where the insects 'mine' their building materials, carefully selecting each grain of sand they use. The termite's nest is contained in the central cavity of the mound, safely protected from the harsh environment outside. The mound itself is formed of an intricate lattice of tunnels, which split into smaller and smaller tunnels, much like a person's blood vessels.

C This complex system of tunnels draws in air from the outside, capturing wind energy to drive it through the mound. It also serves to expel spent respiratory gases from the nest to prevent the termites from suffocating, so ensuring them a continuous provision of fresh, breathable air. So detailed is the design that the nest stays within three degrees of a constant temperature, despite variations on the outside of up to 50℃ , from blistering heat in the daytime to below freezing on the coldest nights. The mound also automatically regulates moisture in the air, by means of its underground 'cellar', and evaporation from the top of the mound. Some colonies even had 'chimneys' at a height of 20m to control moisture in the hottest regions of sub-Saharan Africa.

D Furthermore, the termites have evolved in such a way as to outsource some of their biological functions. Part of their digestive process is carried out by a fungus, which they 'farm' inside the mound. This fungus, which is found nowhere else on earth, thrives in the constant and optimum environment of the mound. The termites feed the fungus with slightly chewed wood pulp, which the fungus then breaks down into a digestible sugary food to provide the insects with energy, and cellulose which they use for building. And, although the termites must generate waste, none ever leaves the structure, indicating that there is also some kind of internal waste-recycling system.

E Scientists are so excited by the mounds that they have labelled them a 'super organism' because, in Soar's word, "they dance on the edge of what we would perceive to cool down, or if you're too cold you need to thrive: that's called homeostasis. What the termites have done is to move homeostatic function away from their body, into the structure in which they live. 'As more information comes to light about the unique features of termite mounds, we may ultimately need to redefine our understanding of what constitutes a 'living' organism."

F To reveal the structure of the mounds, Soar's team begins by filling and covering their plaster of Paris, a chalky white paste based on the mineral gypsum, which becomes rock-solid when dry. The researchers then carve the plaster of Paris into half-millimetre-thick slices, and photograph them sequentially. Once the pictures are digitally scanned, computer technology is able to recreate complex three-dimensional images of the mounds. These models have enabled the team to map termite architecture at a level of detail never before attained.

G Soar hopes that the models will explain how termite mounds create a self-regulating living environment which manages to respond to changing internal and external conditions without drawing on any outside source of power. If they do, the findings could be invaluable in informing future architectural design, and could inspire buildings that are self-sufficient, environmental, and cheap to run. “As we approach a world of climate change, we need temperatures to rise”, he explains, “there will not be enough fuel to drive air conditioners around the world”. It is hoped, says Soar, “that the findings will provide clues that aid the ultimate development of new kinds of human habitats, suitable for a variety of arid, hostile environments not only on the earth but maybe one day on the moon and beyond.”

Questions 27-33

*Reading Passage 3 has seven paragraphs, **A-G**.*

Choose the correct heading for each paragraph from the list below.

*Write the correct number, **i-ix**, in boxes **27-33** on your answer sheet.*

List of Headings

- i. Methods used to investigate termite mound formation
- ii. Challenging our assumptions about the nature of life
- iii. Reconsidering the termite’s reputation
- iv. Principal functions of the termite mound
- v. Distribution of termite mounds in sub-Saharan Africa
- vi. Some potential benefits of understanding termite architecture
- vii. The astonishing physical dimensions of the termite mound
- viii. Termite mounds under threat from global climate change
- ix. Mutually beneficial relationship

27. Paragraph A
28. Paragraph B
29. Paragraph C
30. Paragraph D
31. Paragraph E
32. Paragraph F
33. Paragraph G

Questions 34-37

Lable the diagram below.

*Choose **ONE WORD ONLY** from the passage for each answer.*

*Write your answers in boxes **34-37** on your answer sheet.*

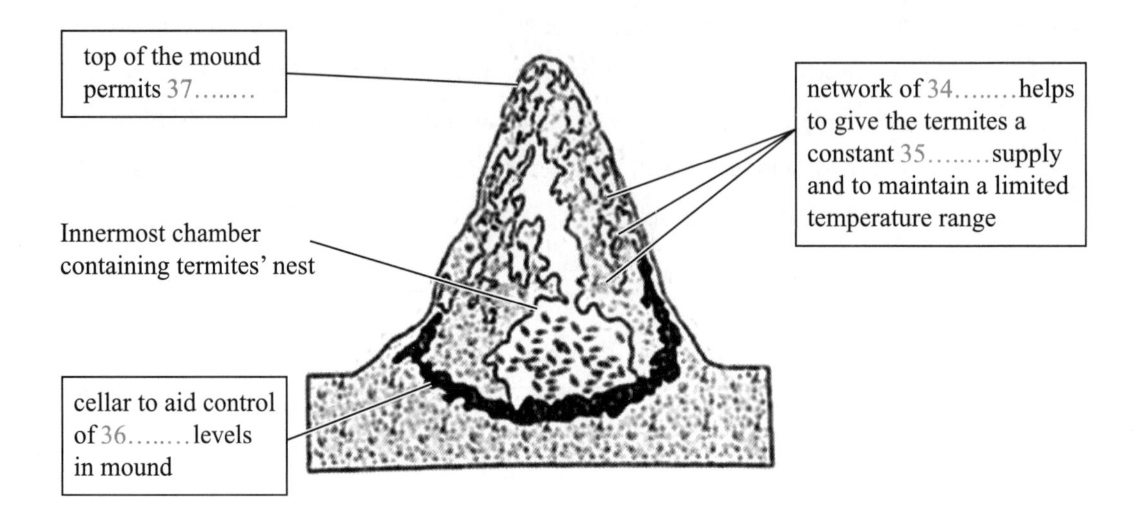

Questions 38-40

Do the following statements agree with the claims of the writer in Reading Passage 3?

*In boxes **38-40** on your sheet, write*

YES	*if the statement agrees with the claims of the writer*
NO	*if the statement contradicts the claims of the writer*
NOT GIVEN	*if it is impossible to say what the writer thinks about this*

38. The termite mound appears to process its refuse material internally.
39. Dr. Soar's reconstruction involves scanning a single photograph of a complete mound into a computer.
40. New information about termite architecture could help people deal with future energy crises.

TEST 3

READING PASSAGE 1

Koalas

A Koalas are just too nice for their own good. And except for the occasional baby taken by birds of prey, koalas have no natural enemies. In an ideal world, the life of an arboreal couch potato would be perfectly safe and acceptable.

B Just two hundred years ago, koalas flourished across Australia. Now they seem to be in decline, but exact numbers are not available as the species would not seem to be "under threat". Their problem, however, has been man, more specifically, the white man. Koala and aborigine had co-existed peacefully for centuries.

C Today koalas are found only in scattered pockets of southeast Australia, where they seem to be at risk on several fronts. The koala's only food source, the eucalyptus tree, has declined. In the past 200 years, a third of Australia's eucalyptus forests have disappeared. Koalas have been killed by parasites, Chlamydia epidemics and a tumour-causing retro-virus. And every year 11000 are killed by cars, ironically most of them in wildlife sanctuaries, and thousands are killed by poachers. Some are also taken illegally as pets. The animals usually soon die, but they are easily replaced.

D Bush fires pose another threat. The horrific ones that raged in New South Wales recently killed between 100 and 1000 koalas. Many that were taken into sanctuaries and shelters were found to have burnt their paws on the glowing embers. But zoologists say that the species should recover. The koalas will be aided by the eucalyptus, which grows quickly and is already burgeoning forth after the fires. So the main problem to their survival is their slow reproductive rate—they produce only one baby a year over a reproductive lifespan of about nine years.

E The latest problem for the species is perhaps more insidious. With plush, grey fur, dark amber eyes and button nose, koalas are cuddliness incarnate. Australian zoos and wildlife parks have taken advantage of their uncomplaining attitudes, and charge visitors to be photographed hugging the furry bundles. But people may not realize how cruel this is. Because of the koala's delicate disposition, constant handling can push an already precariously balanced physiology over the edge.

F Koalas only eat the foliage of certain species of eucalyptus trees, between 600 and 1250 grams a day. The tough leaves are packed with cellulose, tannins, aromatic oils and precursors of toxic cyanides. To handle this cocktail, koalas have a specialized digestive system. Cellulose-digesting bacteria in the caecum break down fibre, while a specially adapted gut and liver process the toxins. To digest their food properly, koalas must sit still for 21 hours every day.

G Koalas are the epitome of innocence and inoffensiveness. Although they are capable of ripping open a man's arm with their needle-sharp claws, or giving a nasty nip, they simply wouldn't. If you upset a koala, it may blink or swallow, or hiccup. But attack? No way! Koalas are just not aggressive. They use their claws to grip the hard smooth bark of eucalyptus trees.

H They are also very sensitive, and the slightest upset can prevent them from breeding, cause them to go off their food, and succumb to gut infections. Koalas are stoic creatures and put on a brave face until they are at death's door. One day they may appear healthy, the next they could be dead. Captive koalas have to be weighed daily to check that they are feeding properly. A sudden loss of weight is usually the only warning keepers have that their charge is ill. Only two keepers plus a vet were allowed to handle London Zoo's koalas, as these creatures are only comfortable with people they know. A request for the koala to be taken to meet the Queen was refused because of the distress this would have caused the marsupial. Sadly, London's Zoo no longer has a koala. Two years ago the female koala died of a cancer caused by a retrovirus. When they come into heat, female koalas become more active, and start losing weight, but after about sixteen days, heat ends and the weight piles back on. London's koala did not. Surgery revealed hundreds of pea-sized tumours.

I Almost every zoo in Australia has koalas—the marsupial has become the Animal

Ambassador of the nation, but nowhere outside Australia would handling by the public be allowed. Koala cuddling screams in the face of every rule of good care. First, some zoos allow koalas to be passed from stranger to stranger, many children who love to squeeze. Secondly, most people have no idea of how to handle the animals; they like to cling on to their handler, all in their own good time and use his or her arm as a tree. For such reasons, the Association of Fauna and Marine parks, an Australian conservation society is campaigning to ban koala cuddling. Policy on koala handling is determined by state government authorities, mostly the Australian Nature Conservation Agency, with the aim of instituting national guidelines. Following a wave of publicity, some zoos and wildlife parks have stopped turning their koalas into photo.

Questions 1-5

Choose the correct letter, A, B, C or D.

Write the correct letter in boxes 1-5 on your answer sheet.

1. The main reason why koalas declined is that they are killed EXCEPT FOR

   A. by poachers.

   B. by diseases they got.

   C. by giving too many birth yet survived little.

   D. by accidents on the road.

2. What can help koalas fully digest their food?

   A. toxic substance in the leaves

   B. organs that dissolve the fibres

   C. remaining inactive for a period to digest

   D. eating eucalyptus trees

3. What would koalas do when facing the dangerous situation?

   A. show signs of being offended

   B. counter attack furiously

   C. use sharp claws to rip the man

   D. use claws to grip the bark of trees

4. In what ways Australian zoos exploit koalas?

   A. encourage people to breed koalas as pets

B. allow tourists to hug the koalas
C. put them on the trees as a symbol
D. establish a koala campaign

5. What would the government do to protect koalas from being endangered?
A. introduce koala protection guidelines
B. close some of the zoos
C. encourage people to resist visiting the zoos
D. persuade the public to learn more knowledge

Questions 6-12

Do the following statements agree with the information given in Reading Passage 1?

*In boxes **6-12** on your answer sheet, write*

YES	*if the statement agrees with the claims of the writer*
NO	*if the statement contradicts the claims of the write*
NOT GIVEN	*if there is no information on this*

6. New coming human settlers caused danger to koalas.
7. Koalas can still be seen in most of the places in Australia.
8. It takes a decade for the eucalyptus trees to recover after the fire.
9. Koalas will fight each other when food becomes scarce.
10. It is not easy to notice that koalas are ill.
11. Koalas are easily infected with human contagious diseases via cuddling.
12. Koalas like to hold a person's arm when they are embraced.

Question 13

*Choose the correct letter, **A, B, C** or **D**.*

Write the correct letter in box 13 on your answer sheet.

From your opinion this article written by
A. a journalist who writes for magazine.
B. a zoo keeper in London Zoo.
C. a tourist traveling back from Australia.
D. a government official who studies koalas to establish a law.

READING PASSAGE 2

Is Graffiti Art or Crime

A The term graffiti derives from the Italian graffito meaning "scratching" and can be defined as uninvited marking or writing scratched or applied to objects, built structures and natural features. It is not a new phenomenon: examples can be found on ancient structures around the world, in some cases predating the Greeks and Romans. In such circumstances it has acquired invaluable historical and archaeological significance, providing a social history of life and events at that time. Graffiti is now a problem that has become pervasive, as a result of the availability of cheap and quick means of mark-making.

B It is usually considered a priority to remove graffiti as quickly as possible after it appears. This is for several reasons. The first is to prevent "copy-cat" emulation which can occur rapidly once a clean surface is defaced. It may also be of a racist or otherwise offensive nature and many companies and councils have a policy of removing this type of graffiti within an hour or two of it being reported. Also, as paints, glues and inks dry out over time they can become increasingly difficult to remove and are usually best dealt with as soon as possible after the incident. Graffiti can also lead to more serious forms of vandalism and, ultimately, the deterioration of an area, contributing to social decline.

C Although graffiti may be regarded as an eyesore, any proposal to remove it from sensitive historic surfaces should be carefully considered: techniques designed for more robust or utilitarian surfaces may result in considerable damage. In the event of graffiti incidents, it is important that the owners of buildings or other structures and their consultants are aware of the approach they should take in dealing with the problem. The police should be informed as there may be other related attacks occurring locally. An incidence pattern can identify possible culprits, as can stylised signatures or nicknames, known as "tags", which may already be familiar to local police. Photographs are useful to record graffiti incidents and may assist the police in bringing a prosecution. Such images are also required for insurance claims and can be helpful in cleaning operatives, allowing them to see the problem area before arriving on site.

D There are a variety of methods that are used to remove graffiti. Broadly these divide between chemical and mechanical systems. Chemical preparations are based on dissolving the media; these solvents can range from water to potentially hazardous chemical "cocktails". Mechanical systems such as wire-brushing and grit-blasting attempt to abrade or chip the media from the surface. Care should be taken to comply with health and safety legislation with regard to the protection of both passers-by and any person carrying out the cleaning. Operatives should follow product guidelines in terms of application and removal, and wear the appropriate protective equipment. Measures must be taken to ensure that run-off, aerial mists, drips and splashes do not threaten unprotected members of the public. When examining a graffiti incident, it is important to assess the ability of the substrate to withstand the prescribed treatment. If there is any doubt regarding this, then small trial areas should be undertaken to assess the impact of more extensive treatment.

E A variety of preventive strategies can be adopted to combat a recurring problem of graffiti at a given site. As no two sites are the same, no one set of protection measures will be suitable for all situations. Each site must be looked at individually. Surveillance systems such as closed-circuit television may also help. In cities and towns around the country, prominently placed cameras have been shown to reduce anti-social behavior of all types including graffiti. Security patrols will also act as a deterrent to prevent recurring attacks. However, the cost of this may be too high for most situations. Physical barriers such as walls, railings, doors or gates can be introduced to discourage unauthorized access to a vulnerable site. However, consideration has to be given to the impact these measures have on the structure being protected. In the worst cases, they can be almost as damaging to the quality of the environment as the graffiti they prevent. In others, they might simply provide a new surface for graffiti.

F One of the most significant problems associated with graffiti removal is the need to remove it from surfaces that are repeatedly attacked. Under these circumstances, the repeated removal of graffiti using even the gentlest methods will ultimately cause damage to the surface material. There may be situations where the preventive strategies mentioned above do not work or are not a viable proposition at a given site. Anti-graffiti coatings are usually applied by brush or spray leaving a thin veneer that essentially serves to isolate the graffiti from the surface.

G Removal of graffiti from a surface that has been treated in this way is much easier, usually using low-pressure water which reduces the possibility of damage. Depending on the type of barrier selected it may be necessary to reapply the coating after each graffiti removal exercise.

Questions 14-19

Reading passage 2 has seven paragraphs, **A-G**.

Which paragraph contains the following information?

Write the correct letter, ***A-G****, in boxes* ***14-19*** *on your answer sheet.*

NB *You may use any letter more than once.*

14. why chemically cleaning graffiti may cause damage
15. the benefit of a precautionary strategy on the gentle removal
16. the damaging and accumulative impact of graffiti on the community
17. the need for different preventive measures being taken to cope with graffiti
18. a legal proposal made to the owner of building against graffiti
19. the reasons for removing graffiti as soon as possible

Questions 20-21

Choose ***TWO*** *letters,* ***A-E****.*

Write your answers in boxes ***20-21*** *on your answer sheet.*

Which **TWO** statements are true concerning the removal of graffiti?

A. Cocktail removal can be safer than water treatment.

B. A small patch trial should be conducted before applying large scale of removing.

C. Chemical treatments are the most expensive way of removing.

D. There are risks for both chemical and mechanical methods.

E. Mechanical removals are much more applicable than chemical treatments.

Questions 22-23

*Choose TWO letters, **A-E**.*

*Write your answers in boxes **22-23** on your answer sheet.*

Which **TWO** of the following preventive measures against graffiti are mentioned effectively in the passage?

A. organise more anti-graffiti movements in the city communities

B. increase police patrols on the street

C. build a new building with material repelling to water

D. install more visible security cameras

E. provide a whole new surface with a chemical coat

Questions 24-27

Complete the sentences below.

Use NO MORE THAN TWO WORDS from the passage for each answer.

*Write your answers in boxes **24-27** on your answer sheet.*

24. Ancient graffiti is of significance and records the...... of life in details for that period.
25. The police can recognize newly committed incidents of graffiti by the signatures called ...... that they are familiar with.
26. Operatives ought to comply with relevant rules during the operation, and put on the suitable ......
27. Removal of graffiti from a new type of coating surface can be much convenient using ......

READING PASSAGE 3

Asian Space Satellite Technology

The space age began with the launch of the Russian artificial satellite Sputnik in 1957 and developed further with the race to the moon between the United States and Russia. This rivalry was characterized by advanced technology and huge budgets. In this process there were spectacular successes, some failures, but also many spin-offs. Europe, Japan, China, and India quickly joined this space club of the superpowers. With the advent of relatively low cost high performance mini-satellites and launchers, the acquisition of indigenous space capabilities by smaller nations in Asia has become possible. How, in what manner, and for what purpose will these capabilities be realized?

A Rocket technology has progressed considerably since the days of "fire arrows" (bamboo poles filled with gunpowder) first used in China around 500 BC, and, during the Sung Dynasty, to repel Mongol invaders at the battle of Kaifeng (Kai-fung fu) in AD 1232.These ancient rockets stand in stark contrast to the present-day Chinese rocket launch vehicles, called the "Long March".

B In the last decade there has been a dramatic growth in space activities in Asia both in the utilization of space-based services and the production of satellites and launchers. This rapid expansion has led many commentators and analysts to predict that Asia will become a world space power. The space age has had dramatic affects worldwide with direct developments in space technology influencing telecommunications, meteorological forecasting, earth resource and environmental monitoring, and disaster mitigation (floods, forest fires, and oil spills). Asian nations have been particularly eager to embrace these developments.

C New and innovative uses for satellites are constantly being explored with potential revolutionary effects, such as in the field of health and telemedicine, distance education, crime prevention (piracy on the high sea), food and agricultural planning and production (rice crop monitoring). Space in Asia is very much influenced by the competitive commercial space sector, the emergence of low cost mini-satellites, and the globalization of industrial and financial markets. It is not evident how Asian space will develop in the coming decades in the face of these trends. It is, however, important to understand and assess the factors and forces that shape Asian space activities and development in determining its possible consequences for the region.

D At present, three Asian nations, Japan, China, and India, have comprehensive end-to-end space capabilities and possess a complete space infrastructure: space technology, satellite manufacturing, rockets, and spaceports. Already self-sufficient in terms of satellite design and manufacturing, South Korea is currently attempting to join their ranks with its plans to develop a launch site and spaceport. Additionally, nations in Southeast Asia as well as those bordering the Indian subcontinent (Nepal, Pakistan, and Bangladesh) have, or are starting to develop, indigenous space programmes. The Association of Southeast Asian Nations (ASEAN) has, in varying degrees, embraced space applications using foreign technology and over the past five years or so its space activities have been expanding. Southeast Asia is predicted to become the largest and fastest growing market for commercial space products and applications driven by telecommunications (mobile and fixed services), the Internet, and remote sensing applications. In the development of this technology, many non-technical factors, such as economics, politics, culture, and history, interact and play important roles, which in turn affect Asian technology.

E Asia, and Southeast Asia in particular, suffers from a long list of recurrent large-scale environmental problems including storms and flooding, forest fires and deforestation, and crop failures. Thus, the space application that has attracted the most attention in this region is remote sensing. Remote sensing satellites equipped with instruments to take photographs of the ground at different wavelengths provide essential information for natural resource accounting, environmental management, disaster prevention and monitoring, land-use mapping, and sustainable development planning. Progress in these applications has been rapid and impressive. ASEAN members, unlike Japan, China, and India, do not have their own remote sensing satellites, however, most of its member nations have facilities to receive, process, and interpret such data from American and European satellites. In particular, Thailand, Malaysia, and Singapore have world-class remote sensing processing facilities and research programmes. ASEAN has plans to develop (and launch) its own satellites and in particular remote sensing satellites. In view of the technological challenges and high risks involved in space activities, a very long, and expensive, learning curve has been followed to obtain successes. Japan's satellite manufacturing was based on the old and traditional defense and military procurement methodologies as practiced in the US and Europe.

F In recent years there have been fundamental changes in the way satellites are designed and built to drastically reduce costs. The emergence of "small satellites" and their quick adoption by Asian countries as a way to develop low-cost satellite technology and rapidly establish a space capability has given these countries the possibility to shorten their learning curve by a decade or more. The global increase of technology transfer mechanisms and use of readily available commercial technology to replace costly space and military standard components may very well result in a highly competitive Asian satellite manufacturing industry.

G The laws of physics are the same in Tokyo as in Toulouse, and the principles of electronics and mechanics know no political or cultural boundaries. However, no such immutability applies to engineering practices and management; they are very much influenced by education, culture, and history. These factors, in turn, have an effect on costs, lead times, product designs and, eventually, international sales. Many Asian nations are sending their engineers to be trained in the West. Highly experienced, they return to work in the growing Asian space industry. Will this acquisition of technical expertise, coupled perhaps with the world-renowned Japanese manufacturing and management techniques, be applied to build world-class satellites and reduce costs?

Questions 28-32

*Reading Passage 3 has seven paragraphs, **A-G**.*

*Choose the correct heading for paragraphs, **A-G**, from the list below.*

*Write the correct number, **i-ix**, in boxes **28-32** on your answer sheet.*

List of Headings

i. Western countries provide essential assistance
ii. Unbalanced development for an essential space technology
iii. Innovative application compelled by competition
iv. An ancient invention which is related to the future
v. Military purpose of satellites
vi. Rockets for application in ancient China
vii. Space development in Asia in the past
viii. Non-technology factors count
ix. Competitive edge gained by more economically feasible satellites
x. Current space technology development in Asia

Example: Paragraph D x

28. Paragraph A
29. Paragraph B
30. Paragraph C
31. Paragraph E
32. Paragraph F

Questions 33-36

Match the following reasons for each question according to the information given in the passage.

Write the correct letter, ***A-F****, in boxes* ***33-36*** *on your answer sheet.*

A. Because it helps administrate the crops.
B. Because there are some unapproachable areas.
C. Because the economic level in that area is low.
D. Because there are influences from some other social factors.
E. Because it can be used in non-peaceful purpose.
F. Because disasters such as bush fire happen in Southeast Asia.

33. Why remote-photographic technology is used to resolve environment problems?
34. Why satellite technology is used in the medicine area?
35. Why Asian countries' satellite technology is limited for development?
36. Why satellite technology is deployed in the agricultural area?

Questions 37-40

Do the following statements agree with the information given in Reading Passage 3?

In boxes ***37-40*** *on your answer sheet, write*

TRUE *if the statement agrees with the information*
FALSE *if the statement contradicts the information*
NOT GIVEN *if there is no information on this*

37. Ancient China had already deployed rockets as a military purpose as early as 500 years ago.
38. Space technology has enhanced literacy of Asia.
39. Photos taken by satellites with certain technology help natural catastrophes prevention and surveillance.
40. Commercial competition constitutes a boosting factor to Asian technology development.

TEST 4

READING PASSAGE 1

Multitasking Debate:
Can you do them at the same time?

A Talking on the phone while driving isn't the only situation where we're worse at multitasking than we might like to think we are. New studies have identified a bottleneck in our brains that some say it means we are fundamentally incapable of true multitasking. If experimental findings reflect real-world performance, people who think they are multitasking are probably just underperforming in all—or at best, all but one—of their parallel pursuits. Practice might improve your performance, but you will never be as good as when focusing on one task at a time.

B The problem, according to René Marois, a psychologist at Vanderbilt University in Nashville, Tennessee, is that there's a sticking point in the brain. To demonstrate this, Marois devised an experiment to locate it. Volunteers watch a screen and when a particular image appears, a red circle, say, they have to press a key with their index finger. Different coloured circles require presses from different fingers. Typical response time is about half a second, and the volunteers quickly reach their peak performance. Then they learn to listen to different recordings and respond by making a specific sound. For instance, when they hear a bird chirp, they have to say "ba"; an electronic sound should elicit a "ko", and so on. Again, no problem. A normal person can do that in about half a second, with almost no effort.

C The trouble comes when Marios shows the volunteers an image, and then almost immediately plays them a sound. Now they're flummoxed. "If you show an image and play a sound at the same time, one task is postponed," he says. In fact, if the second task is introduced within the half-second or so it takes to process and react to the first, it will simply be delayed until the first one is done. The largest dual-task delays occur when the two tasks are presented simultaneously; delays progressively shorten as the interval between presenting the tasks lengthens.

D There are at least three points where we seem to get stuck, says Marois. The first is in simply identifying what we're looking at. This can take a few tenths of a second, during which time we are not able to see and recognize a second item. This limitation is known as the "attentional blink": experiments have shown that if you're watching out for a particular event and a second one shows up unexpectedly any time within this crucial window of concentration, it may register in your visual cortex but you will be unable to act upon it. Interestingly, if you don't expect the first event, you have no trouble responding to the second. What exactly causes the attentional blink is still a matter for debate.

E A second limitation is our short-term visual memory. It's estimated that we can keep track of about four items at a time, fewer if they are complex. This capacity shortage is thought to explain, in part, our astonishing inability to detect even huge changes in scenes that are otherwise identical, so-called "change blindness". Show people pairs of near-identical photos—say, aircraft engines in one picture have disappeared in the other—and they will fail to spot the differences. Here again, though, there is disagreement about what the essential limiting factor really is. Does it come down to a dearth of storage capacity, or is it about how much attention a viewer is paying?

F A third limitation is that choosing a response to a stimulus—braking when you see a child in the road, for instance, or replying when your mother tells you over the phone that she's thinking of leaving your dad—also takes brainpower. Selecting a response to one of these things will delay by some tenths of a second your ability to respond to the other. This is called the "response selection bottleneck" theory, first proposed in 1952.

G But David Meyer, a psychologist at the University of Michigan, Ann Arbor, doesn't buy the bottleneck idea. He thinks dual-task interference is just evidence of a strategy used by the brain to prioritise multiple activities. Meyer is known as something of an optimist by his peers. He has written papers with titles like "Virtually perfect time-sharing in dual-task performance: Uncorking the central cognitive bottleneck". His experiments have shown that with enough practice—at least 2000 tries—some people can execute two tasks simultaneously as competently as if they were doing them one after the other. He suggests that there is a central cognitive processor that coordinates all this and, what's more, he thinks it uses discretion: sometimes it chooses to delay one task while completing another.

H Marois agrees that practice can sometimes erase interference effects. He has found that with just 1 hour of practice each day for two weeks, volunteers show a huge improvement at managing both his tasks at once. Where he disagrees with Meyer is in what the brain is doing to achieve this. Marois speculates that practice might give us the chance to find less congested circuits to execute a task—rather like finding trusty back streets to avoid heavy traffic on main roads—effectively making our response to the task subconscious. After all, there are plenty of examples of subconscious multitasking that most of us routinely manage: walking and talking, eating and reading, watching TV and folding the laundry.

I It probably comes as no surprise that, generally speaking, we get worse at multitasking as we age. According to Art Kramer at the University of Illinois at Urbana-Champaign, who studies how aging affects our cognitive abilities, we peak in our 20s. Though the decline is slow through our 30s and on into our 50s, it is there; and after 55, it becomes more precipitous. In one study, he and his colleagues had both young and old participants do a simulated driving task while carrying on a conversation. He found that while young drivers tended to miss background changes, older drivers failed to notice things that were highly relevant. Likewise, older subjects had more trouble paying attention to the more important parts of a scene than young drivers.

J It's not all bad news for over-55s, though. Kramer also found that older people can benefit from practice. Not only did they learn to perform better, brain scans showed that underlying that improvement was a change in the way their brains become active. While it's clear that practice can often make a difference, especially as we age, the basic facts remain sobering. "We have this impression of an almighty complex brain," says Marois, "and yet we have very humbling and crippling limits." For most of our history, we probably never needed to do more than one thing at a time, he says, and so we haven't evolved to be able to. Perhaps we will in the future, though. We might yet look back one day on people like Debbie and Alun as ancestors of a new breed of true multitaskers.

Questions 1-5

Reading Passage 1 has ten paragraphs, **A-J.**

Which paragraph contains the following information?

*Write the correct letter, **A-J**, in boxes **1-5** on your answer sheet.*

1. a theory explained delay happens when selecting one reaction.
2. different age groups respond to important things differently.
3. conflicts happened when visual and audio element emerge simultaneously.
4. an experiment designed to demonstrate the critical part in brain for multitasking.
5. a viewpoint favors the optimistic side of multitask performance.

Questions 6-8

*Choose the correct letter, **A, B, C** or **D**.*

*Write your answers in boxes **6-8** on your answer sheet.*

6. Which one is correct about the experiment conducted by René Marois?

   A. Participants performed poorly on listening task solely.

   B. Volunteers press a different key on different color.

   C. Participants need use different fingers on different colored objects.

   D. They did a better job on mixed image and sound information.

7. Which statement is correct about the first limitation of Marois's experiment?

   A. "Attentional blink" takes about ten seconds.

   B. Lag occurs if we concentrate on one object while the second one appears.

   C. We always have trouble in reacting the second one.

   D. First limitation can be avoided by certain measures.

8. Which one is **NOT** correct about Meyer's experiments and statements?

   A. Just after failure in several attempts can people execute dual-task.

   B. Practice can overcome dual-task interference.

   C. Meyer holds a different opinion on Marois's theory.

   D. An existing processor decides whether delay another task or not.

Questions 9-13

Do the following statements agree with the information given in Reading Passage 1?

*In boxes **9-13** on your answer sheet, write*

YES	*if the statement is true*
NO	*if the statement is false*
NOT GIVEN	*if the information is not given in the passage*

9. Longer gap between two presenting tasks means shorter delay toward the second one.
10. Incapable of human memory causes people to sometimes miss the differences when presented two similar images.
11. Marois has different opinion on the claim that training removes bottleneck effect.
12. Art Kramer proved there is a correlation between multitasking performance and genders.
13. The author doesn't believe that the effect of practice could bring any variation.

READING PASSAGE 2

The Cacao: A Sweet History

A Chapter 1

Most people today think of chocolate as something sweet to eat or drink that can be easily found in stores around the world. It might surprise you that chocolate was once highly treasured. The tasty secret of the cacao (Kah Kow) tree was discovered 2,000 years ago in the tropical rainforests of the Americas. The story of how chocolate grew from a local Mesoamerican beverage into a global sweet encompasses many cultures and continents.

B Chapter 2

Historians believe the Maya people of Central America first learned to farm cacao plants around two thousand years ago. The Maya took cacao trees from the rainforests and grew them in their gardens. They cooked cacao seeds, then crushed them into a soft paste. They mixed the paste with water and flavorful spices to make an unsweetened chocolate drink. The Maya poured the chocolate drink back and forth between two containers so that the liquid would have a layer of bubbles, or foam.

Cacao and chocolate were an important part of Maya culture. There are often images of cacao plants on Maya buildings and art objects. Ruling families drank chocolate at special ceremonies. And, even poorer members of the society could enjoy the drink once in a while. Historians believe that cacao seeds were also used in marriage ceremonies as a sign of the union between a husband and a wife.

The Aztec culture in current-day Mexico also prized chocolate. But, cacao plants could not grow in the area where the Aztecs lived. So, they traded to get cacao. They even used cacao seeds as a form of money to pay taxes. Chocolate also played a special role in both Maya and Aztec royal and religious events. Priests presented cacao seeds and offerings to the gods and served chocolate drinks during sacred ceremonies. Only the very wealthy in Aztec societies could afford to drink chocolate because cacao was so valuable. The Aztec ruler Montezuma was believed to drink fifty cups of chocolate every day. Some experts believe the word for chocolate came from the Aztec word “xocolatl” which in the Nahuatl language means “bitter water”. Others believe the word “chocolate” was created by combining Mayan and Nahuatl words.

C Chapter 3

The explorer Christopher Columbus brought cacao seeds to Spain after his trip to Central America in 1502. But it was the Spanish explorer Hernando Cortes who understood that chocolate could be a valuable investment. In 1519, Cortes arrived in current-day Mexico. He believed the chocolate drink would become popular with Spaniards. After the Spanish soldiers defeated the Aztec empire, they were able to seize the supplies of cacao and send them home. Spain later began planting cacao in its colonies in the Americas in order to satisfy the large demand for chocolate. The wealthy people of Spain first enjoyed a sweetened version of chocolate drink. Later, the popularity of the drink spread throughout Europe. The English, Dutch and French began to plant cacao trees in their own colonies. Chocolate remained a drink that only wealthy people could afford to drink until the eighteenth century. During the period known as the Industrial Revolution, new technologies helped make chocolate less costly to produce.

D Chapter 4

Farmers grow cacao trees in many countries in Africa, Central and South America. The trees grow in the shady areas of the rainforests near the Earth's equator. But these trees can be difficult to grow. They require an exact amount of water, warmth, soil and protection. After about five years, cacao trees start producing large fruits called pods, which grow near the trunk of the tree. The seeds inside the pods are harvested to make chocolate. There are several kinds of cacao trees. Most of the world's chocolate is made from the seed of the forastero tree. But farmers can also grow criollo or trinitario cacao plants. Cacao trees grown on farms are much more easily threatened by diseases and insects than wild trees. Growing cacao is very hard work for farmers. They sell their harvest on a futures market. This means that economic conditions beyond their control can affect the amount of money they will earn. Today, chocolate industry officials, activists, and scientists are working with farmers. They are trying to make sure that cacao can be grown in a way that is fair to the farmers and safe for the environment.

E Chapter 5

To become chocolate, cacao seeds go through a long production process in a factory. Workers must sort, clean and cook the seeds. Then they break off the covering of the seeds so that only the inside fruit, or nibs, remain. Workers crush the nibs into a soft substance called chocolate liquor. This gets separated into cocoa solids and a fat called cocoa butter. Chocolate makers have their own special recipes in which they combine chocolate liquor with exact amounts of sugar, milk and cocoa fat. They finely crush this 'crumb' mixture in order to make it smooth. The mixture then goes through two more processes before it is shaped into a mold form.

Chocolate making is a big business. The market value of the yearly cacao crop around the world is more than five billion dollars. Chocolate is especially popular in Europe and the United States. For example, in 2005, the United States bought 1.4 billion dollars worth of cocoa products. Each year, Americans eat an average of more than five kilograms of chocolate per person. Specialty shops that sell costly chocolates are also very popular. Many offer chocolate lovers the chance to taste chocolates grown in different areas of the world.

Questions 14-18

Reading Passage 2 has five chapters.

Which chapter contains the following information?

*Write your answers in boxes **14-18** on your answer sheet.*

***NB** You may use any letter more than once.*

14. the part of cacao trees used to produce chocolate
15. average chocolate consumption by people in the US per person per year
16. risks faced by farmers in the cacao business
17. where the first sweetened chocolate drink appeared
18. how ancient American civilizations obtained cacao

Questions 19-23

Do the following statements agree with the information given in Reading Passage 2?

*In boxes **19-23** on your answer sheet, write*

TRUE	*if the statement is true*
FALSE	*if the statement is false*
NOT GIVEN	*if the information is not given in the passage*

19. Using cacao and chocolate in ceremonies was restricted to Maya royal families.
20. The Spanish explorer Hernando Cortes invested in chocolate and chocolate drinks.
21. The forastero tree produces the best chocolate.
22. Some parts in cacao seeds are got rid of during the chocolate process.
23. Chocolate is welcomed more in some countries or continents than other parts around the world.

Questions 24-27

The flow chart below shows the steps in chocolate making.

*Complete the flow chart using **NO MORE THAN THREE WORDS** from the passage for each blank.*

*Write your answers in boxes **24-27** on your answer sheet.*

cacao seeds

↓ sorting, cleaning and cooking, riddling seeds of their **24** ....

nibs

↓ crushing

25 ....

↓ add sugar, milk and **26** ....

crumb mixture

↓ crush finely and then come into a shape in a **27** ....

chocolate

READING PASSAGE 3

Australia's Lost Giants

What happened to Australia's megafauna, the giant animals that once existed across this enormous continent?

A In 1969, a fossil hunter named Rod Wells came to Naracoorte in South Australia to explore what was then known as Victoria Cave. Wells clawed through narrow passages, and eventually into a huge chamber. Its floor of red soil was littered with strange objects. It took Wells a moment to realize what he was looking at: the bones of thousands of creatures that must have fallen through holes in the ground above and become trapped. Some of the oldest belonged to mammals far larger than any found today in Australia. They were the ancient Australian megafauna—huge animals of the Pleistocene epoch. In boneyards across the continent, scientists have found the fossils of a giant snake, a huge flightless bird, and a seven-foot-tall kangaroo, to name but a few. Given how much ink has been spilled on the extinction of the dinosaurs, it's a wonder that even more hasn't been devoted to megafauna. Prehistoric humans never threw spears at Tyrannosaurus rex but really did hunt mammoths and mastodons.

B The disappearance of megafauna in the Americas—mammoths, saber-toothed cats, giant sloths, among others—happened relatively soon after the arrival of human beings, about 13,000 years ago. In the 1960s, paleoecologist Paul Martin developed what became known as the blitzkrieg hypothesis. Modern humans, Martin said, created havoc as they spread through the Americas, wielding spears to annihilate animals that had never faced a technological predator. But this period of extinction wasn't comprehensive. North America kept its deer, black bears and a small type of bison, and South America kept its jaguars and llamas.

C What happened to Australia's large animals is baffling. For years scientists blamed the extinctions on climate change. Indeed, Australia has been drying out for over a million years, and the megafauna were faced with a continent where vegetation began to disappear. Australian paleontologist Tim Flannery suggests that people, who arrived on the continent around 50,000 years ago, used fire to hunt, which led to deforestation. Something dramatic happened to Australia's dominant land creatures—somewhere around 46,000 years ago, strikingly soon after the invasion of a tool-wielding, highly intelligent predator. In Flannery's 1994 book called *The Future Eaters,* he sets out his thesis that human beings are a new kind of animal on the planet, and are in general, one prone to ruining ecosystems. Flannery's book was proved highly controversial. Some viewed it as critical of the Aborigines, who pride themselves on living in harmony with nature. The more basic problem with Flannery's thesis is that there is no direct evidence that they killed any Australian megafauna. It would be helpful if someone uncovered a Diprotodon skeleton with a spear point embedded in a rib—or perhaps Thylacoleo bones next to the charcoal of a human campfire. Such kill sites have been found in the Americas but not in Australia.

D The debate about megafauna pivots to a great degree on the techniques for dating old bones and the sediments in which they are buried. If scientists can show that the megafauna died out fairly quickly and that this extinction event happened within a few hundred, or even a couple thousand years, of the arrival of people, that's a strong case—even if a purely circumstantial one—that the one thing was the direct result of the other. As it happens, there is one place where there may be such evidence: Cuddie Springs in New South Wales. Today the person most vocal about the site is archeologist Judith Field. In 1991, she discovered megafauna bones directly adjacent to stone tools—a headline-making find. She says there are two layers showing the association, one about 30,000 years old, the other 35,000 years old. If that dating is accurate, it would mean humans and megafauna coexisted in Australia for something like 20,000 years. "What Cuddie Springs demonstrates is that you have an extended overlap of humans and megafauna," Field says. Nonsense, say her critics. They say the fossils have been moved from their original resting places and redeposited in younger sediments.

E Another famous boneyard in the same region is a place called Wellington Caves, where Diprotodon, the largest known marsupial—an animal which carries its young in a pouch like kangaroos and koalas—was first discovered. Scientist Mike Augee says that: "This is a sacred site in Australian paleontology." Here's why. In 1830 a local official named George Rankin lowered himself into the cave on a rope tied to a protrusion in the cave wall. The protrusion turned out to be a bone. A surveyor named Thomas Mitchell arrived later that year, explored the caves in the area, and shipped fossils off to Richard Owen, the British paleontologist who later gained fame for revealing the existence of dinosaurs. Owen recognized that the Wellington cave bones belonged to an extinct marsupial. Later, between 1909 and 1915 sediments in Mammoth Cave that contained fossils were hauled out and examined in a chaotic manner that no scientist today would approve. Still, one bone in particular has drawn extensive attention: a femur with a cut in it, possibly left there by a sharp tool.

F Unfortunately, the Earth preserves its history haphazardly. Bones disintegrate, the land erodes, the climate changes, forests come and go, rivers change their course—and history, if not destroyed, is steadily concealed. By necessity, narratives are constructed from limited data. Australia's first people expressed themselves in rock art. Paleontologist Peter Murray has studied a rock painting in far northern Australia that shows what looks very much like a megafauna marsupial known as Palorchestes. In Western Australia another site shows what appears to be a hunter with either a marsupial lion or a Tasmanian tiger—a major distinction, since the marsupial lion went extinct and the much smaller Tasmanian tiger survived into the more recent historical era. But as Murray says, "Every step of the way involves interpretation. The data doesn't just speak for itself."

Questions 28-32

Reading Passage 3 has six paragraphs, A-F.

Which paragraph contains the following information?

Write your answers in boxes 28-32 on your answer sheet.

NB You may use any letter more than once.

28. descriptions of naturally occurring events that make the past hard to trace

29. an account of the discovery of a particular animal which had died out

30. the reason why a variety of animals all died in the same small area

31. the suggestion that a procedure to uncover fossilised secrets was inappropriate

32. examples of the kinds of animals that did not die out as a result of hunting

Questions 33-34

*Choose TWO letters, **A-E**.*

*Write the correct letters in boxes **33-34** on your answer sheet.*

Which TWO of these possible reasons for Australian megafauna extinction are mentioned in the text?

A. human activity
B. disease
C. loss of habitat
D. a drop in temperature
E. the introduction of new animal species

Questions 35-36

*Choose TWO letters, **A-E**.*

*Write the correct letters in boxes **35-36** on your answer sheet.*

The list below shows possible forms of proof for humans having contact with Australian megafauna.

Which TWO possible forms of proof do the Writer say have been found in Australia?

A. bone injury caused by a man-made object
B. bones near to early types of weapons
C. man-made holes designed for trapping animals
D. preserved images of megafauna species
E. animal remains at campfires

Questions 37-40

Do the following statements agree with the claims of the writer in Reading Passage 3?

*In boxes **37-40** on your answer sheet, write*

YES *if the statement agrees with the claims of the writer*
NO *if the statement contradicts the claims of the writer*
NOT GIVEN *if it is impossible to say what the writer thinks about this*

37. Extinct megafauna should receive more attention than the extinction of the dinosaurs.
38. There are problems with Paul Martin's "blitzkrieg" hypothesis for the Americas.
39. The Aborigines should have found a more effective way to protest about Flannery's book.
40. There is sufficient evidence to support Tim Flannery's ideas about megafauna extinction.

TEST 5

READING PASSAGE 1

Animal Minds: Parrot Alex

A In 1977 Irene Pepperberg, a recent graduate of Harvard University, did something very bold. At a time when animals still were considered automatons, she set out to find what was on another creature's mind by talking to it. She brought a one-year-old African gray parrot she named Alex into her lab to teach him to reproduce the sounds of the English language. "I thought if he learned to communicate, I could ask him questions about how he sees the world."

B When Pepperberg began her dialogue with Alex, who died last September at the age of 31, many scientists believed animals were incapable of any thought. They were simply machines, robots programmed to react to stimuli but lacking the ability to think or feel. Any pet owner would disagree. We see the love in our dogs' eyes and know that, of course, they have thoughts and emotions. But such claims remain highly controversial. Gut instinct is not science, and it is all too easy to project human thoughts and feelings onto another creature. How, then, does a scientist prove that an animal is capable of thinking—that it is able to acquire information about the world and act on it? "That's why I started my studies with Alex," Pepperberg said. They were seated—she at her desk, he on top of his cage—in her lab, a windowless room about the size of a boxcar, at Brandeis University. Newspapers lined the floor; baskets of bright toys were stacked on the shelves. They were clearly a team—and because of their work, the notion that animals can think is no longer so fanciful.

C Certain skills are considered key signs of higher mental abilities: good memory, a gasp of grammar and symbols, self-awareness, understanding others' motives, imitating others, and being creative. Bit by bit, in ingenious experiments, researchers have documented these talents in other species, gradually chipping away at what we thought made human beings distinctive while offering a glimpse of where our own abilities came from. Scrub jays know that other jays are thieves and that stashed food can spoil; sheep can recognize faces; chimpanzees use a variety of tools to probe termite mounds and even use weapons to hunt small mammals; dolphins can imitate human postures; the archerfish, which stuns insects with a sudden blast of water, can learn how to aim its squirt simply by watching an experienced fish perform the task. And Alex the parrot turned out to be a surprisingly good talker.

D Thirty years after the Alex studies began, Pepperberg and a changing collection of assistants were still giving him English lessons. The humans, along with two younger parrots, also served as Alex's flock, providing the social input all parrots crave. Like any flock, this one—as small as it was—had its share of drama. Alex dominated his fellow parrots, acted huffy at times around Peeperberg, tolerated the other female humans, and fell to pieces over a male assistant who dropped by for a visit. Pepperberg bought Alex in a Chicago pet store where she let the store's assistant pick him out because she didn't want other scientists saying later that she'd particularly chosen an especially smart bird for her work. Given that Alex's brain was the size of a shelled walnut, most researchers thought Pepperberg's interspecies communication study would be futile.

E "Some people actually called me crazy for trying this," she said. "Scientists thought that chimpanzees were better subjects, although, of course, chimps can't speak." Chimpanzees, bonobos, and gorillas have been taught to use sign language and symbols to communicate with us, often with impressive results. The bonobo Kanzi, for instance, carries his symbol-communication board with him so he can "talk" to his human researchers, and he has invented combinations of symbols to express his thoughts. Nevertheless, this is not the same thing as having an animal look up at you, open his mouth, and speak. Under Pepperberg's patient tutelage, Alex learned how to use his vocal tract to imitate almost one hundred English words, including the sounds for various foods, although he calls an apple a "banerry". "Apples taste a little bit like bananas to him, and they look a little bit like cherries, so Alex made up that word for them," Pepperberg said.

F It sounded a bit mad, the idea of a bird having lessons to practice, and willingly doing it. But after listening to and observing Alex, it was difficult to argue with Pepperberg's explanation for his behaviors. She wasn't handing him treats for the repetitious work or rapping him on the claws to make him say the sounds. "He has to hear the words over and over before he can correctly imitate them," Pepperberg said, after pronouncing "seven" for Alex a good dozen times in a row. "I'm not trying to see if Alex can learn a human language," she added. "That's never been the point. My plan always was to use his imitative skills to get a better understanding of avian cognition."

G In other words, because Alex was able to produce a close approximation of the sounds of some English words, Pepperberg could ask him questions about a bird's basic understanding of the world. She couldn't ask him what he was thinking about, but she could ask him about his knowledge of numbers, shapes, and colors. To demonstrate, Pepperberg carried Alex on her arm to a tall wooden perch in the middle of the room. She then retrieved a green key and a small green cup from a basket on a shelf. She held up the two items to Alex's eye. "What's same?" she asked. Without hesitation, Alex's beak opened: "Co-lor." "What's different?" Pepperberg asked. "Shape," Alex said. His voice had the digitized sound of a cartoon character. Since parrots lack lips (another reason it was difficult for Alex to pronounce some sounds, such as ba), the words seemed to come from the air around him, as if a ventriloquist were speaking. But the words—and what can only be called the thoughts—were entirely his.

H For the next 20 minutes, Alex ran through his tests, distinguishing colors, shapes, sizes, and materials (wool versus wood versus metal). He did some simple arithmetic, such as counting the yellow toy blocks among a pile of mixed hues. And, then, as if to offer final proof of the mind inside his bird's brain, Alex spoke up. "Talk clearly!" he commanded, when one of the younger birds Pepperberg was also teaching talked with wrong pronunciation. "Talk clearly!" "Don't be a smart aleck," Pepperberg said, shaking her head at him. "He knows all this, and he gets bored, so he interrupts the others, or he gives the wrong answer just to be obstinate. At this stage, he's like a teenager; he's moody, and I'm never sure what he'll do."

Questions 1-6

Do the following statements agree with the information given in Reading Passage 1?

*In boxes **1-6** on your answer sheet, write*

TRUE *if the statement agrees with the information*

FALSE *if the statement contradicts the information*

NOT GIVEN *if there is no information*

1. Firstly Alex grasped quite a lot of vocabulary.
2. At the beginning of study, Alex felt frightened in the presence of humans.
3. Previously, many scientists realized that animals possess the ability of thinking.
4. It has taken a long time before people get to know cognition existing in animals.
5. As Alex could approximately imitate the sounds of English words, he was capable of roughly answering Irene's questions regarding the world.
6. By breaking in other parrots as well as producing the incorrect answers, Alex tried to be focused.

Questions 7-10

*Complete the following summary of the paragraphs of Reading Passage 1, using **NO MORE THAN THREE WORDS** from the passage for each answer.*

*Write your answers in boxes **7-10** on your answer sheet.*

After the training of Irene, parrot Alex can use his vocal tract to pronounce more than **7**............, while other scientists believe that animals have no this advanced ability of thinking, they would rather teach **8**............ Pepperberg clarified that she wanted to conduct a study concerning **9**............ but not to teach him to talk. The store's assistant picked out a bird at random for her for the sake of avoiding other scientists saying that the bird is **10**............ afterwards.

Questions 11-13

*Answer the questions **11-13** below.*

*Choose **NO MORE THAN THREE WORDS AND/OR A NUMBER** from the passage for each answer.*

*Write your answers in boxes **11-13** on your answer sheet.*

11. What did Alex reply regarding the similarity of the subjects showed to him?
12. What is the problem of the young parrots except Alex?
13. To some extent, through the way he behaved, what can we call Alex?

READING PASSAGE 2

Brunel: The Practical Prophet

A In the frontispiece of his book on Brunel, Peter Hay quotes from Nicholson's *British Encyclopedia* of 1909 as follows: "Engineers are extremely necessary for these purposes; wherefore it is requisite that, besides being ingenious, they should be brave in proportion" . His father, Sir Marc Isambard Brunel (1769-1849), was himself a famous engineer, of French parents. He was sent to France at the age of 14 to study mathematics and science and was only 16 when he returned to England to work with his father. Sir Marc was then building his famous tunnel under the River Thames. Isambard was recuperating near Bristol from injuries received in a tunnel cave—in when he became involved with his own first major project.

The Suspension Bridge on the Avon Gorge

B The span of Brunel's bridge was over 700ft, longer than any existing when it was designed, and the height above water about 245ft. The technical challenges of this engineering project were immense, and Brunel dealt with them with his usual thoroughness and ingenuity. Two design competitions were held, and the great bridge designer Thomas Telford was the committee's expert. Brunel presented four designs. He went beyond technicalities to include arguments based on, among other things, the grace of his tower design. Unfortunately, he only got so far as to put up the end piers in his lifetime. The Clifton Suspension Bridge was completed in his honor by his engineering friends in 1864, and is still in use.

The Great Western Railway

C While Brunel was still in Bristol, and with the Avon Bridge project stopped or going slowly, he became aware that the civic authorities saw the need for a railway link to London. Railway location was controversial, since private landowners and towns had to be dealt with. Mainly, the landed gentry did not want a messy, noisy railway anywhere near them. The Duke of Wellington (of Waterloo fame) was certainly against it. Again Brunel showed great skill in presenting his arguments to the various committees and individuals. Brunel built his railway with a broad gauge (7ft) instead of the standard 4ft $8\frac{1}{2}$ in, which had been used for lines already installed. There is

TEST 5

no doubt that the broad gauge gave superior ride and stability, but it was fighting a standard.

Atmospheric Railway

D Brunel's ready acceptance of new ideas overpowered good engineering judgment (at least in hindsight) when he advocated the installation of an atmospheric railway in South Devon. It had the great attraction of doing away with the locomotive, and potentially could deal with steeper gradients. Since this connecting arm had to run along the slit, it had to be opened through a flap as the train progressed, but closed airtight behind it. Materials were not up to it, and this arrangement was troublesome and expensive to keep in repair. After a year of frustration, the system was abandoned. Brunel admitted his failure and took responsibility. He also took no fee for his work, setting a good professional example.

Brunel's Ships

E The idea of using steam to power ships to cross the ocean appealed to Brunel. When his GWR company directors complained about the great length of their railway (it was only about 100 miles), Isambard jokingly suggested that they could even make it longer—why not go all the way to New York, and call the link the "Great Western". The Great Western was the first steamship to engage in transatlantic service. Brunel formed the Great Western Steamship Company, and construction started on the ship in Bristol in 1836. Built of wood and 236ft long, the Great Western was launched in 1837, and powered by sail and paddle wheels. The first trip to New York took just 15 days, and 14 days to return. This was a great success; a one way trip under sail would take more than a month. The Great Western was the first steamship to engage in transatlantic service and made 74 crossings to New York.

F Having done so well with the Great Western, Brunel immediately got to work on an even bigger ship. The Great Britain was made of iron and also built in Bristol, 322ft in length. The initial design was for the ship to be driven by paddle wheels, but Brunel had seen one of the first propeller driven ships to arrive in Britain, and he abandoned his plans for paddle wheel propulsion. The ship was launched in 1843 and was the first screw-driven iron ship to cross the Atlantic. The Great Britain ran aground early in its career, but was repaired, sold, and sailed for years to Australia, and other parts of the world, setting the standard for ocean travel. In the early 1970s the old ship was rescued from the Falklands, and is now under restoration in Bristol.

G Conventional wisdom in Brunel's day was that steamships could not carry enough coal to make long ocean voyages. But he correctly figured out that this was a case where size mattered. He set out to design the biggest ship ever, five times larger than any ship built up to that time. Big enough to carry fuel to get to Australia without refueling, in addition it would carry 4,000 passengers. The Great Eastern was 692ft long, with a displacement of about 32,000 tons. Construction began in 1854 on the Thames at Millwall. Brunel had chosen John Scott Russell to build the ship. He was a well-established engineer and naval architect, but the contract did not go well. Among other things, Scott Russell was very low in his estimates and money was soon a problem.

Construction came to a standstill in 1856 and Brunel himself had to take over the work. But Brunel was nothing if not determined, and by September, 1859, after a delayed and problem ridden launch, the Great Eastern was ready for the maiden voyage. Brunel was too sick to go, but it was just as well, because only a few hours out there was an explosion in the engine room which would have destroyed a lesser ship. Brunel died within a week or so of the accident. The great ship never carried 4,000 passengers (among other things, the Suez Canal came along) and although it made several transatlantic crossings, it was not a financial success. Shortly after the Great Eastern began working life, the American entrepreneur Cyrus Field and his backers were looking for a ship big enough to carry 5,000 tons of telegraphic cables, which was to be laid on the ocean floor from Ireland to Newfoundland. Although Brunel did not have it in mind, the Great Eastern was an excellent vessel for this work. On July 27, 1866 it successfully completed the connection and a hundred years of transatlantic communication by cable began. The ship continued this career for several years, used for laying cables in many parts of the world.

Questions 14-19

*Use the information in the passage to match the project Brunel did (listed **A-G**) with opinions or deeds below.*

*Write the appropriate letter, **A-G**, in boxes **14-19** on your answer sheet.*

***NB** You may use any letter more than once.*

A. River Thames Tunnel
B. Clifton Suspension Bridge
C. Atmospheric Railway
D. Great Britain
E. The Great Western
F. Great Western Railway
G. The Great Eastern

14. It was a project of construction that I.K Brunel was not responsible for.
15. The project had stopped due to inconvenience and high maintaining cost.
16. The project was honored to yet not completed by Brunel himself.
17. The project had budget problem although built by a famous engineer.
18. Serious problems happened and delayed repeatedly.
19. The project was the first one to cross Atlantic Ocean in mankind history.

Questions 20-22

Reading Passage 2 has seven paragraphs, **A-G**.

Which paragraph contains the following information?

*Write the correct letter, **A-G**, in boxes **20-22** on your answer sheet.*

***NB** You may use any letter more than once.*

20. There was a great ship setting the criteria for the journey of the ocean.
21. An ambitious project which seemed to be applied in an unplanned service later.
22. Brunel showed his talent of interpersonal skills with landlords and finally the project had been gone though.

Questions 23-26

*Complete the following summary of the paragraphs of Reading Passage 2 using **NO MORE THAN TWO WORDS** from the passage for each answer.*

*Write your answers in boxes **23-26** on your answer sheet.*

The Great Eastern was specially designed as the **23**.........for carrying more fuels and was to take long voyage to **24**..........; however, due to physical condition, Brunel couldn't be able to go with the maiden voyage. Actually, the Great Eastern was unprofitable because the construction of **25**........... But soon after there was an ironic opportunity for the Great Eastern which was used to carry and to lay huge **26**.......in Atlantic Ocean floor.

READING PASSAGE 3

Memory Decoding

Try this memory test: Study each face and compose a vivid image for the person's first and last name. Rose Leo, for example, could be a rosebud and a lion. The Examinations School at Oxford University is an austere building of oak-paneled rooms, large Gothic windows, and looming portraits of eminent dukes and earls. It is where generations of Oxford students have tested their memory on final exams, and it is where, last August, 34 contestants gathered at the World Memory Championships to be examined in an entirely different manner.

A In timed trials, contestants were challenged to look at and then recite a two-page poem, memorize rows of 40-digit numbers, recall the names of 110 people after looking at their photographs, and perform seven other feats of extraordinary retention. Some tests took just a few minutes; others lasted hours. In the 14 years since the World Memory Championships was founded, no one has memorized the order of a shuffled deck of playing cards in less than 30 seconds. That nice round number has become the four-minute mile of competitive memory, a benchmark that the world's best "mental-athletes," as some of them like to be called, are closing in on. Most contestants claim to have just average memories, and scientific testing confirms that they're not just being modest. Their feats are based on tricks that capitalize on how the human brain encodes information. Anyone can learn them.

B Psychologists Elizabeth Valentine and John Wilding, authors of the monograph *Superior Memory*, recently teamed up with Eleanor Maguire, a neuroscientist at University College London to study eight people, including Karsten, who had finished near the top of the World Memory Championships. They wondered if the contestants' brains were different in some way. The researchers put the competitors and a group of control subjects into an MRI machine and asked them to perform several different memory tests while their brains were being scanned. When it came to memorizing sequences of three-digit numbers, the difference between the memory contestants and the control subjects was, as expected, immense. However, when they were shown photographs of magnified snowflakes, images that the competitors had never tried to memorize before, the champions did no better than the control group. When the researchers analyzed the brain scans, they found that the memory champions were activating some brain regions that were different from those the control subjects were using. These regions, which included the right posterior hippocampus, are known to be involved in visual memory and spatial navigation.

C It might seem odd that the memory contestants would use visual imagery and spatial navigation to remember numbers, but the activity makes sense when their techniques are revealed. Cooke, a 23-year-old cognitive-science graduate student with a shoulder-length mop of curly hair, is a grand master of brain storage. He can memorize the order of 10 decks of playing cards in less than an hour or one deck of cards in less than a minute. He is closing in on the 30-second deck. In the Lamb and Flag, Cooke pulled out a deck of cards and shuffled it. He held up three cards—the 7 of spades, the queen of clubs, and the 10 of spades. He pointed at a fireplace and said, "Destiny's Child is whacking Franz Schubert with handbags." The next three cards were the king of hearts, the king of spades, and the jack of clubs.

D How did he do it? Cooke has already memorized a specific person, verb, and object that he associates with each card in the deck. For example, for the 7 of spades, the person (or, in this case, persons) is always the singing group Destiny's Child, the action is surviving a storm, and the image is dinghy. The queen of clubs is always his friend Henrietta, the action is whacking with a handbag, and the image is of wardrobes filled with designer clothes. When Cooke commits a deck to memory, he does three cards at a time. Every three-card group forms a single image of a person doing something to an object. The first card in the triplet becomes the person, the second the verb, the third the object. He then places those images along a specific familiar route, such as the one he took through the Lamb and Flag. In competitions, he uses an imaginary route that he has designed to be as smooth and downhill as possible. When it comes time to recall, Cooke takes a mental walk along his route and translates the images into cards. That's why the MRIs of the memory contestants showed activation in the brain areas associated with visual imagery and spatial navigation.

E The more resonant the images are, the more difficult they are to forget. But even meaningful information is hard to remember when there's a lot of it. That's why competitive memorizers place their images along an imaginary route. That technique, known as the loci method, reportedly originated in 477 B.C. with the Greek poet Simonides of Ceos. Simonides was the sole survivor of a roof collapse that killed all the other guests at a royal banquet. The bodies were mangled beyond recognition, but Simonides was able to reconstruct the guest list by closing his eyes and recalling each individual around the dinner table. What he had discovered was that our brains are exceptionally good at remembering images and spatial information. Evolutionary psychologists have offered an explanation: Presumably our ancestors found it important to recall where they found their last meal on the way back to the cave. After Simonides' discovery, the loci method became popular across ancient Greece as a trick for memorizing speeches and texts. Aristotle wrote about it, and later a number of treatises on the art of memory were published in Rome. Before printed books, the art of memory was considered a staple of classical education, on a par with grammar, logic, and rhetoric.

F The most famous of the naturals was the Russian journalists S.V. Shereshevski, who could recall long lists of numbers memorized decades earlier, as well as poems, strings of nonsense syllables, and just about anything else he was asked to remember. "The capacity of his memory had no distinct limits," wrote Alexander Luria, the Russian psychologist who studied Shereshevski from the 1920s to the 1950s. Shereshevski also had synesthesia, a rare condition in which the senses become intertwined. For example, every number may be associated with a color or every word with a taste. Synesthetic reactions evoke a response in more areas of the brain, making memory easier.

G K. Anders Ericsson, a Swedish-born psychologist at Florida State University, thinks anyone can acquire Shereshevski's skills. He cites an experiment with S. F., an undergraduate who was paid to take a standard test of memory called the digit span for one hour a day, two or three days a week. When he started, he could hold, like most people, only about seven digits in his head at any given time (conveniently, the length of a phone number). Over two years, S. F. completed 250 hours of testing. By then, he had stretched his digit span from 7 to more than 80. The study of S. F. led Ericsson to believe that innately superior memory doesn't exist at all. When he reviewed original case studies of naturals, he found that exceptional memorizers were using techniques—sometimes without realizing it—and lots of practice. Often, exceptional memory was only for a single type of material, like digits. "If we look at some of these memory tasks, they're the kind of thing most people don't even waste one hour practicing, but if they wasted 50 hours, they'd be exceptional at it," Ericsson says. "It would be remarkable," he adds, "to find a person who is exceptional across a number of tasks. I don't think that there's any compelling evidence that there are such people."

Questions 27-31

Reading Passage 3 has seven paragraphs, *A-G*.

Which paragraph contains the following information?

*Write the correct letter, **A-G**, in boxes **27-31** on your answer sheet.*

27. the reason why competence of super memory is significant in academic settings
28. mention of a contest for extraordinary memory held in consecutive years
29. a demonstrative example of an extraordinary person did an unusual recalling game
30. a belief that extraordinary memory can be gained though enough practice
31. a depiction of a rare ability which assists the extraordinary memory reactions

Questions 32-36

*Complete the following summary of the paragraphs of Reading Passage 3, using **NO MORE THAN THREE WORDS** from the passage for each answer.*

*Write your answers in boxes **32-36** on your answer sheet.*

Using visual imagery and spatial navigation to remember numbers is investigated and explained. A man called Ed Cooke in a pub, spoke a string of odd words when he held 7 of the spades (the first one of the any cards group was remembered as he encoded it to a **32**..........) and the card deck to memory are set to be one time of an order of **33**..................; when it comes time to recall, Cooke took a **34**............along his way and interpreted the imaginary scene into cards. This superior memory skill can be traced back to Ancient Greece, and the strategy was called **35**............which had been a major subject in ancient **36**............

Questions 37-38

*Choose TWO correct letters, **A-E**.*

*Write your answers in boxes **37-38** on your answer sheet.*

According to World Memory Championships, what activities need good memory?

A. order for a large group of each digit

B. recall people's face

C. recite a long Greek poem

D. match names with pictures and features

E. recall what people ate and did yesterday

Questions 39-40

*Choose TWO correct letters, **A-E**.*

*Write your answers in boxes **39-40** on your answer sheet.*

What did psychologists Elizabeth Valentine and John Wilding's MRI Scan experiment find out?

A. The champions' brains are different in some way from common people's.

B. There are differences in the brain scans of champions compared to control subjects when they are memorizing sequences of three-digit numbers.

C. The champions did much worse when they were asked to remember photographs.

D. The memory champions activated more brain regions than the control subjects.

E. Some parts in the brain coping with visual and spatial memory were activated in the memory champions.

TEST 6

READING PASSAGE 1

Foot Pedal Irrigation

A Until now, governments and development agencies have tried to tackle the problem through large-scale projects: gigantic dams, sprawling irrigation canals and vast new fields of high-yield crops introduced during the Green Revolution, the famous campaign to increase grain harvests in developing nations. Traditional irrigation, however, has degraded the soil in many areas, and the reservoirs behind dams can quickly fill up with silt, reducing their storage capacity and depriving downstream farmers of fertile sediments. Furthermore, although the Green Revolution has greatly expanded worldwide farm production since 1950, poverty stubbornly persists in Africa, Asia and Latin America. Continued improvements in the productivity of large farms may play the main role in boosting food supply, but local efforts to provide cheap, individual irrigation systems to small farms may offer a better way to lift people out of poverty.

B The Green Revolution was designed to increase the overall food supply, not to raise the incomes of the rural poor, so it should be no surprise that it did not eradicate poverty or hunger. India, for example, has been self-sufficient in food for 15 years, and its granaries are full, but more than 200 million Indians— one fifth of the country's population—are malnourished because they cannot afford the food they need and because the country's safety nets are deficient. In 2000, 189 nations committed to the Millennium Development Goals, which called for cutting world poverty in half by 2015. With business as usual, however, we have little hope of achieving most of the Millennium goals, no matter how much money rich countries contribute to poor ones.

C The supply-driven strategies of the Green Revolution, however, may not help subsistence farmers, who must play to their strengths to compete in the global marketplace. The average size of a family farm is less than four acres in India, 1.8

acres in Bangladesh. Combines and other modem farming tools are too expensive to be used on such small areas. An Indian farmer selling surplus wheat grown on his one-acre plot could not possibly compete with the highly efficient and subsidized Canadian wheat farms that typically stretch over thousands of acres. Instead subsistence farmers should exploit the fact that their labor costs are the lowest in the world, giving them a comparative advantage in growing and selling high-value, intensely farmed crops.

D Paul Polak saw firsthand the need for a small-scale strategy in 1981 when he met Abdul Rahman, a farmer in the Noakhali district of Banqladesh. From his three quarter-acre plots of rain-fed rice fields, Abdul could grow only 700 kilograms of rice each year—300 kilograms less than what he needed to feed his family. During the three months before the October rice harvest came in, Abdul and his wife had to watch silently while their three children survived on one meal a day or less. As Polak walked with him through the scattered fields he had inherited from his father, Polak asked what he needed to move out of poverty. "Control of water for my crops," he said, "at a price I can afford."

E Soon Polak learned about a simple device that could help Abdul achieve his goal: the treadle pump. Developed in the late 1970s by Norwegian engineer Gunnar Barnes, the pump is operated by a person walking in place on a pair of treadles and two handle arms made of bamboo. Properly adjusted and maintained, it can be operated several hours a day without tiring the users. Each treadle pump has two cylinders which are made of engineering plastic. The diameter of a cylinder is 100.5mm and the height is 280mm. The pump is capable of working up to a maximum depth of 7 meters. Operation beyond 7 meters is not recommended to preserve the integrity of the rubber components. The pump mechanism has piston and foot valve assemblies. The treadle action creates alternate strokes in the two pistons that lift the water in pulses.

F The human-powered pump can irrigate half an acre of vegetables and costs only $25 (including the expense of drilling a tube well down to the groundwater). Abdul heard about the treadle pump from a cousin and was one of the first farmers in Bangladesh to buy one. He borrowed the $25 from an uncle and easily repaid the loan four months later. During the five-month dry season, when Bangladeshis typically farm very little, Abdul used the treadle pump to grow a quarter-acre of chili peppers, tomatoes, cabbage and eggplants. He also improved the yield of one of his rice plots by irrigating it. His family ate some of the vegetables and sold the rest at the village market, earning a net profit of $100. With his new income, Abdul was able to buy rice for his family to eat, keep his two sons in school until they were 16 and set aside a little money for his daughter's dowry. When Polak visited him again in 1984, he had doubled the size of his vegetable plot and replaced the thatched roof on his house with corrugated tin. His family was raising a calf and some chickens. He told me that the treadle pump was a gift from God.

G Bangladesh is particularly well suited for the treadle pump because a huge reservoir of ground water lies just a few meters below the farmers' feet. In the early 1980s IDE initiated a campaign to market the pump, encouraging 75 small private-sector companies to manufacture the devices and several thousand village dealers and tube-well drillers to sell and install them. Over the next 12 years one and a half million farm families purchased treadle pumps, which increased the farmers' net income by a total of $150 million a year. The cost of IDE's market-creation activities was only $12 million, leveraged by the investment of $37.5 million from the farmers themselves. In contrast, the expense of building a conventional dam and canal system to irrigate an equivalent area of farmland would be in the range of $2, 000 per acre, or $1.5 billion.

Questions 1-6

Do the following statements agree with the information given in Reading Passage 1?

*In boxes **1-6** on your answer sheet, write*

TRUE *if the statement agrees with the information*

FALSE *if the statement contradicts the information*

NOT GIVEN *if there is no information*

1. It is more effective to resolve poverty or food problem in large scale rather than in small scale.
2. Construction of gigantic dams costs more time in developing countries.
3. Green revolution failed to increase global crop production from the mid of 20th century.
4. Agricultural production in Bangladesh declined in last decade.
5. Farmer Abdul Rahman knew how to increase production himself.
6. The small pump spread into a big project in Bangladesh in the past decade.

Questions 7-10

Filling the blanks in diagram of treadle pump's each parts.

*Choose **NO MORE THAN THREE WORDS AND/OR A NUMBER** from the passage for each answer.*

*Write your answers in boxes **7-10** on your answer sheet.*

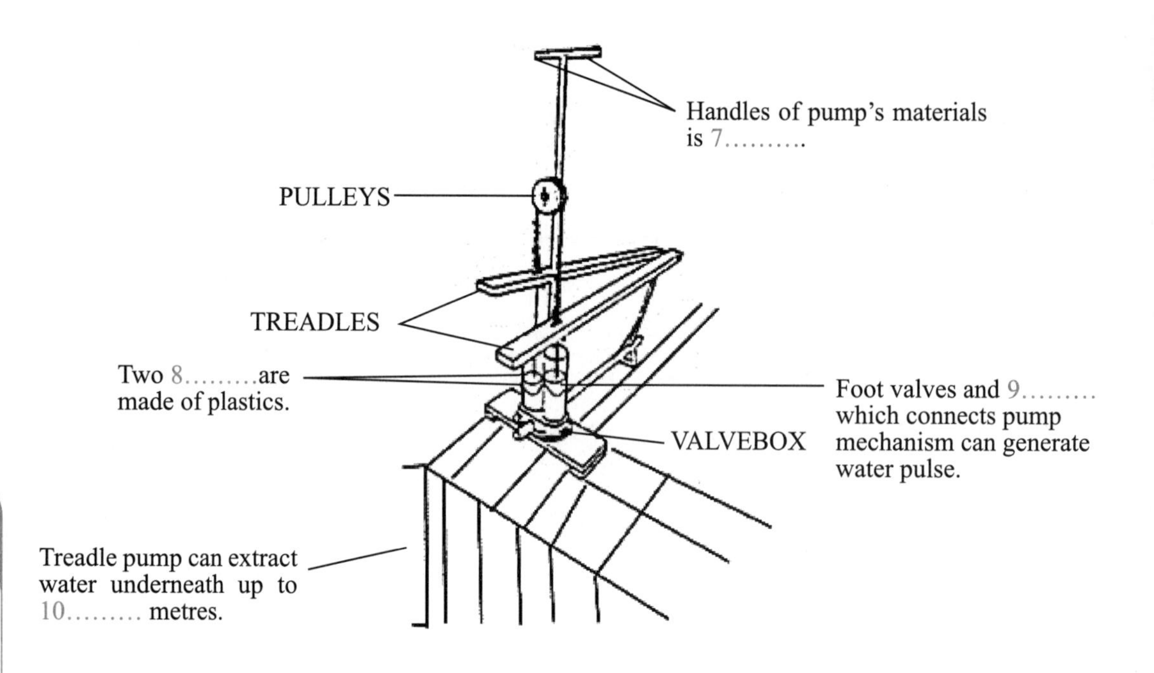

Questions 11-13

Answer the questions below.

*Choose **NO MORE THAN THREE WORDS AND/OR A NUMBER** from the passage for each answer.*

*Write your answers in boxes **11-13** on your answer sheet.*

11. What size of area can a treadle pump irrigate at a low level of expense?

12. What is Abdul's new roof made of?

13. How much did farmers in Bangladesh invest due to IDE's initiatives?

READING PASSAGE 2

The Secret of The Yawn

A When a scientist began to study yawning in the 1980s, it was difficult to convince some of his research students of the merits of "yawning science". Although it may appear quirky, his decision to study yawning was a logical extension to human beings of his research in developmental neuroscience, reported in such papers as "Wing-flapping during Development and Evolution". As a neurobehavioral problem, there is not much difference between the wing-flapping of birds and the face-and body-flapping of human yawners.

B Yawning is an ancient, primitive act. Humans do it even before they are born, opening wide in the womb. Some snakes unhinge their jaws to do it. One species of penguins yawns as part of mating. Only now are researchers beginning to understand why we yawn, when we yawn and why we yawn back. A professor of cognitive neuroscience at Drexel University in Philadelphia, Steven Platek, studies the act of contagious yawning, something done only by people and other primates.

C In his first experiment, he used a psychological test to rank people on their empathic feelings. He found that participants who did not score high on compassion did not yawn back. "We literally had people saying, 'Why am I looking at people yawning?'" Professor Platek said. "It just had no effect."

D For his second experiment, he put 10 students in a magnetic resonance imaging machine as they watched video tapes of people yawning. When the students watched the videos, the part of the brain which reacted was the part scientists believe controls empathy—the posterior cingulate, in the brain's middle rear. "I don't know if it's necessarily that nice people yawn more, but I think it's a good indicator of a state of mind," said Professor Platek. "It's also a good indicator if you're empathizing with me and paying attention."

E His third experiment is studying yawning in those with brain disorders, such as autism and schizophrenia, in which victims have difficulty connecting emotionally with others. A psychology professor at the University of Maryland, Robert Provine, is one of the few other researchers into yawning. He found the basic yawn lasts about six seconds and they come in bouts with an interval of about 68 seconds. Men and women yawn or half-yawn equally often, but men are significantly less likely to cover their mouths which may indicate complex distinction in genders. "A watched yawner never yawns," Professor Provine said. However, the physical root of yawning remains a mystery. Some researchers say it's coordinated within the hypothalamus of the brain, the area that also controls breathing.

F Yawning and stretching also share properties and may be performed together as parts of a global motor complex. But they do not always co-occur—people usually yawn when we stretch, but we don't always stretch when we yawn, especially before bedtime. Studies by J.I.P, G.H.A. Visser and H.F. Prechtl in the early 1980s, charting movement in the developing fetus using ultrasound, observed not just yawning but a link between yawning and stretching as early as the end of the first prenatal trimester.

G The most extraordinary demonstration of the yawn-stretch linkage occurs in many people paralyzed on one side of their body because of brain damage caused by a stroke. The prominent British neurologist Sir Francis Walshe noted in 1923 that when these hemiplegics yawn, they are startled and mystified to observe that their otherwise paralyzed arm rises and flexes automatically in what neurologists term an "associated response". Yawning apparently activates undamaged, unconsciously controlled connections between the brain and the cord motor system innervating the paralyzed limb. It is not known whether the associated response is a positive prognosis for recovery, nor whether yawning is therapeutic for reinnervation or prevention of muscular atrophy.

H Clinical neurology offers other surprises. Some patients with "locked-in" syndrome, who are almost totally deprived of the ability to move voluntarily, can yawn normally. The neural circuits for spontaneous yawning must exist in the brain stem near other respiratory and vasomotor centers, because yawning is performed by anencephalic who possess only the medulla oblongata. The multiplicity of stimuli of contagious yawning, by contrast, implicates many higher brain regions.

Questions 14-18

Complete the summary paragraph described below.

*In boxes **14-18** on your answer sheet, write the correct answer with NO MORE THAN THREE WORDS.*

A psychology professor obseved that it takes about six seconds to complete an average yawning, and it takes 14..........before the next one occurs. Men and women yawn or half-yawn with similar frequency, but behavior accompanied with their yawning shows a 15..........in genders. While the exact cause of yawning remains uncertain, some researchers believe it is coordinated in the area of the brain that also manages 16..........Another finding is that, even before a baby was born, there is already a link between yawning and 17..........The connection is there even among people whose 18..........is damaged.

Questions 19-23

Reading Passage 2 has eight paragraphs, **A-H.**

Which paragraph contains the following information?

*Write the correct letter, **A-H**, in boxes **19-23** on your answer sheet.*

19. The rate for yawning shows some regular pattern.
20. Yawning is an inherent ability that appears in both animals and humans.
21. Stretching and yawning are not always going together.
22. Yawning may suggest people are having positive notice or response in communicating.
23. Some superior areas in brain may deal with the infectious feature of yawning.

Questions 24-26

Do the following statements agree with the information given in Reading Passage 2?

*In boxes **24-26** on your answer sheet, write*

TRUE *if the statement is true*

FALSE *if the statement is false*

NOT GIVEN *if the information is not given in the passage*

24. Several students in Platek's experiment did not comprehend why their tutor ask them to yawn back.
25. Some results from certain experiment indicate the link between yawning and compassion.
26. Yawning can show an affirmative impact on the recovery from brain damage brought by a stroke.

READING PASSAGE 3

Thomas Harriot—The Discovery of Refraction

A When light travels from one medium to another, it generally bends, or refracts. The law of refraction gives us a way of predicting the amount of bending. Refraction has many applications in optics and technology. A lens uses refraction to form an image of an object for many different purposes, such as magnification. A prism uses refraction to form a spectrum of colors from an incident beam of light. Refraction also plays an important role in the formation of a mirage and other optical illusions. The law of refraction is also known as Snell's Law, named after Willbrord Snell, who discovered the law in 1621. Although Snell's sine law of refraction is now taught routinely in undergraduate courses, the quest for it spanned many centuries and involved many celebrated scientists. Perhaps the most interesting thing is that the first discovery of the sine law, made by the sixteenth-century English scientist Thomas Harriot (1560-1621), has been almost completely overlooked by physicists, despite much published material describing his contribution.

B A contemporary of Shakespeare, Elizabeth I, Johannes Kepler and Galilei Galileo, Thomas Harriot (1560-1621) was an English scientist and mathematician. His principal biographer, J. W. Shirley, was quoted saying that in his time he was "England's most profound mathematician, most imaginative and methodical experimental scientist". As a mathematician, he contributed to the development of algebra, and introduced the symbols of ">" and "<" for "more than" and "less than." He also studied navigation and astronomy. On September 17, 1607, Harriot observed a comet, later identified as Hailey-s. With his painstaking observations, later workers were able to compute the comer's orbit. Harriot was also the first to use a telescope to observe the heavens in England. He made sketches of the moon in 1609, and then developed lenses of increasing magnification. By April 1611, he had developed a lens with a magnification of 32. Between October 17, 1610 and February 26, 1612, he observed the moons of Jupiter, which had already discovered by Galileo. While observing Jupiter's moons, he made a discovery of his own: sunspots, which he viewed 199 times between December 8, 1610 and January 18, 1613. These observations allowed him to figure out the sun's period of rotation.

C He was also an early English explorer of North America. He was a friend of the English courtier and explorer Sir Walter Raleigh, and travelled to Virginia as a scientific observer on a colonising expedition in 1585. On June 30, 1585, his ship anchored at Roanoke Island, off Virginia. On shore, Harriot observed the topography, flora and fauna, made many drawings and maps, and met the native people who spoke a language the English called Algonquian. Harriot worked out a phonetic transcription of the native people's speech sounds and began to learn the language, which enabled him to converse to some extent with other natives the English encountered. Harriot wrote his report for Raleigh and published it as *A Briefe and True Report of the New Found Land of Virginia* in 1588. Raleigh gave Harriot his own estate in Ireland, and Harriot began a survey of Raleigh's Irish holdings. He also undertook a study of ballistics and ship design for Raleigh in advance of the Spanish Armada's arrival.

D Harriot kept regular correspondence with other scientists and mathematicians, especially in England but also in mainland Europe, notably with Johannes Kepler. About twenty years before Snell's discovery, Johannes Kepler (1571-1630) had also looked for the law of refraction, but used the early data of Ptolemy. Unfortunately, Ptolemy's data was in error, so Kepler could obtain only an approximation which he published in 1604. Kepler later tried to obtain additional experimental results on refraction, and corresponded with Thomas Harriot from 1606 to 1609 since Kepler had heard Harriot had carried out some detailed experiments. In 1606, Harriot sent Kepler some tables of refraction data for different materials at a constant incident angle, but didn't provide enough detail for the data to be very useful. Kepler requested further information, but Harriot was not forthcoming, and it appears that Kepler eventually gave up the correspondence, frustrated with Harriot's reluctance.

E Apart from the correspondence with Kepler, there is no evidence that Harriot ever published his detailed results on refraction. His personal notes, however, reveal extensive studies significantly predating those of Kepler, Snell and Descartes. Harriot carried out many experiments on refraction in the 1590s, and from his notes it is clear that he had discovered the sine law at least as early as 1602. Around 1606, he had studied dispersion in prisms (predating Newton by around 60 years), measured the refractive indices of different liquids placed in a hollow glass prism, studied refraction in crystal spheres, and correctly understood refraction in the rainbow before Descartes.

F As his studies of refraction, Harriot's discoveries in other fields were largely unpublished during his lifetime, and until this century, Harriot was known only for an account of his travels in Virginia published in 1588, and for a treatise on algebra published posthumously in 1631. The reason why Harriot kept his results unpublished is unclear. Harriot wrote to Kepler that poor health prevented him from providing more information, but it is also possible that he was afraid of the sevententh century's English religious establishment which was suspicious of the work carried out by mathematicians and scientists.

G After the discovery of sunspots, Harriot's scientific work dwindled. The cause of his diminished productivity might have been a cancer discovered on his nose. Hariot died on July 2, 1621, in London, but his story did not end with his death. Recent research has revealed his wide range of interests and his genuinely original discoveries. What some writers describe as his "thousands upon thousands of sheets of mathematics and of scientific observations" appeared to be lost until 1784, when they were found in Henry Percy's country estate by one of Percy's descendants. She gave them to Franz Xaver Zach, her husband's son's tutor. Zach eventually put some of the papers in the hands of the Oxford University Press, but much work was required to prepare them for publication, and it has never been done. Scholars have begun to study them, and an appreciation of Harriot's contribution started to grow in the second half of the twentieth century. Harriot's study of refraction is but one example where his work overlapped with independent studies carried out by others in Europe, but in any historical treatment of optics his contribution rightfully deserves to be acknowledged.

Questions 27-31

Reading Passage 3 has seven paragraphs, **A-G**.

*Choose the correct heading for paragraphs **B-D** and **F-G** from the list below.*

*Write the correct number, **ii-x**, in boxes **27-31** on your answer sheet.*

List of Headings

i.	A misunderstanding in the history of science
ii.	Thomas Harriot's biography
iii.	Unknown reasons for his unpublished works
iv.	Harriot's 1588 publication on North America studies
v.	Expedition to the New World
vi.	Reluctant cooperation with Kepler
vii.	Belated appreciation of Harriot's contribution
viii.	Religious pressures keeping him from publishing
ix.	Correspondence with Kepler
x.	Interests and researches into multiple fields of study

Example Answer: Paragraph A i

27. Paragraph B

28. Paragraph C

29. Paragraph D

30. Paragraph F

31. Paragraph G

Questions 32-36

*Answer the questions below using **NO MORE THAN THREE WORDS** from the passage for each answer.*

*Write your answers in boxes **32-36** on your answer sheet.*

Various modern applications base on an image produced by lens using refraction, such as **32**........... And a spectrum of colors from a beam of light can be produced with **33**.......... Harriot travelled to Virginia and mainly did research which focused on two subjects of American **34**........... After, he also entered upon a study of flight dynamics and **35**.......... for one of his friends much ahead of major European competitors. He undertook extensive other studies which were only noted down personally yet predated many other great scientists. One result, for example, corrected the misconception about the idea of **36**.........

Questions 37-40

*Look at the following researchers (listed **A-E**) and findings.*

Match each researcher with the correct finding.

*Write your answers in boxes **37-40** on your answer sheet.*

***NB** You may use any letter more than once.*

A. Willobrord Snell
B. Johannes Kepler
C. Ptolemy
D. Galileo
E. Harriot

37. discovered the moons of Jupiter
38. distracted by experimental calculation on refraction
39. the discovery of sunspots
40. the person whose name the snell's Law was attributed to

READING

02

Section 2

逐题精讲

READING

TEST 1 解析

READING PASSAGE 1

Undersea Movement

文章结构

体裁	说明文
题材	生物类
主题	鱼如何在水下运动
段落概括	A 段：水下运动具有很大的挑战，这导致水下动物们采用不同的方式来运动。 B 段：鱼的骨骼功能。 C 段：鱼的肌肉是如何提供动能的。 D 段：两种类型肌肉的不同功能。 E 段：鱼鳍的功能。 F 段：不同位置的鱼鳍用途不同。 G 段：根据鱼的游泳速度对其进行分类。 H 段：鱼的大小和游泳能力之间的关联。

重点词汇

A 段							
单词	音标	词性	释义	单词	音标	词性	释义
challenge	[ˈtʃælɪndʒ]	*n.*	挑战，难题	aquatic	[əˈkwætɪk]	*adj.*	水生的，水栖的
a variety of		*phr.*	各种各样的	method	[ˈmeθəd]	*n.*	方法
B 段							
单词	音标	词性	释义	单词	音标	词性	释义
skeleton	[ˈskelɪtn]	*n.*	骨骼，骨架	function	[ˈfʌŋkʃn]	*n.*	功能，职责
aid	[eɪd]	*v.*	帮助，援助	skull	[skʌl]	*n.*	颅骨，头骨
spine	[spaɪn]	*n.*	脊椎，脊柱	vertebrae	[ˈvɜːtɪbriː]	*n.*	椎骨，脊椎

C 段							
单词	音标	词性	释义	单词	音标	词性	释义
muscle	[ˈmʌsl]	*n.*	肌肉	contract	[kənˈtrækt]	*v.*	收缩
frequency	[ˈfriːkwənsi]	*n.*	出现次数，频率	vary	[ˈveəri]	*v.*	（使）呈现差异；（根据情况）变化
pronounced	[prəˈnaʊnst]	*adj.*	明显的，显著的	perceptible	[pəˈseptəbl]	*adj.*	可察觉的，可感知的

D 段							
单词	音标	词性	释义	单词	音标	词性	释义
bulk	[bʌlk]	*n.*	主体，大部分	be composed of		*phr.*	由……组成
ample	[ˈæmpl]	*adj.*	充足的，充裕的	storage	[ˈstɔːrɪdʒ]	*n.*	储存，贮藏
threaten	[ˈθretn]	*v.*	威胁，恐吓				

E 段							
单词	音标	词性	释义	单词	音标	词性	释义
fin	[fɪn]	*n.*	鳍	distinctive	[dɪˈstɪŋktɪv]	*adj.*	独特的，与众不同的
feature	[ˈfiːtʃə(r)]	*n.*	特点，特征	serve as		*phr.*	起……作用，充当
emphasize	[ˈemfəsaɪz]	*v.*	强调，着重	stability	[stəˈbɪləti]	*n.*	稳定（性）

F 段							
单词	音标	词性	释义	单词	音标	词性	释义
forward	[ˈfɔːwəd]	*adv.*	向前	thrust	[θrʌst]	*n.*	猛推；（飞机、火箭等的）驱动力
be responsible for		*phr.*	对……负责				

G 段							
单词	音标	词性	释义	单词	音标	词性	释义
aquaria	[əˈkweəriːə]	*n.*	水族馆，养鱼池	accurate	[ˈækjərət]	*adj.*	精确的，准确的
measurement	[ˈmeʒəmənt]	*n.*	测量	various	[ˈveəriəs]	*adj.*	各种各样的
distance	[ˈdɪstəns]	*n.*	距离	determine	[dɪˈtɜːmɪn]	*v.*	决定，查明
performance	[pəˈfɔːməns]	*n.*	表演，表现	categorise	[ˈkætəgəraɪz]	*v.*	将……分类

H 段							
单词	音标	词性	释义	单词	音标	词性	释义
consider	[kənˈsɪdə(r)]	*v.*	考虑，认为	species	[ˈspiːʃiːz]	*n.*	物种，种类
excess	[ɪkˈses]	*n.*	超过，过量	capability	[ˌkeɪpəˈbɪləti]	*n.*	能力，才能

题目精解

Questions 1-6

题型：段落信息配对题

解析：段落信息配对题属于乱序题，考查的是题干中每句话对应原文的段落出处，考生在寻找答案时必须先精读所有题干，再回到原文逐段寻找；此类题目的定位非常分散，且多为同义替换，因此难度系数较大。

Question 1

题干定位词 / 关键词	categorizations; swimming speed
原文定位	G 段第三、四句 Many people have attempted to make accurate measurements of the speed at which various fish swim, either by timing them over known distances in their natural environment or by determining their performance in man-made swimming channels. From these studies, we can broadly categorise fish into four groups...
题目解析	题干：根据鱼的游泳速度对其进行分类。 本题的关键词一个是 categorizations（分类），另一个是 swimming speed。G 段第三句说许多人试图精确测量各种鱼类的游泳速度，方法或是计算这些鱼在自然环境中游过特定距离需要的时间，或是测定它们在人造游泳通道中的表现，紧接着下一句说根据这些研究，我们可以把鱼分成四类。categorise 正好对应定位词 categorizations。
答案	G

Question 2

题干定位词 / 关键词	an example of fish; fast swimming; for a long time
原文定位	H 段第一句 One type of sailfish is considered to be the fastest species of fish over short distances, achieving 68 mph over a three-second period, and anglers have recorded speeds in excess of 40 mph over longer periods for several species of tuna.
题目解析	题干：一个能够长时间保持快速游动的鱼的例子。 H 段第一句的前半句提到旗鱼（sailfish）在较短的距离内游得很快，紧接着 and 连接的后半句提到垂钓者记录的几种金枪鱼（tuna）在较长时间内（over longer periods）的速度超过每小时 40 英里，正好对应题干。
答案	H

Question 3

题干定位词 / 关键词	control stability
原文定位	E 段最后一句 Their main function is to control the stability and direction of the fish: as water passes over its body, a fish uses its fins to thrust in the direction it wishes to go.
题目解析	题干：鱼是如何保持稳定的。 E 段第一句首先介绍鳍（fins）是鱼类最独特的特征。第二句提到鱼鳍的一个常用功能是辅助鱼游动。最后一句说它们（指鱼鳍）的主要功能是控制鱼的稳定和方向，这就解答了题干的问题，即鱼是通过鱼鳍来保持稳定的。
答案	E

Question 4

题干定位词 / 关键词	frequency; muscle movement
原文定位	C 段第四至六句 The muscles on each side of the spine contract in a series from head to tail and down each side alternately, causing a wave-like movement to pass down the body. Such a movement may be very pronounced in fish such as eels, but hardly perceptible in others, e.g. mackerel. The frequency of the waves varies from about 50/min in the dogfish to 170/min in the mackerel.
题目解析	题干：鱼的肌肉运动的频率。 题干问的是频率，故答案应对应数字。首先 C 段第一句就提到鱼的肌肉提供动能，由此可知本段和肌肉有关。接着往下读，第四句提到脊柱两侧的肌肉从头部到尾部依次向下交替收缩，然后交替向两侧收缩，使身体像波浪般移动。第六句提到这种波动的频率（也就是肌肉运动的频率）是 50 ～ 170/min，所以 C 段包含了这些信息。
答案	C

Question 5

题干定位词 / 关键词	a mechanical model; skeleton
原文定位	B 段 Fish rely on their skeleton, fins, and muscles to move. The primary function of the skeleton is to aid movement of other parts. Their skull acts as a fulcrum and their vertebrae act as levers. The vertebral column consists of a series of vertebrae held together by ligaments, but not so tightly as to prevent slight sideways movement between each pair of vertebrae. The whole spine is, therefore, flexible. The skull is the only truly fixed part of a fish. It does not move in and off itself but acts as a point of stability for other bones. These other bones act as levers that cause movement of the fish's body.
题目解析	题干：鱼骨骼的力学模型。 B 段第一句说鱼类依靠骨骼、鳍和肌肉运动。第二句说骨骼的主要功能是辅助其他部位运动。后面具体介绍骨骼的构造和各类骨头的功能，如第三句说头骨起到支点的作用，脊椎则充当杠杆，随后开始具体讲解这个构造，也就是鱼骨骼的力学模型。由此可知，答案为 B 段。
答案	B

Question 6

题干定位词 / 关键词	energy storage devices
原文定位	D 段第三、四句 The red muscle receives a good supply of blood and contains ampler quantities of fat and glycogen, the storage form of glucose, which is used for most day-to-day swimming movements. In contrast, the white muscle has a poor blood supply and few energy stores, and it is used largely for short-term, fast swimming.
题目解析	题干：鱼体内的能量储存装置。 D 段第三句提到红肌能接收良好的血液供应，并含有大量的脂肪和糖原，即葡萄糖的储存形式，可用于大多数的日常游泳运动。一开始考生可能无法把葡萄糖和能量联系在一起，但是后面提到用于大多数的日常游泳运动，据此可以肯定该段和能量有关。后文提到白肌的血液供应差，能量储存也少，主要用于短时间的快速游动，该句也和能量储存有关，所以可以肯定答案是 D 段。
答案	D

Questions 7-10

题型：图表填空题

解析：图表填空题需要考生在审题的时候注意空格前后的词，明确定位的目标，要思考所填单词的词性、含义以及与前后单词的逻辑关系；空格所指的图片信息可以用来辅助理解和确定定位信息；与其他填空题一样，考生需要注意所填单词的字数限制。

Question 7

题干定位词 / 关键词	tail fin
原文定位	F 段第二句 The tail fin, in its final lash, may contribute as much as 40 percent of the forward thrust.
题目解析	题干：鱼的尾鳍，提供部分的 ________。 利用 tail fin 定位，F 段第一句主旨句提到鱼身上不同位置的鳍有不同的用途，据此可以判断图表填空题从 F 段开始出题。本段第二句提到 tail fin 在它最后的甩尾中可以贡献多达 40% 的 forward thrust（向前推力），也就是提供部分的 forward thrust，40% 对应 part of。
答案	forward thrust

Question 8

题干定位词 / 关键词	dorsal fin; movements
原文定位	F 段第三句 The median fins, that is, the dorsal, anal and ventral fins, control the rolling and yawing movements of the fish by increasing the vertical surface area presented to the water.
题目解析	题干：背鳍，________ 运动。 用 dorsal fin 定位到 F 段第三句，该句提到中间鳍，即背鳍、臀鳍和腹鳍，控制鱼的滚动和偏航运动（rolling and yawing movements），by 引出通过什么方式，所以答案就是 rolling and yawing。
答案	rolling and yawing

TEST 1 解析

Question 9

题干定位词 / 关键词	fins; pushing up and down
原文定位	F 段第四句 The paired fins, pectoral and pelvic, act as hydroplanes and control the pitch of the fish, causing it to swim downwards or upwards according to the angle to the water at which they are held by their muscles.
题目解析	题干：________ 鳍，推动向上和向下。 F 段第四句提到偶鳍，即胸鳍和腹鳍，充当水平舵，控制鱼的俯仰，使它向下或向上游动，也就是说，pectoral and pelvic (paired fins) 推动鱼上下游动。
答案	pectoral and pelvic/paired

Question 10

题干定位词 / 关键词	paired fins
原文定位	F 段第六句 The paired fins are also the means by which the fish slows down and stops.
题目解析	题干：偶鳍，也用于 ________ 运动。 用 paired fins 定位到 F 段最后一句，该句提到它们也是鱼减速并且停下来的手段，也就是说，paired fins 也可以用于 slows and stops 这两个动作。
答案	slows and stops

Questions 11-13

题型：摘要填空题

解析：摘要填空题通常为文中一个段落或几个段落的概括或总结。首先，考生需要通过空格前后的信息定位到文章中的某个句子，然后根据句意选取文中的某个原词作为答案。

Question 11

题干定位词 / 关键词	the majority of a fish’s body; red muscle
原文定位	D 段第二句 The bulk of a fish’s body is composed of the so-called white muscle, while the much smaller areas at the roots of the fins and in a strip along the centre of each flank comprise red muscle.
题目解析	题干：鱼类游泳时涉及两种类型的肌肉。鱼身体的大部分由 _____ 组成，红肌只长在鳍的根部，沿着两侧的肋腹呈带状分布。 D 段第一句说参与游泳的肌肉有两类，由此可以判断第 11 题的出题位置在 D 段。该段第二句说鱼身体的大部分是由所谓的白肌组成的，其中 bulk（大部分）对应题干中的 the majority，所以答案就是 white muscle。
答案	white muscle

Question 12

题干定位词 / 关键词	routine movements; saved in body
原文定位	D 段第三句 The red muscle receives a good supply of blood and contains ampler quantities of fat and glycogen, the storage form of glucose, which is used for most day-to-day swimming movements.
题目解析	题干：对于大部分的日常运动，鱼使用很多储存在身体里的 ______。 由于 routine movements 对应 day-to-day swimming movements，故可定位到 D 段第三句，答案应为储存在身体里的某种东西。第三句提到红肌能接收良好的血液供应，并含有大量的脂肪和糖原，这是葡萄糖的储存形式，可用于日常游泳运动，由此可知，鱼使用了很多脂肪和糖原。有的考生可能会填 glucose 这个词，但是要注意 the storage form of glucose 是前面 glycogen 的同位语，只是起解释说明的作用。
答案	fat and glycogen

Question 13

题干定位词 / 关键词	short-term, fast swimming; escaping from
原文定位	D 段第四句至本段结束 In contrast, the white muscle has a poor blood supply and few energy stores, and it is used largely for short-term, fast swimming. It might seem odd that the body of an animal which adapts so efficiently to its environment should be composed almost entirely of a type of muscle it rarely uses. However, this huge auxiliary power pack carried by a fish is of crucial significance if the life of the fish is threatened by a predator, for instance, because it enables the fish to swim rapidly away from danger.
题目解析	题干：白肌主要用于短期的快速游动，例如逃离 ______。 本题的定位点有两个：一个是白肌的功能，另一个是“逃离 ______”。D 段第四句提到白肌主要用于短期的快速游动，但没有提到逃离什么，需要继续往下阅读，最后一句说“然而，如果鱼的生命受到威胁，例如，受到捕食者的威胁，鱼身上的这个巨大的辅助能量包就具有至关重要的意义，因为它能使鱼迅速游离危险”。也就是说，逃离捕食者（a predator）或者危险（danger），填这两个答案都可以。
答案	a predator/danger

长难句分析

D 段：However, this huge auxiliary power pack carried by a fish is of crucial significance if the life of the fish is threatened by a predator, for instance, because it enables the fish to swim rapidly away from danger.

思路分析：本句的重点是把握句子的主语和谓语，以及逻辑关系词。这个句子的主语是 this huge auxiliary power pack，动词是 is，而 carried by a fish 是分词作定语，修饰前面的主语，即鱼携带的巨大的辅助能量包，of crucial significance 作表语；逻辑关系词有 if（引导条件状语从句）和 because（引出原因）。

参考翻译：然而，如果鱼的生命受到威胁，例如，受到捕食者的威胁，鱼身上的这个巨大的辅助能量包就具有至关重要的意义，因为它能使鱼迅速游离危险。

E 段：But it must be emphasized that the swimming movements are produced by the whole of the muscular body, and in only a few fish do the fins contribute any propulsive force!

思路分析：it 在本句中作形式主语，真正的主语是 that 引导的名词性从句；另外，后半句为了表示强调，把介词短语 in only a few fish 提前了，句子要部分倒装，所以助动词 do 提前到了主语 the fins 前。

参考翻译：但必须强调的是，游动的动作是由整个肌肉发达的身体完成的，只有少数鱼类的鳍能提供推进力！

参考译文

海底运动

A 海底世界面临很多挑战。其中最基本的挑战就是运动。水的密度使动物很难移动。向前的运动是各种水下力量的复杂相互作用的结果。此外，水本身也在运动。强劲的水流携带着不可思议的力量，可以轻易地将生物卷走。水的运动带来的挑战导致动物使用的游泳方式各式各样。结果呈现出一场令人眼花缭乱的水下芭蕾表演。

B 鱼类依靠骨骼、鳍和肌肉运动。骨骼的主要功能是辅助其他部位运动。它们的头骨起到支点的作用，脊椎则充当杠杆。脊柱由一系列由韧带连接在一起的脊椎骨组成，但这些脊椎骨不会太过紧密，以防止每对脊椎骨之间的微小侧向移动。因此，整个脊柱都是灵活的。头骨是鱼类唯一真正固定的部位。它本身不移动，而是作为其他骨头的稳定点。这些其他的骨头就像杠杆一样，能引起鱼身体的运动。

C 鱼的骨骼使鱼能够运动，而肌肉则提供了动能。一条鱼全身通常有数百块向各个方向伸展的肌肉。这就是鱼可以快速转动、扭转和改变方向的原因。脊柱两侧的肌肉从头部到尾部依次向下交替收缩，然后交替向两侧收缩，导致身体像波浪般移动。这种运动在鳗鱼等鱼类中可能非常明显，但在其他鱼类（如鲭鱼）中却很难察觉。波动的频率从角鲨的每分钟约 50 次到鲭鱼的每分钟 170 次不等。鱼的头部和身体对水的侧向和向后推力产生了水的阻力，进而将鱼推向与推力方向相反的侧面和前方。当另一侧相应的一组肌肉收缩时，鱼会在另一侧经历类似的水力作用。这两个侧向的力是相等且相反的，除非鱼在转弯，否则这两个力就可以相互抵消，只剩下两个向前的合力。

D 参与游泳的肌肉主要有两种类型。鱼身体的大部分是由所谓的白肌组成的，而鳍根部以及两侧肋腹间的狭长地带的小得多的区域则由红肌组成。红肌能接收良好的血液供应，并含有大量的脂肪和糖原，即葡萄糖的储存形式，可用于大多数的日常游泳运动。相比之下，白肌的血液供应较差，能量储存较少，主要用于短期的快速游动。一种能如此高效地适应环境的动物，其身体却几乎完全由一种它很少用到的肌肉组成，这似乎有些奇怪。然而，如果鱼的生命受到威胁，例如，受到捕食者的威胁，鱼身上的这个巨大的辅助能量包就具有至关重要的意义，因为它能使鱼迅速游离危险。

E 鳍是鱼类最独特的特征，由从身体突出的骨刺组成，有皮肤包裹并将它们连接在一起。它们要么像大多数硬骨鱼那样呈蹼状，要么像鲨鱼那样更类似于鳍状肢。它们通常充当一种鱼游泳的手段。但必须强调的是，游动的动作是由整个肌肉发达的身体完成的，只有少数鱼类的鳍能提供推进力！鱼鳍的主要功能是控制鱼的稳定和方向：当水经过鱼的身体时，鱼就用它的鳍朝着它想去的方向推进。

F 鱼身上不同位置的鳍有不同的用途，例如向前移动、转弯和保持直立。尾鳍，在它最后一下摆动的过程中，可以贡献多达 40% 的向前推力。中间鳍，即背鳍、臀鳍和腹鳍，通过增加呈现在水中的垂直表面积来控制鱼的滚动和偏航运动。偶鳍，即胸鳍和腹鳍，充当水平舵，控制鱼的俯仰，使鱼根据肌肉所控制的与水的角度向下或向上游动。胸鳍位于重心的前面，易于移动，主要负责将鱼向上或向下移动。偶鳍也是鱼减速并且停下来的手段。

G 鱼的游泳速度并不如人们在水族馆或池塘里看到它们快速移动时所想的那么快。金枪鱼似乎游得最快，能达到每小时 44 英里，鳟鱼的记录是每小时 23 英里，梭子鱼能短暂地游到每小时 20 英里，拟鲤大约为每小时 10 英里，而大多数小鱼可能不超过每小时 2 或 3 英里。许多人试图精确测量各种鱼类的游泳速度，他们或是计算这些鱼在自然环境中游过特定距离需要的时间，或是测定它们在人造游泳通道中的表现。从这些研究中，我们可以大致将鱼类分为四类："潜行者"，例如鳗鱼，它们只能以较慢的速度游泳，但具有一定的耐力；"耐力者"，可以在很长一段时间内游得很快；"短跑者"，可以产生快速爆发的速度（如梭子鱼）；以及缓慢游泳的"爬行者"，尽管它们可以轻微加速（如鲷鱼）。

H 有一种旗鱼被认为是短距离内速度最快的鱼类，它在 3 秒内可以达到每小时 68 英里，而垂钓者记录的几种金枪鱼在较长时间内的速度超过了每小时 40 英里。人们可能会认为鱼的游泳能力与它的大小有关。然而，通常情况下，体型小的鱼比体型大的鱼游泳能力更强。另一方面，就每小时英里的速度而言，在所有其他条件相同的情况下，大鱼会比小鱼游得快。

READING PASSAGE 2

Coral Reefs

文章结构

体裁	说明文
题材	生物和环境
主题	珊瑚礁带来的好处以及所面临的危害
段落概括	A 段：珊瑚礁的分布。 B 段：珊瑚礁对全球的经济价值。 C 段：珊瑚礁对当地经济的价值。 D 段：珊瑚礁面临的各种危险。 E 段：旅游业对珊瑚礁造成的危害。 F 段：科学家分析影响珊瑚礁的因素。 G 段：澳大利亚的保护方案。

重点词汇

A 段							
单词	音标	词性	释义	单词	音标	词性	释义
coral reef		*phr.*	珊瑚礁	cover	[ˈkʌvə(r)]	*v.*	覆盖，遮盖；涉及
account for		*phr.*	占比	marine	[məˈriːn]	*adj.*	海洋的，海产的
species	[ˈspiːʃiːz]	*n.*	物种，种类	flourish	[ˈflʌrɪʃ]	*v.*	繁荣；(植物或动物) 长势好
B 段							
单词	音标	词性	释义	单词	音标	词性	释义
ecosystem	[ˈiːkəʊsɪstəm]	*n.*	生态系统	tourism	[ˈtʊərɪzəm]	*n.*	旅游业
fishery	[ˈfɪʃəri]	*n.*	渔业；渔场	economic	[ˌiːkəˈnɒmɪk]	*adj.*	经济的，经济学的
estimate	[ˈestɪmeɪt]	*v.*	估计，判断，评价				

C 段							
单词	音标	词性	释义	单词	音标	词性	释义
biodiverse	[ˌbaɪəʊdaɪˈvɜːs]	*adj.*	生物多样的	region	[ˈriːdʒən]	*n.*	地区，区域
worth	[wɜːθ]	*adj.*	价值……的，值得的	intact	[ɪnˈtækt]	*adj.*	完好无损的
reserve	[rɪˈzɜːv]	*n.*	储备（量）；保护区	tourist	[ˈtʊərɪst]	*n.*	旅行者，观光客
employment	[ɪmˈplɔɪmənt]	*n.*	雇用；工作，就业	livelihood	[ˈlaɪvlihʊd]	*n.*	生计，营生
generate	[ˈdʒenəreɪt]	*v.*	产生，引起				

D 段							
单词	音标	词性	释义	单词	音标	词性	释义
unfortunately	[ʌnˈfɔːtʃənətli]	*adv.*	不幸地，遗憾地	localize	[ˈləʊkəlaɪz]	*v.*	使地方化；使局部化
threat	[θret]	*n.*	威胁，恐吓	greenhouse gas		*phr.*	温室气体
emission	[ɪˈmɪʃn]	*n.*	排放（物）	practice	[ˈpræktɪs]	*n.*	实践，做法
destructive	[dɪˈstrʌktɪv]	*adj.*	破坏性的，毁灭性的	unsustainable	[ˌʌnsəˈsteɪnəbl]	*adj.*	破坏生态平衡的，不可持续的
overfishing	[ˌəʊvəˈfɪʃɪŋ]	*n.*	过度捕捞	degradation	[ˌdegrəˈdeɪʃn]	*n.*	损害，恶化，衰退

E 段							
单词	音标	词性	释义	单词	音标	词性	释义
tourist resort		*phr.*	观光胜地	sewage	[ˈsuːɪdʒ]	*n.*	污水，污物
contribute to		*phr.*	有助于，促成	damage	[ˈdæmɪdʒ]	*v.*	损坏，损害
grab	[græb]	*v.*	攫取，抓住	kick	[kɪk]	*v.*	踢，踢腿
sediment	[ˈsedɪmənt]	*n.*	沉淀物	harm	[hɑːm]	*v.*	危害，损害
anchor	[ˈæŋkə(r)]	*n.*	锚				

F 段							
单词	音标	词性	释义	单词	音标	词性	释义
factor	[ˈfæktə(r)]	*n.*	因素，要素	impact	[ˈɪmpækt]	*v./n.*	冲击，撞击；（对……）产生影响
carbon dioxide		*phr.*	二氧化碳	ultraviolet light		*phr.*	紫外线
ocean acidification		*phr.*	海洋酸化	virus	[ˈvaɪrəs]	*n.*	病毒

G 段							
单词	音标	词性	释义	单词	音标	词性	释义
The Great Barrier Reef		*phr.*	大堡礁	legislation	[ˌledʒɪsˈleɪʃn]	*n.*	法规，法律
inhabitant	[ɪnˈhæbɪtənt]	*n.*	居民	restrict	[rɪˈstrɪkt]	*v.*	限制，控制
lagoon	[ləˈguːn]	*n.*	环礁湖，咸水湖				

题目精解

Questions 14-19

题型：段落信息配对题

Question 14

题干定位词 / 关键词	geographical location
原文定位	A 段第一至四句 Coral reefs are estimated to cover 284,300 km² just under 0.1% of the oceans' surface area, about half the area of France. The Indo-Pacific region accounts for 91.9% of this total area. Southeast Asia accounts for 32.3% of that figure, while the Pacific including Australia accounts for 40.8%. Atlantic and Caribbean coral reefs account for 7.6%.
题目解析	题干：世界上珊瑚礁的地理位置。 A 段第一句说明珊瑚礁的覆盖面积，从第二句开始分别介绍在印太地区、东南亚地区、太平洋地区、大西洋和加勒比地区的珊瑚礁面积占比，也就是它的分布。
答案	A

Question 15

题干定位词 / 关键词	how; benefit economy locally
原文定位	C 段全段
题目解析	题干：珊瑚礁对当地经济有何益处。 C 段是总分结构。第一句提到在生物多样的地区，珊瑚礁的价值甚至更高。接着分别介绍珊瑚礁给印度尼西亚、加勒比地区、澳大利亚带来的经济利益。第六句（Further, reef tourism is an important source of employment...）提到珊瑚礁旅游带来了就业。第七句提到珊瑚礁为发展中国家渔民带来了生计，并以菲律宾为例。因此，本段提到了珊瑚礁给各个国家当地经济带来的好处。
答案	C

Question 16

题干定位词 / 关键词	statistics; coral reefs, economic significance
原文定位	C段第二句 In parts of Indonesia and the Caribbean where tourism is the main use, reefs are estimated to be worth US$1 million per square kilometer, based on the cost of maintaining sandy beaches and the value of attracting snorkelers and scuba divers.
题目解析	题干：珊瑚礁对经济重要性的数据。 本题和上一题都是关于珊瑚礁对当地的经济意义的，区别在于本题的重点在数据上（statistics），所以应到文中去找对应的数字。C段第二句提到在印度尼西亚和加勒比地区，珊瑚礁的估计价值为每平方公里100万美元，这就是珊瑚礁对经济意义的数据体现。
答案	C

Question 17

题干定位词 / 关键词	dangerous situation
原文定位	D段第一至四句 Unfortunately, coral reefs are dying around the world. In particular, coral mining, agricultural and urban runoff, pollution (organic and inorganic), disease, and the digging of canals and access into islands and bays are localized threats to coral ecosystems. Broader threats are sea temperature rise, sea level rise and pH changes from ocean acidification, all associated with greenhouse gas emissions. Some current fishing practices are destructive and unsustainable.
题目解析	题干：珊瑚礁面临的危险状况。 D段主旨句提到"不幸的是，世界各地的珊瑚礁正在死亡"。第二至四句具体说明了有哪些危险的状况，如有来自当地的威胁，包括珊瑚开采、农业和城市径流、污染、疾病、挖掘运河等；更广泛的威胁来自海洋的温度上升、海平面升高和pH值变化；另外，目前的捕鱼方法也具有破坏性。这些都是珊瑚礁面对的dangerous situation。
答案	D

Question 18

题干定位词 / 关键词	physical approach; tourists
原文定位	E 段最后两句 Whenever people grab, kick, and walk on, or stir up sediment in the reefs, they contribute to coral reef destruction. Corals are also harmed or killed when people drop anchors on them or when people collect coral.
题目解析	题干：游客对珊瑚礁的身体上的接近。 本题的重点是 physical approach（身体上的接近），E 段最后两句提到人们在珊瑚礁上抓、踢、行走、搅动沉积物，以及把锚扔在珊瑚上或者收集珊瑚，这些都是身体上的接近。
答案	E

Question 19

题干定位词 / 关键词	unsustainable fishing methods
原文定位	D 段第四、五句 Some current fishing practices are destructive and unsustainable. These include cyanide fishing, overfishing and blast fishing.
题目解析	题干：世界上一些地区使用不可持续的捕鱼方法。 本题的重点在于不可持续的捕鱼方法。D 段第四句说当前一些捕鱼方法是破坏性的，而且是不可持续的，下一句具体提到了这些方法是什么。原文中的 fishing practices 对应题干中的 fishing methods。
答案	D

Questions 20-25

题型：判断题

解析：判断题为顺序题，一般按照其在原文中出现的顺序排列，确定了第一个题目对应原文中的具体位置后，即可向后直接寻找其他题目的答案；审题时需标记定位词，通常以实义名词为主，但也要注意动词及形容词。

需要特别说明的是，NOT GIVEN 这个选项容易与 FALSE 混淆。其实该选项的判断原则在官方的说明部分已经说得很清楚了：一是 there is no information on this，即文中没有关于题干的信息；二是 it is impossible to say what the writer thinks about this，即你可以定位到答案句，但信息不足，无法进行判断。

Question 20

题干定位词 / 关键词	habitat; a variety of marine life
原文定位	A 段第六句 They provide a home for 25% of all marine species, including fish, mollusks, worms, crustaceans, echinoderms, sponges, tunicates and other cnidarians.
题目解析	题干：珊瑚礁给多种海洋生物提供了栖息地。 本题的考点在于珊瑚礁是否给多种海洋生物提供了栖息地。通过 habitat 和 marine life 可以定位到 A 段第六句：它们（珊瑚礁）为 25% 的海洋物种提供了家园，包括 fish（鱼类）、mollusks（软体动物）、worms（蠕虫）、crustaceans（甲壳类动物）、echinoderms（棘皮动物）、sponges（海绵动物）、tunicates（被囊动物）和 other cnidarians（其他刺胞动物）。由此可知，答案为 TRUE。这里 home 对应 habitat，marine species 对应 marine life。
答案	TRUE

Question 21

题干定位词 / 关键词	distribute; disproportionally
原文定位	A 段第八句到最后 They are most commonly found at shallow depths in tropical waters, but deep water and cold water corals also exist on smaller scales in other areas. Although corals exist both in temperate and tropical waters, shallow-water reefs form only in a zone extending from 30°N to 30°S of the equator. Deep water coral can exist at greater depths and colder temperatures at much higher latitudes, as far north as Norway. Coral reefs are rare along the American and African west coasts. This is due primarily to upwelling and strong cold coastal currents that reduce water temperatures in these areas (respectively the Peru, Benguela and Canary streams). Corals are seldom found along the coastline of South Asia from the eastern tip of India (Madras) to the Bangladesh and Myanmar borders. They are also rare along the coast around northeastern South America and Bangladesh due to the freshwater release from the Amazon and Ganges Rivers, respectively.
题目解析	题干：珊瑚礁在海洋中分布不均匀。 本题的考点在于珊瑚礁在海洋中的分布是否均匀。A 段第八句提到它们（珊瑚礁）最常见于热带水域的浅水处，但深水和冷水珊瑚也小规模存在于其他地区。这里已经体现“分布不均匀”了。后面还具体说了很多分布不均匀的例子，如在不同温度带分布不均匀，在美洲和非洲西海岸、南亚海岸线、南美洲东北部等也很少见等。由此可知，珊瑚礁的分布是不均匀的，答案为 TRUE。
答案	TRUE

Question 22

题干定位词 / 关键词	important; scientific purpose
原文定位	无
题目解析	题干：珊瑚礁在科学研究中越来越重要。 无法定位到原文，所以答案是 NOT GIVEN。
答案	NOT GIVEN

Question 23

题干定位词 / 关键词	exchanged; exported
原文定位	无
题目解析	题干：珊瑚礁在其他国家之间进行了大量的交换，并出口到其他国家。 无法定位到原文，所以答案是 NOT GIVEN。
答案	NOT GIVEN

Question 24

题干定位词 / 关键词	economic essence; some poor people
原文定位	C 段第六句 Further, reef tourism is an important source of employment, especially for some of the world's poorest people.
题目解析	题干：珊瑚礁旅游通常对一些穷人来说具有经济意义。 根据 poor people 定位到 C 段第六句：此外，珊瑚礁旅游是重要的就业来源，特别是对世界上一些最贫穷的人来说。通过这句话可以判断，珊瑚礁旅游对于穷人来说是有重要经济意义的，所以答案是 TRUE。
答案	TRUE

Question 25

题干定位词 / 关键词	coral fishery; women and children
原文定位	无
题目解析	题干：与其他渔业一样，珊瑚渔业不适合妇女和儿童。 无法定位到原文，所以答案是 NOT GIVEN。
答案	NOT GIVEN

Question 26

题型：单选题

解析：单选题考查的是考生在文中寻找细节信息的能力，此类题型为顺序题，可以通过题干或者选项中的某些特殊信息来确定出题段落，通常情况下，出题句是文章中的 1 ~ 2 个句子，偶尔也会遇到全文出题的题目。

Question 26

题干定位词 / 关键词	main purpose; passage
原文定位	全文
题目解析	题干：这篇文章的主要目的是什么？ A：展示了珊瑚是如何在海里生长的 B：告诉我们珊瑚礁作为一个科研项目被广泛应用 C：展示了珊瑚礁总体的好处以及面临的令人担忧的局面 D：澳大利亚为了保护珊瑚礁做出的重大努力 主旨类单选题在做完其他题以后就比较好解答了，因为至此考生已经基本了解了文章的主旨和结构。文章 A 段介绍了珊瑚礁在全球的分布，B 段、C 段介绍了珊瑚礁在经济上的好处，D 段到 F 段介绍了珊瑚礁面对的危险，G 段介绍了澳大利亚的保护措施。因此，这篇文章的重点一是珊瑚礁带来的经济利益，二是它所面对的危险，所以答案为选项 C。
答案	C

长难句分析

C 段：In parts of Indonesia and the Caribbean where tourism is the main use, reefs are estimated to be worth US$1 million per square kilometer, based on the cost of maintaining sandy beaches and the value of attracting snorkelers and scuba divers.

思路分析：这个句子包含一个由 where 引导的定语从句，修饰前面的地点；based on... 为分词状语。

参考翻译：在以旅游业为主的印度尼西亚和加勒比地区，根据维护沙滩的成本和吸引浮潜者和水肺潜水员的价值计算，珊瑚礁的估计价值为每平方公里 100 万美元。

C 段：UNEP says that of the estimated 30 million small-scale fishers in the developing world, most are dependent to a greater or lesser extent on coral reefs.

思路分析：of 在本句中表示“在……中”，这里的 of the estimated 30 million small-scale fisheries in the developing world 指的是“在发展中国家估计有 3000

万小规模渔民”。

参考翻译： 联合国环境规划署说，在发展中国家估计有3000万小规模渔民，其中大多数或多或少地依赖珊瑚礁。

参考译文

珊瑚礁

珊瑚礁是由珊瑚分泌的碳酸钙组成的水下结构。珊瑚礁是在海水中发现的含有少量营养物质的微小生物的群落。大多数珊瑚礁是由石珊瑚组成的，而石珊瑚又由成群聚集的珊瑚虫组成。

A 据估计，珊瑚礁覆盖的面积有28.43万平方公里，略低于海洋表面积的0.1%，约为法国面积的一半。印度洋－太平洋地区的珊瑚占其总面积的91.9%。其中东南亚地区占32.3%，包括澳大利亚在内的太平洋地区占40.8%。大西洋和加勒比地区的珊瑚礁占7.6%。珊瑚礁通常被称为“海洋中的热带雨林”，形成了一些地球上最多样化的生态系统。它们为25%的海洋物种提供了家园，包括鱼类、软体动物、蠕虫、甲壳类动物、棘皮动物、海绵动物、被囊动物和其他刺胞动物。然而，与珊瑚礁的繁荣相悖的是，它们周围的海水提供的营养物质却很少。虽然珊瑚礁最常见于热带水域的浅水处，但深水和冷水珊瑚也小规模存在于其他地区。虽然珊瑚在温带和热带水域都存在，但浅水珊瑚礁只在赤道南北30° 内的区域形成。深水珊瑚可以在远至挪威以北的更高纬度的更深处和更冷的温度下生存。在美洲和非洲西海岸，珊瑚礁非常罕见。这主要是由于上升流和强冷海岸流降低了这些地区（分别是秘鲁河、本格拉河和加那利河）的水温。南亚海岸线从印度东端（马德拉斯）到孟加拉国和缅甸边境沿线的珊瑚也很少见。由于亚马孙河和恒河的淡水流出，它们在南美洲东北部和孟加拉国沿岸也很罕见。

B 珊瑚礁为旅游业、渔业和海岸线保护提供生态系统服务。据估计，珊瑚礁的全球经济价值每年高达3750亿美元。珊瑚礁通过吸收波浪能来保护海岸线，如果没有珊瑚礁的保护，许多小岛就不会存在。

C 在生物多样的地区，珊瑚礁的价值甚至更高。在以旅游业为主的印度尼西亚和加勒比地区，根据维护沙滩的成本和吸引浮潜者和水肺潜水员的价值计算，珊瑚礁的估计价值为每平方公里100万美元。与此同时，最近对澳大利亚大堡礁的一项研究发现，作为一个完整的生态系统，珊瑚礁对该国的价值比作为渔业开采保护区的更大。每年有超过180万名游客来大堡礁旅游，他们在潜水、租船、豪华岛屿度假等珊瑚礁相关产业上的支出据估计达到了 43 亿澳元。联合国环境规划署说，2000 年加勒比地区潜水旅游的年净收益为 20 亿美元，其中 6.25 亿美元直接来自珊瑚礁潜水。此外，珊瑚礁旅游是重要的就业来源，特别是对世界上一些最贫穷的人来说。联合国环境规划署说，在发展中国家估计有 3000 万小规模渔民，其中大多数或多或少地依赖珊瑚礁。例如，在菲律宾，有 100 多万小规模渔民直接依靠珊瑚礁为生。报告估计，珊瑚礁渔业每年的价值在每平方公里 1.5 万至 15 万美元之间，而为水族馆捕捞的鱼每公斤价值 500 美元，作为食物捕捞的鱼每公斤价值 6 美元。在斯里兰卡，水族鱼出口业养活了大约 5 万人，每年产生的收入约为 550 万美元。

D 不幸的是，世界各地的珊瑚礁正在死亡。特别是，珊瑚开采、农业和城市径流、污染（有机和无机）、疾病以及挖掘运河和进入岛屿和海湾的通道都对珊瑚生态系统造成了局部威胁。更广泛的威胁来自海洋温度上升、海平面上升和海洋酸化导致的 pH 值变化，所有这些都与温室气体排放有关。目前的一些捕鱼活动是破坏性的，是不可持续的。其中包括氰化物捕捞、过度捕捞和爆破捕捞。虽然氰化物捕捞为热带水族馆市场提供活礁鱼，但大多数用这种方法捕获的鱼都在以亚洲为主的餐馆里出售，那里的活鱼以新鲜著称。为了用氰化物捕鱼，渔民们潜入珊瑚礁，在珊瑚裂缝中和快速移动的鱼身上喷射氰化物，使鱼昏迷，使它们更容易被捕获。过度捕捞是导致珊瑚礁退化的另一个主要原因。通常的做法是，从一个珊瑚礁上捕捞过多的鱼来维持该地区的人口。糟糕的捕鱼方法，如用棍子敲打珊瑚礁 (muro-ami)，破坏了通常作为鱼类栖息地的珊瑚结构。在某些情况下，人们用炸药捕鱼（爆破捕鱼），这会将周围的珊瑚炸开。

E 旅游胜地将污水直接排入珊瑚礁周围的水域，导致珊瑚礁退化。堆存在维护不善的化粪池中的废物也会泄漏到周围的地下水中，最终渗入珊瑚礁。不加注意的划船、潜水、浮潜和钓鱼也会破坏珊瑚礁。人们在珊瑚礁上抓、踢、行走，或搅动沉积物时，都会对珊瑚礁造成破坏。人们在珊瑚上抛锚或收集珊瑚时，珊瑚也会受到伤害或死亡。

F 为了解决这些问题，科学家和研究人员研究了影响珊瑚礁的各种因素。这些因素包括海洋作为二氧化碳汇的作用、大气变化、紫外线、海洋酸化、病毒、携带病原体的沙尘暴对遥远珊瑚礁的影响、污染物、藻华等。珊瑚礁受到的威胁远远超出了沿海地区。概算显示，世界上大约有 10% 的珊瑚礁已经死亡。由于人类的破坏性活动，世界上约 60% 的珊瑚礁正处于危险之中。在东南亚地区，珊瑚礁受到的健康威胁尤其严重，其中 80% 的珊瑚礁处于濒危状态。

G 在澳大利亚，大堡礁受到大堡礁海洋公园管理局的保护，它同样也是许多立法的对象，包括生物多样性行动计划。巴布亚新几内亚马努斯省阿胡斯岛（Ahus Island）的居民沿袭了几代人的古老习俗，在其珊瑚礁泻湖的六个区域限制捕鱼。他们的文化传统允许垂线捕鱼，但不允许网捕或用鱼叉捕鱼。结果是，珊瑚礁生物量和个体鱼的大小都明显大于捕鱼不受限制的地方。

READING PASSAGE 3

Sand Dunes

文章结构

体裁	说明文
题材	生物与环境
主题	沙丘的构成、形成原因和特征
段落概括	A 段：沙丘带来的坏处和好处。 B 段：沙子的构成。 C 段：最常见的沙丘形式。 D 段：其他形式的沙丘。 E 段：沙丘形成的原因。 F 段：沙丘的循环前进。 G 段：沙丘会唱歌。 H 段：科学家们在实验室建造沙丘的模型。

重点词汇

A 段							
单词	音标	词性	释义	单词	音标	词性	释义
encroachment	[ɪnˈkrəʊtʃmənt]	*n.*	侵入，侵犯；侵蚀	niche	[niːʃ]	*n.*	生态位
crop	[krɒp]	*n.*	庄稼	prevent	[prɪˈvent]	*v.*	阻止，阻碍
overwhelm	[ˌəʊvəˈwelm]	*v.*	压垮，淹没	priority	[praɪˈɒrəti]	*n.*	优先事项，最重要的事
B 段							
单词	音标	词性	释义	单词	音标	词性	释义
be composed of		*phr.*	由……组成	mineral	[ˈmɪnərəl]	*n.*	矿物质
quartz	[kwɔːts]	*n.*	石英	shade	[ʃeɪd]	*n.*	（色彩的）浓淡深浅，色度
presence	[ˈprezns]	*n.*	存在	compound	[ˈkɒmpaʊnd]	*n..*	混合物

C 段							
单词	音标	词性	释义	单词	音标	词性	释义
form	[fɔ:m]	*n.*	形式，形状	mound	[maʊnd]	*n.*	土堆，石堆
blow	[bləʊ]	*v.*	（风）刮，吹	consistently	[kənˈsɪstəntli]	*adv.*	一贯地，始终地
direction	[dəˈrekʃn] [daɪˈrekʃn]	*n.*	方向				

D 段							
单词	音标	词性	释义	单词	音标	词性	释义
radically	[ˈrædɪkli]	*adv.*	根本上，彻底地	symmetrical	[sɪˈmetrɪkl]	*adj.*	对称的，匀称的
radiate	[ˈreɪdieɪt]	*v.*	辐射，向周围伸展	accumulate	[əˈkju:mjəleɪt]	*v.*	积累，积攒
laterally	[ˈlætərəli]	*adv.*	旁边地；在侧面	dominate	[ˈdɒmɪneɪt]	*v.*	统治，支配
margin	[ˈmɑ:dʒɪn]	*n.*	边缘	ridge	[rɪdʒ]	*n.*	山脊，山脉；隆起部分
merge	[mɜ:dʒ]	*v.*	（使）合并，（使）融合	extend	[ɪkˈstend]	*v.*	延伸；扩大，延长

E 段							
单词	音标	词性	释义	单词	音标	词性	释义
pile	[paɪl]	*n.*	一堆，一叠	pile up		*phr.*	积累，堆放起来
ripple	[ˈrɪpl]	*n.*	涟漪	steep	[sti:p]	*adj.*	（路、山等）陡峭的
collapse	[kəˈlæps]	*v.*	倒塌，坍塌	steepness	[ˈsti:pnəs]	*n.*	险峻；陡度
stable	[ˈsteɪbl]	*adj.*	稳定的，牢固的	angle	[ˈæŋgl]	*n.*	角；倾斜；角度
property	[ˈprɒpəti]	*n.*	性质，特性	material	[məˈtɪəriəl]	*n.*	材料，原料

F 段							
单词	音标	词性	释义	单词	音标	词性	释义
repeating	[rɪˈpi:tɪŋ]	*adj.*	重复出现的	cycle	[ˈsaɪkl]	*n.*	循环
inch	[ɪntʃ]	*v.*	（使）缓慢移动	crest	[krest]	*n.*	顶，峰
internal	[ɪnˈtɜ:n(ə)l]	*adj.*	内部的	structure	[ˈstrʌktʃə(r)]	*n.*	结构，构造

G 段							
单词	音标	词性	释义	单词	音标	词性	释义
decibel	[ˈdesɪbel]	*n.*	分贝	avalanche	[ˈævəlɑːnʃ]	*n.*	崩塌
resonate	[ˈrezəneɪt]	*v.*	发出回响；引起共鸣	flute	[fluːt]	*n.*	长笛
collision	[kəˈlɪʒn]	*n.*	碰撞，相撞	grain	[greɪn]	*n.*	谷物，谷粒
synchronize	[ˈsɪŋkrənaɪz]	*v.*	（使）同步	layer	[ˈleɪə(r)] [leə(r)]	*n.*	层；层次
vibrate	[vaɪˈbreɪt]	*v.*	（使）震动，（使）颤动	tone	[təʊn]	*n.*	音质，音色
depend on		*phr.*	依靠；取决于				

H 段							
单词	音标	词性	释义	单词	音标	词性	释义
perform	[pəˈfɔːm]	*v.*	执行	simulation	[ˌsɪmjuˈleɪʃn]	*n.*	模拟
dynamics	[daɪˈnæmɪks]	*n.*	动力学，力学；动力	laboratory	[ləˈbɒrətri]	*n.*	实验室
pattern	[ˈpætn]	*n.*	模式，方式	reproduce	[ˌriːprəˈdjuːs]	*v.*	复制；模拟

题目精解

Questions 27-34

题型：标题题

解析：标题题的考查重点是段落的主旨，所以必须找到段落的主题句，通常是每段的第一句、第二句或最后一句，然后根据主题句的意思在选项列表中找到与其对应的选项。考生在解答此类题型时，一个常见的误区是：根据段落中一些描述细节信息的词，在选项中直接寻找这些细节信息词的同义替换词。

小标题	译文
i. Potential threat to buildings and crops despite of benefit	尽管有益，但对建筑物和农作物有潜在威胁
ii. The cycle of sand moving forward with wind	沙子随风循环前进
iii. Protection method in various countries	各国的保护方法
iv. Scientists simulate sand move and build model in lab	科学家们在实验室模拟沙子移动并建立模型

续表

小标题	译文
v. Sand composition explanation	沙子的成分说明
vi. Singing sand dunes	唱歌的沙丘
vii. Other types of sand dunes	其他类型的沙丘
viii. The personal opinion on related issues	个人对相关问题的看法
ix. Reasons why sand dunes form	沙丘的形成原因
x. The most common sand type	最常见的沙丘类型

Question 27

题干定位词 / 关键词	threat to buildings and crops; benefit
原文定位	A 段
题目解析	A 段第一句就提到沙丘造成的主要问题之一是对人类栖息地的侵占。第三句说沙丘威胁着建筑物和农作物，这里对应小标题中的 potential threat to buildings and crops。最后一句又说沙丘栖息地为一些稀有和濒危的动植物提供了生态位，正好对应小标题中的 benefit，所以 A 段选 i。
答案	i

Question 28

题干定位词 / 关键词	sand composition
原文定位	B 段第一至四句 Sand is usually composed of hard minerals such as quartz that cannot be broken down into silt or clay. Yellow, brown and reddish shades of sand indicate their presence of iron compounds. Red sand is composed of quartz coated by a layer of iron oxide. White sands are nearly pure gypsum.
题目解析	B 段第一至四句都在说沙子的成分。第一句说沙子通常由坚硬的矿物构成，如石英。第二句说黄色、棕色和略带红色的沙子表明它们含有铁化合物。第三句说红色的沙子由石英组成，石英表面覆盖了一层氧化铁。第四句说白沙几乎是纯石膏。显然，B 段讲的是沙子的成分(composition)，所以选 v。
答案	v

Question 29

题干定位词 / 关键词	the most common sand type
原文定位	C 段首句和尾句 The most common dune form on Earth and on Mars is the crescentic. The largest crescentic dunes on Earth, with mean crest-to-crest widths of more than 3 kilometres, are in China's Taklamakan Desert.
题目解析	C 段的主旨句很明显，第一句说地球和火星上最常见的沙丘形式是新月形沙丘，最后一句说地球上最大的新月形沙丘位于中国的塔克拉玛干沙漠，平均峰顶宽度超过 3 公里。显然，这一段都在讲最常见的沙丘形式——新月形沙丘，所以选 x。
答案	x

Question 30

题干定位词 / 关键词	other types of sand dunes
原文定位	D 段
题目解析	D 段第一句介绍星形沙丘 (star dunes)，再看第二至六句的主语，分别是 they, star dunes, they, they, the star dunes，显然这部分讲的都是星形沙丘。第七句开始讲线形沙丘（linear dunes），其后的五个句子的主语分别是 they, some linear dunes, many, the long axes of these dunes, linear loess hills，显然，这些都是围绕线形沙丘展开的。因此，这一段主要介绍了另外的两种沙丘形式，对应 other types of sand dunes，所以选 vii。
答案	vii

Question 31

题干定位词 / 关键词	reasons; sand dunes form
原文定位	E 段第一句 Once sand begins to pile up, ripples and dunes can form.
题目解析	E 段主旨句很清晰，直接指出一旦沙子开始堆积，就会形成波纹和沙丘。正好对应 ix，后面讲解了沙丘的具体形成过程。
答案	ix

Question 32

题干定位词 / 关键词	cycle; moving forward; wind
原文定位	F 段第一句 The repeating cycle of sand inching up the windward side to the dune crest, then slipping down the dune's slip face allows the dune to inch forward, migrating in the direction the wind blows.
题目解析	F 段第一句提到沙子从迎风的一侧一点点上升到沙丘顶部，然后从沙丘的滑落面滑落，这样的重复循环让沙丘慢慢向前移动，朝着风吹的方向移动。这正好对应 the cycle of sand moving forward with wind，所以 F 段选 ii。
答案	ii

Question 33

题干定位词 / 关键词	singing
原文定位	G 段第一句 Sand dunes can "sing" at a level up to 115 decibels and generate sounds in different notes.
题目解析	G 段第一句说沙丘可以以高达 115 分贝的声音"唱歌"，并发出不同音符的声音。这句正好对应 singing，所以选 vi。
答案	vi

Question 34

题干定位词 / 关键词	scientists; simulate; model; lab
原文定位	H 段第一句 Scientists performed a computer simulation on patterns and dynamics of desert dunes in laboratory.
题目解析	H 段第一句说科学家们在实验室对沙漠沙丘的模式和动态进行了计算机模拟，这正好对应 scientists simulate sand move and build model in lab。simulation 对应 simulate, laboratory 对应 lab, patterns 对应 model，所以选 iv。
答案	iv

Questions 35-36

题型：单选题

Question 35

题干定位词 / 关键词	main composition; white sand
原文定位	B 段第四句 White sands are nearly pure gypsum.
题目解析	题干：根据文章，白沙的主要成分是什么？ A：石英 B：石膏 C：石灰 D：铁 首先 B 段第一句就提到沙子通常是由坚硬的矿物构成的，据此可以判断本题大概出自这一段落，再往下阅读用 white sands 定位，就找到了第四句 White sands are nearly pure gypsum（白沙几乎是纯的石膏），所以答案选 B。
答案	B

Question 36

题干定位词 / 关键词	not mentioned; a sand dunes type
原文定位	C 段第一句，D 段第一和第七句 The most common dune form on Earth and on Mars is the crescentic. Radially symmetrical, star dunes are pyramidal sand mounds with slipfaces on three or more arms that radiate from the high center of the mound. Straight or slightly sinuous sand ridges typically much longer than they are wide are known as linear dunes.
题目解析	题干：这篇文章没有提到哪一种沙丘类型？ A：线形 B：新月形 C：重叠形 D：星形 C 段第一句 The most common dune form ...is the crescentic，提到了最常见的沙丘形式是新月形沙丘。 D 段第一句 Radially symmetrical, star dunes... 提到了星形沙丘。 D 段第七句 Straight or slightly sinuous sand ridges... are known as linear dunes，提到了线形沙丘。 由于选项 A、B、D 中的沙丘类型都提到了，所以选 C。
答案	C

Questions 37-40

题型：摘要填空题

Question 37

题干定位词 / 关键词	crescentic; Earth and Mars
原文定位	C 段第一句 The most common dune form on Earth and on Mars is the crescentic.
题目解析	题干：在地球和火星上，新月形是常见的 ______，除此之外，还有其他类型的沙丘。 首先分析题干，题干问的是常见的什么，答案应该是名词。用 crescentic, Earth and Mars 定位，很容易定位到 C 段第一句：地球和火星上最常见的沙丘形式是新月形沙丘。ordinary 对应 common, 所以答案应该是 dune form，在给出的列表中找 dune form 的同义词，即 B shape（形状）。
答案	B

Question 38

题干定位词 / 关键词	color; clay
原文定位	B 段第一句 Sand is usually composed of hard minerals such as quartz that cannot be broken down into silt or clay.
题目解析	题干：不同颜色的沙子反映出不同的成分，其中一些富含不容易碎成黏土的 ______。 首先分析题干，空格处要填的是不容易碎成黏土的某种东西，答案应该是名词。用 color 和 clay 定位，结合前面做过的标题题可知，B 段提到了很多颜色，再进一步用 clay 定位，答案范围就缩小到了 B 段第一句，原文说沙子通常由坚硬的矿物构成，如 quarts（石英），后面 that 引导的定语从句修饰的是 hard minerals，说它不能分解成淤泥或黏土，所以答案是 hard minerals，给出的列表中正好 G 选项原词重现。
答案	G

Question 39

题干定位词 / 关键词	sound intensity
原文定位	G 段第一句 Sand dunes can "sing" at a level up to 115 decibels and generate sounds in different notes.
题目解析	题干：沙丘可以以一定的声音强度 _______。 首先分析题干，题干问沙丘在一定的声音强度下可以做什么事，be able to 后面只能跟动词原形。看一下给出的列表，只有 H 选项是动词，所以可以直接根据词性确定选 H。 考生也可以按常规做法解题，用 sound intensity 可以定位到 G 段第一句：沙丘可以以高达 115 分贝的声音"唱歌"，并发出不同音符的声音。题干中的 a certain level of sound intensity 正好对应 115 分贝（decibels），这就是一个声音强度。沙丘可以以 115 分贝的声音唱歌，也就是说沙丘能够在一定的声音强度下"唱歌"，由此也可以确定选 H。
答案	H

Question 40

题干定位词 / 关键词	different size of grains
原文定位	G 段最后一句 The tone of the sounds depended primarily on the size of the grains.
题目解析	题干：不同大小的颗粒会产生不同 _____ 的声音。 用 size of grains 定位到 G 段最后一句：声音的音调主要取决于沙粒的大小，也就是说不同沙粒会产生不同的音调（tone），列表中 D 选项原词重现。
答案	D

长难句分析

A 段：One of the main problems posed by sand dunes is their encroachment on human habitats.

思路分析：这个句子的主语是 one of the main problems，谓语是 is，主语和谓语中间的 posed by sand dunes 是分词作定语，修饰前面的主语，可理解为沙丘造成的主要问题之一。

参考翻译：沙丘造成的主要问题之一是它们对人类栖息地的侵占。

F段：The repeating cycle of sand inching up the windward side to the dune crest, then slipping down the dune's slip face allows the dune to inch forward, migrating in the direction the wind blows.

思路分析：遇到再复杂的句子也要先找出句子的谓语，首先找在句子里可以作谓语的动词，inching up，slipping down 和 migrating 都是动词的 ing 形式，不可以作谓语，所以谓语只能是 allows，前面的 the repeating cycle of sand inching up the windward side to the dune crest, then slipping down the dune's slip face 是句子的主语，也就是主语所说的这件事情使得沙丘向前移动，朝着风吹的方向移动。inching up... 和 slipping down... 是分词定语，而 migrating... 是分词状语。

参考翻译：沙子从迎风的一侧一点点上升到沙丘顶部，然后从沙丘的滑落面滑落，这样的重复循环让沙丘慢慢向前移动，朝着风吹的方向移动。

参考译文

沙丘

A 沙丘造成的主要问题之一是它们对人类栖息地的侵占。沙丘移动的方式各不相同，但都得到了风的帮助。在非洲、中东和中国，沙丘威胁着建筑物和农作物。防止沙丘淹没城市和农业地区已经成为联合国环境规划署的重中之重。另一方面，沙丘栖息地为极为特殊的植物和动物提供了生态位，包括许多稀有和濒危物种。

B 沙子通常由不能分解成淤泥或黏土的坚硬矿物构成，如石英。黄色、棕色和略带红色的沙子表明铁化合物的存在。红色的沙子是由被一层氧化铁覆盖的石英组成的。白沙几乎是纯石膏。硅酸盐含量高的沙子可用于玻璃制造。砂岩是由沙子与石灰、白垩或其他一些起黏结剂作用的物质混合而成的，这些物质成层地沉积在海底或其他地区的底部，经过数千年或数百万年，在其上方的沉积物的巨大压力下被压成岩石。

C 地球和火星上最常见的沙丘形式是新月形沙丘。新月形状的沙丘一般都是宽边大于长边的。滑落面位于沙丘的凹面上。这些沙丘在从一个方向持续吹来的风的作用下形成，它们也被称为新月形沙丘，或横向沙丘。某些类型的新月形沙丘比其他类型的沙丘在沙漠表面移动得更快。1954 年至 1959 年间，中国宁夏的一组沙丘每年移动超过 100 米，埃及西部沙漠也有类似的速度记录。地球上最大的新月形沙丘位于中国的塔克拉玛干沙漠，平均峰顶宽度超过 3 公里。

D 星形沙丘呈放射状对称，是金字塔状的沙丘，滑落面位于从丘的高中心向外辐射的三条或多条支臂上。它们倾向于在多向风区聚集。星形沙丘向上生长，而非横向生长。它们主宰着撒哈拉沙漠的东方大尔格。在其他沙漠中，它们出现在沙海的边缘，特别是靠近地形屏障的地方。在中国巴丹吉林沙漠东南部，星形沙丘高达 500 米，可能是地球上最高的沙丘。直的或略弯曲的沙脊通常长度大于宽度，被称为线形沙丘。它们可能超过 160 公里（99 英里）长。一些线形沙丘合并形成 Y 形复合沙丘。它们中的许多形成于双向风区。这些沙丘的长轴在沙子运动引起的方向上延伸。被称为 pahas 的线形黄土丘陵外表上与其相似。

E 一旦沙子开始堆积，就会形成波纹和沙丘。风继续把沙子吹到沙堆的顶部，直到沙堆变得非常陡峭，在自身的重量下坍塌。坍塌的沙子达到合适的陡度时就会停下来，以保持沙丘的稳定。这个角度，通常在 30° ~ 34° 左右，被称为休止角。每一堆松散的颗粒都有一个独特的休止角，这取决于组成它的材料的性质，如颗粒大小和圆度。随着风沙输入量的增加，波纹会成长为沙丘。

F 沙子从迎风的一侧一点点上升到沙丘顶部，然后从沙丘的滑落面滑落，这样的重复循环让沙丘慢慢向前移动，朝着风吹的方向移动。正如你可能猜到的那样，所有这些攀爬和滑落都会在沙丘的内部结构上留下印记。这张照片（略）显示了保存在金门国家娱乐区芬斯顿堡的默塞德地层中的沙丘结构化石。你看到的倾斜线条或叠片结构，是保存下来的一个迁移沙丘的滑落面。这种结构被称为交错层理，可能是风或水流的结果。然而，交错层理结构越大，它越有可能是由风而不是水形成的。

G 沙丘可以以高达 115 分贝的声音“唱歌”，并发出不同音符的声音。内华达州沙山的沙丘通常会唱低 C 调，但也会唱升 B 调 和升 C 调。智利的沙丘之海（La Mar de Dunas）用 F 调哼唱，而摩洛哥的 Ghord Lahmar 用升 G 调哼唱。这些声音是由风吹起的沙子崩塌而发出的。有一段时间，人们认为崩塌使整个沙丘产生了像长笛或小提琴一样的共鸣，但如果这是真的，那么不同大小的沙丘会发出不同的音符。21 世纪中期，美国、法国和摩洛哥的科学家参观了摩洛哥、智利、中国和阿曼的沙丘，并在《物理评论快报》上发表了一篇论文，确定了这些声音是由沙粒之间的碰撞产生的，这种碰撞导致沙粒的运动变得同步，导致沙丘的外层像扬声器的锥体一样振动，进而产生声音。声音的音调主要取决于沙粒的大小。

H 科学家们在实验室对沙漠沙丘的模式和动态进行了计算机模拟。重现了在沙漠中观察到的沙丘的模式。从最初的随机状态，到后来风向的变化产生了星形和线形沙丘。在沙丘的发展过程中计算了沙粒的输送效率。科学家们发现，线形横向沙丘的沙粒输送效率最高。沙粒输送效率在演化过程中始终呈递增趋势，且递增的方式是阶梯式的。他们还发现，阴影区，即沙子不怎么移动的区域，在演化过程中会缩小，这极大地帮助了他们建立模拟沙子移动的模型。

TEST 2 解析

READING PASSAGE 1

Bondi Beach

文章结构

体裁	说明文
题材	历史与发展
主题	邦迪海滩的历史与发展
段落概括	A 段：介绍邦迪海滩的方位和邦迪这个名称的含义。 B 段：关于当地土著人的不同理论，以及邦迪这个名称的来历。 C 段：邦迪海滩从最初建造到成为公共海滩的历史。 D 段：电车的开通使邦迪海滩变得更受欢迎。 E 段：邦迪海滩变得更受欢迎。海水浴的流行引发了对公众生命安全的担忧，因此建立了冲浪救生俱乐部。 F 段：随着各种活动的举办，邦迪海滩吸引来更多的人，随之出现了房屋紧缺的问题。 G 段：邦迪海滩的建筑特点。 H 段：邦迪海滩举办了 2000 年夏季奥运会的沙滩网球比赛，为此建了很多体育场所。活动人士对此表示反对。 I 段：人们对建体育场所可能带来的环境、健康问题表达了担忧。

重点词汇

A 段							
单词	音标	词性	释义	单词	音标	词性	释义
be located in		*phr.*	位于……	suburb	[ˈsʌbɜːb]	*n.*	城郊
aboriginal	[ˌæbəˈrɪdʒənl]	*adj.*	原始的，土著的				

B 段							
单词	音标	词性	释义	单词	音标	词性	释义
indigenous	[ɪnˈdɪdʒənəs]	*adj.*	本土的	settlement	[ˈsetlmənt]	*n.*	殖民
theory	[ˈθɪəri]	*n.*	学说，理论	language	[ˈlæŋgwɪdʒ]	*n.*	语言
distinct	[dɪˈstɪŋkt]	*adj.*	不同的，有区别的	roam	[rəʊm]	*v.*	漫步，闲逛
derive from		*phr.*	源于，来自	be based on		*phr.*	根据，以……为基础

C 段							
单词	音标	词性	释义	单词	音标	词性	释义
outing	[ˈaʊtɪŋ]	*n.*	短途旅游，远足	grant	[grɑ:nt]	*n.*	（政府给予的）土地
hectare	[ˈhekteə(r)] [ˈhektɑ:(r)]	*n.*	公顷	residential	[ˌrezɪˈdenʃl]	*adj.*	住宅区的，居民区的
purchase	[ˈpɜ:tʃəs]	*v.*	购买，采购	embrace	[ɪmˈbreɪs]	*v.*	包括，涉及
frontage	[ˈfrʌntɪdʒ]	*n.*	前方，正面	available to sb.		*phr.*	对某人可用
threaten	[ˈθretn]	*v.*	威胁，恐吓；危及	intervene	[ˌɪntəˈvi:n]	*v.*	干预，干涉

D 段							
单词	音标	词性	释义	单词	音标	词性	释义
be/become associated with		*phr.*	和……有关 / 有联系	leisure	[ˈleʒə(r)]	*n.*	闲暇；休闲活动
democracy	[dɪˈmɒkrəsi]	*n.*	民主	migrant	[ˈmaɪgrənt]	*adj.*	移民的
comprise	[kəmˈpraɪz]	*v.*	包括，包含，构成	tram	[træm]	*n.*	有轨电车
public transportation		*phr.*	公共交通	alternative	[ɔ:lˈtɜ:nətɪv]	*n.*	可供选择的事物，替代物
refer to as		*phr.*	把……称作				

E 段							
单词	音标	词性	释义	单词	音标	词性	释义
trend	[trend]	*n.*	趋势，动态	popularity	[ˌpɒpjuˈlærəti]	*n.*	流行，受欢迎
raise	[reɪz]	*v.*	引起，提高	safety	[ˈseɪfti]	*n.*	安全，安全性
prevent	[prɪˈvent]	*v.*	阻止，阻碍	drown	[draʊn]	*v.*	（使）淹死
document	[ˈdɒkjumənt]	*v.*	记录，记载	surf	[sɜ:f]	*v.*	冲浪
reinforce	[ˌri:ɪnˈfɔ:s]	*v.*	加强，强化（观点、思想或感觉）	rescue	[ˈreskju:]	*v./n.*	营救，援救

F 段							
单词	音标	词性	释义	单词	音标	词性	释义
carnival	[ˈkɑ:nɪvl]	*n.*	狂欢节，嘉年华会	instill	[ɪnˈstɪl]	*v.*	逐渐灌输
destination	[ˌdestɪˈneɪʃn]	*n.*	目的地，终点	royal	[ˈrɔɪəl]	*adj.*	王室的
in addition to		*phr.*	除……之外	wealthy	[ˈwelθi]	*adj.*	富有的，丰富的
shortage	[ˈʃɔ:tɪdʒ]	*n.*	短缺，不足	satisfied	[ˈsætɪsfaɪd]	*adj.*	满意的，满足的
G 段							
单词	音标	词性	释义	单词	音标	词性	释义
commercial	[kəˈmɜ:ʃl]	*adj.*	商业的，商务的	contemporary	[kənˈtemprəri]	*adj.*	当代的，现代的
depict	[dɪˈpɪkt]	*v.*	描述，描绘	unique	[juˈni:k]	*adj.*	独一无二的，独特的
scent	[sent]	*n.*	香味，芳香	architecture	[ˈɑ:kɪtektʃə(r)]	*n.*	建筑设计，建筑风格
H 段							
单词	音标	词性	释义	单词	音标	词性	释义
competition	[ˌkɒmpəˈtɪʃn]	*n.*	竞争；比赛	tournament	[ˈtʊənəmənt]	*n.*	锦标赛，联赛
construct	[kənˈstrʌkt]	*v.*	建造，修建	divide	[dɪˈvaɪd]	*v.*	（使）分开，
restrict	[rɪˈstrɪkt]	*v.*	限制，控制，约束	access	[ˈækses]	*n.*	入口，通道
protest	[ˈprəʊtest]	*v.*	（公开）反对，抗议				
I 段							
单词	音标	词性	释义	单词	音标	词性	释义
risk	[rɪsk]	*v.*	冒……的危险	acidify	[əˈsɪdɪfaɪ]	*v.*	（使）成酸，（使）酸化
surface	[ˈsɜ:fɪs]	*n.*	表面				

题目精解

Questions 1-5

题型：判断题

Question 1

题干定位词 / 关键词	name; Bondi beach; first called; British settlers
原文定位	B 段最后一句 A number of place names within Waverley, most famously Bondi, have been based on words derived from Aboriginal languages of the Sydney region.
题目解析	题干：邦迪海滩的名字最初是由英国殖民者命名的。 本题的考点在于 Bondi 这个名字是谁命名的。用 name 和 Bondi beach 可以定位到 B 段最后一句，最后一句说韦弗利的许多地名，包括最著名的邦迪，都是基于悉尼地区土著语言的词汇。由此可知，Bondi 这个名字是土著词汇，并不是英国人命名的，所以答案是 FALSE。对于这道题需要掌握 derive from（源自，出自）这个短语的含义。
答案	FALSE

Question 2

题干定位词 / 关键词	aboriginal culture ; European culture
原文定位	无
题目解析	题干：澳大利亚的土著文化与欧洲文化不同。 无法定位到原文，所以答案是 NOT GIVEN。
答案	NOT GIVEN

Question 3

题干定位词 / 关键词	contemporary hotels
原文定位	G 段第一、二句 Bondi Beach has a commercial area along Campbell Parade and adjacent side streets, featuring many popular cafes, restaurants, and hotels, with views of the contemporary beach. It is depicted as wholly modern and European.

题目解析	题干：邦迪海滩地区有许多当代酒店。 本题的考点在于邦迪海滩是否有很多当代酒店。用 contemporary hotels 可以定位到 G 段第一、二句：邦迪海滩沿着坎贝尔广场和邻近的街道有一个商业区，以许多受欢迎的咖啡馆、餐馆和酒店为特色，可以看到当代海滩的景色。它被描绘为完全的现代和欧洲风格。 可以发现 contemporary 和 hotels 这两个词都出现了，但是并不能就此判断答案是 TRUE。原文说的是有很多 hotels，可以看到 contemporary beach 的景色，但没有说这些酒店是否是 contemporary 的风格，后一句说商业街是完全的现代和欧洲风格，也没有提到酒店是否是 contemporary 的风格，所以答案是 NOT GIVEN。这是典型的生拉硬拽题，看上去信息都出现了，但其实是把信息杂糅在了一起。
答案	NOT GIVEN

Question 4

题干定位词 / 关键词	British culture; red color
原文定位	G 段最后两句 The valley running down to the beach is famous world over for its view of distinctive red tiled roofs. Those architectures are deeply influenced by British costal town.
题目解析	题干：邦迪海边小镇具有特色的红色屋顶是受英国文化影响的。 本题考查具有特色的红色屋顶是否受英国文化影响。用 red color 和 British culture 定位到 G 段最后两句，原文先说通往海滩的山谷因其独特的红色瓦片屋顶而闻名于世，再说这些建筑深受英国沿海城镇的影响。因此，可以判断答案是 TRUE。
答案	TRUE

Question 5

题干定位词 / 关键词	not beneficial for health
原文定位	H 段最后一句 People protest for their human rights of having a pure seaside and argue for health life in Bondi.
题目解析	题干：住在邦迪海滨附近不利于健康。 用 health 可以定位到 H 段最后一句：人们为享有一个纯净海滨的人权而抗议，并呼吁健康的邦迪生活。也就是说，在邦迪海滩生活是对健康有益的。此外，D 段最开始也提到在 20 世纪初，海滩与健康、休闲和民主联系在一起，所以本题的答案是 FALSE。
答案	FALSE

Questions 6-9

题型：简答题

解析：简答题本质上是填空题，因此考生需要注意题目要求中的字数限制。答题的时候要看清题目问的是什么，注意那些特殊疑问词，如 when 要回答“时间”，who 要填入“人名”等；此外，了解整个句子的内容有助于定位。该题型对考生把握特殊疑问句的能力要求比较高。

Question 6

题干定位词 / 关键词	end of 19th century; public transport
原文定位	D 段第三、四句 The first tramway reached the beach in 1884. Following this, tram became the first public transportation in Bondi.
题目解析	题干：在 19 世纪末，人们乘坐哪种公共交通工具去邦迪？ 分析题干可知，答案应是一种公共交通工具。本题用 19th century 和 public transport 定位到 D 段第三、四句：第一条有轨电车于 1884 年来到海滩。此后，有轨电车成为邦迪的第一种公共交通工具。由此可知，在 19 世纪末（对应 1884 年），人们乘坐 tram（电车）去邦迪海滩。
答案	tram

Question 7

题干定位词 / 关键词	British Royalty; first visit
原文定位	F 段第三句 A royal Surf Carnival was held at Bondi Beach for Queen Elizabeth Il during her first visit in Australia in 1954.
题目解析	题干：英国皇室第一次访问邦迪是在什么时候？ 本题问英国皇室第一次访问邦迪的时间，所以答案应该是表示时间的词。用 British Royalty 定位到 F 段第三句：1954 年，女王伊丽莎白二世首次访问澳大利亚时，邦迪海滩举行了皇家冲浪嘉年华。这里提到了 Elizabeth II（伊丽莎白二世）和她第一次访问澳大利亚的时间，所以答案就是 1954。
答案	(in) 1954

Question 8

题干定位词 / 关键词	2000 Sydney Olympic games
原文定位	H 段第一句 Bondi Beach hosted the beach volleyball competition at the 2000 Summer Olympics.
题目解析	题干：邦迪在 2000 年悉尼奥运会上举办了哪个奥运项目？ 用 Sydney Olympic games 定位到 H 段第一句：邦迪海滩举办了 2000 年夏季奥运会的沙滩排球比赛。由此可知，答案就是 beach volleyball（沙滩排球）。
答案	beach volleyball

Question 9

题干定位词 / 关键词	stadium; Olympic event
原文定位	I 段第一句 "They're prepared to risk lives and risk the Bondi Beach environment for the sake of eight days of volleyball", said Stephen Unicake, a construction lawyer involved in the campaign.
题目解析	题干：如果为了奥运会项目而建造体育馆，什么会被损坏？ 首先分析题干，that Olympic event 指的是上题中的沙滩排球项目，在 H 段继续找 stadium，会发现从第二句开始就出现了这个词，但需要明确的是，题干问的是如果这个体育场建立起来了，什么会被破坏。带着这个问题往下阅读，直到 I 段第一句引述建筑律师斯蒂芬 • 尤尼凯克的话"他们为了 8 天的排球比赛，冒着生命危险以及破坏邦迪海滩环境的风险"，由此可知，被破坏的（be damaged）就只有环境了，所以答案是 environment。
答案	environment

Questions 10-13

题型：摘要填空题

Question 10

题干定位词 / 关键词	feature sport activities; holidays
原文定位	F 段第六句 Many wealthy people spend Christmas Day at the beach.
题目解析	题干：邦迪海滩每年都会举办特色体育活动，吸引了很多选择假期住在这里的 ______。 首先分析题干，体育活动吸引了很多什么，空格后面的分词定语为选择假期住在这里，那么答案一定是表示人的名词。用 feature sport activities 可以定位到 F 段第一句，这里提到了 Surf Fun Run，算是一种特色体育活动。接着找 holidays 的对应词，就看到了第六句，该句提到许多富人会在海滩上过圣诞节，这里的 Christmas Day 对应 holidays，spend Christmas Day at the beach 对应 choosing to live at this place during holidays。由此可知，邦进海滩吸引了很多选择假期住在这里的富人，答案是 wealthy people。
答案	wealthy people

Question 11

题干定位词 / 关键词	local accommodation; expanding population; a nearby town
原文定位	F 段第七、八句 However, the shortage of houses occurs when lots of people crush to seaside. Manly is the seashore town which solved this problem.
题目解析	题干：但是当地住宿无法满足不断增长的人口，一个附近的城镇 ____ 是第一个提供解决方案的郊区。 由题干可知，空格处应为一个城镇的名字。根据 expanding population 可以定位到 F 段第七句，该句提到当大量的人涌入海边时，房子就紧缺了，the shortage of houses 对应题干中的 cannot meet with，lots of people crushed to seaside 对应 expanding population，紧接着后面一句就提出了解决方案，Manly 这个海滨小镇解决了这个问题。因此，空格处城镇的名字就是 Manly。
答案	Manly

Question 12

题干定位词 / 关键词	yet people prefer; best choice
原文定位	F 段最后一句 However, people still choose Bondi as the satisfied destination rather than Manly.
题目解析	题干：但是人们更偏爱 ______ 作为他们的最佳选择。 当填空题的一个句子里出了两道题时，考生要两道题一起看。第 11 题说郊区城镇 Manly 帮助解决了住房短缺的问题，第 12 题问人们更偏爱什么作为最佳选择，其实也就是问人们更偏爱住在哪里，所以空格处要填的大概率还是地名。顺着第 11 题的定位句往下阅读，F 段最后一句指出人们仍然选择邦迪作为心仪的目的地，而不是 Manly，其中 satisfied destination 对应 best choice，所以答案就是 Bondi。
答案	Bondi

Question 13

题干定位词 / 关键词	seaside buildings; special scenic colored
原文定位	G 段第四句 The valley running down to the beach is famous world over for its view of distinctive red tiled roofs.
题目解析	题干：它的海滨建筑以其位于建筑上的风景独特的彩色 ____ 和来自大海的快乐气息而闻名。 分析题干可知，空格处应填位于建筑上的某种彩色的东西，答案应该是名词。根据 special scenic 和 colored 定位到 G 段第四句：通往海滩的山谷因其独特的红色瓦片屋顶而闻名于世。distinctive 对应 special，colored 对应 red，答案就是 tiled roofs。roofs 这个词正好也对应题干中的 on buildings。
答案	(tiled) roofs

长难句分析

B 段：A number of place names within Waverley, most famously Bondi, have been based on words derived from Aboriginal languages of the Sydney region.

思路分析： 这个句子的主语是 a number of place names，谓语是 have been based on，most famously Bondi 是插入语，derived from 引导的是分词定语，修饰前面的 words。

参考翻译： 韦弗利的许多地名，包括最著名的邦迪，都是基于悉尼地区土著语言的词汇。

G 段：Bondi Beach has a commercial area along Campbell Parade and adjacent side streets, featuring many popular cafes, restaurants, and hotels, with views of the contemporary beach.

思路分析： 这个句子的难点在于 feature 这个单词，它通常被用作名词，表示“特点”，但是在这个句子里 feature 被用作动词，表示“以……为特色”，并且在语法上作状语。

参考翻译： 邦迪海滩沿着坎贝尔广场和邻近的街道有一个商业区，以许多受欢迎的咖啡馆、餐馆和酒店为特色，可以看到当代海滩的景色。

参考译文

邦迪海滩

A 邦迪海滩是澳大利亚最著名的海滩，位于邦迪郊区——韦弗利地方政府区域，距离悉尼市中心 7 公里。“Bondiu”或“Boondi”是一个土著单词，意为水冲破岩石或海浪碎裂的声音。澳大利亚博物馆记载，邦迪是指木棍飞行发生的地方。在本 · 巴克勒海滩北端和靠近麦肯齐斯海滩的邦迪海滩南部的海岸步道上，有土著的岩雕。

B 在欧洲殖民时期，该地区的土著居民通常被称为悉尼人或伊欧拉（Eora 的意思是“人民”）。一种理论将伊欧拉描述为达鲁格语系的一个分支，该语系居住在蓝山以西的坎伯兰平原。然而，另一种理论认为，他们是一个不同的语言群体。目前没有明确的证据表明在韦弗利区域漫游的伊欧拉族特定部落的名称。韦弗利的许多地名，包括最著名的邦迪，都是基于悉尼地区土著语言的词汇。

C 从 19 世纪中期开始，邦迪海滩成为家庭出游和野餐的最爱。该郊区的起源可以追溯到 1809 年，当时早期的道路建设者威廉·罗伯茨从布莱总督那里获得了 81 公顷的土地，这些土地构成了现在的邦迪海滩商业和住宅区的大部分。1851 年，爱德华·史密斯·霍尔和弗朗西斯·奥布莱恩购买了邦迪地区的 200 英亩土地，几乎包括了邦迪海滩的整个海岸线，这片土地被命名为“邦迪庄园”(The Bondi Estate)。在 1855 年到 1877 年期间，奥布莱恩购买了霍尔的土地份额，将这块土地重新命名为“奥布莱恩庄园”，并将海滩及周边土地作为野餐场所和游乐场所向公众开放。随着海滩越来越受欢迎，奥布莱恩威胁说要停止对公众开放海滩。然而，市政委员会认为政府需要介入，使海滩成为公共区域。

D 在 20 世纪初，海滩与健康、休闲和民主联系在一起，它是一个每个人都可以平等享受的游乐场。在 20 世纪的大部分时间里，邦迪海滩是一个工人阶级的郊区，来自新西兰的移民占了当地人口的大多数。第一条有轨电车于 1884 年来到海滩。此后，有轨电车成为邦迪的第一种公共交通工具。另外，这一行动也改变了只有富人才能享受海滩的规则。到了 20 世纪 30 年代，邦迪吸引的不只有当地游客，还有澳大利亚其他地方和海外的游客。当时的广告将邦迪海滩称为“太平洋游乐场”。

E 人们更喜欢在海边放松，而不是在城市里不健康地生活，这种趋势日益增长。在 19 世纪末和 20 世纪初，海水浴越来越流行，这引发了人们对公共安全和如何防止人们溺水的担忧。作为回应，世界上第一个正式记录在案的冲浪救生俱乐部——邦迪冲浪游泳救生俱乐部于 1907 年成立了。1938 年，邦迪“黑色星期天”这一戏剧性事件有力地巩固了该俱乐部的地位。当时海滩上大约有 35000 人，一大群救生员正准备开始一场冲浪比赛，突然三股反常的海浪打在海滩上，把数百人卷到了海里。救生员救出了 300 人。这是冲浪浴史上规模最大的一次大规模救援，它确认了救生员在国民想象中的地位。

F 邦迪海滩是每年 8 月举行的“城市冲浪趣味跑”的终点。澳大利亚冲浪嘉年华进一步强化了这一形象。1954 年，女王伊丽莎白二世首次访问澳大利亚时，邦迪海滩举行了皇家冲浪嘉年华。自 1867 年以来，英国王室成员访问澳大利亚的次数已超过 50 次。除了许多活动，邦迪海滩市场每个星期天都开放。许多富人会在海滩上过圣诞节。然而，当大量的人涌入海边时，房子就紧缺了。海滨小镇曼利解决了这一问题。然而，邦迪仍然是人们心仪的目的地，而不是曼利。

G 邦迪海滩沿着坎贝尔广场和邻近的街道有一个商业区，以许多受欢迎的咖啡馆、餐馆和酒店为特色，可以看到当代海滩的景色。它被描绘为完全的现代和欧洲风格。在过去的十年里，邦迪海滩的独特位置见证了以海景和大海的气息为优势的房屋和公寓的急剧增加。通往海滩的山谷因其独特的红色瓦片屋顶而闻名于世。这些建筑深受英国沿海城镇的影响。

H 邦迪海滩举办了 2000 年夏季奥运会的沙滩排球比赛。为了举办比赛，海滩建造了一个可容纳 10000 人的临时大型体育场、一个很小的体育场、2 个热身场和 3 个训练场。专门建造的邦迪海滩排球场只矗立了六个星期。活动人士对这一行为的社会和环境后果表示反对。体育场将把海滩一分为二，并严格限制公众游泳、散步和其他形式的户外娱乐活动。人们为享有一个纯净海滨的人权而抗议，并呼吁健康的邦迪生活。

I 参与该活动的建筑律师斯蒂芬 · 尤尼凯克说，“他们为了 8 天的排球比赛，冒着生命危险以及破坏邦迪海滩环境的风险。”其他环境问题还包括，从沙子下面挖出来的土壤被带到水面后可能会酸化。

READING PASSAGE 2

When the Tulip Bubble Burst

文章结构

体裁	说明文
题材	金融类
主题	郁金香热的历史
段落概括	A 段：介绍一种名为“永远的奥古斯都”的郁金香。 B 段：一名阿姆斯特丹人拒绝了以 3000 荷兰盾购买他的一株球茎的提议。 C 段：达什讲述“郁金香热”的历史。 D 段：16 世纪，郁金香的传播。 E 段：17 世纪初，阿姆斯特丹商人们在贸易中获得暴利。 F 段：丰厚的利润引起了郁金香热，商人们开始寻找花卉爱好者和投机者。 G 段：郁金香成为流通手段，出现了郁金香期货市场，郁金香贸易达到了顶峰。 H 段：郁金香市场的崩塌。 I 段：郁金香热和互联网热的区别。

重点词汇

A 段							
单词	音标	词性	释义	单词	音标	词性	释义
stock	[stɒk]	*n.*	股票	bond	[bɒnd]	*n.*	债券
B 段							
单词	音标	词性	释义	单词	音标	词性	释义
specimen	[ˈspesɪmən]	*n.*	样品，标本	bulb	[bʌlb]	*n.*	（植物的）球茎
accurate	[ˈækjərət]	*adj.*	准确的，精确的	render	[ˈrendə(r)]	*v.*	表达；使成为
greenback	[ˈgriːnbæk]	*n.*	美钞	sum	[sʌm]	*n.*	总数，金额
annual	[ˈænjuəl]	*adj.*	一年一度的；年度的	income	[ˈɪnkʌm]	*n.*	收入，收益
merchant	[ˈmɜːtʃənt]	*n.*	商人，批发商	nix	[nɪks]	*v.*	阻止，拒绝

C段							
单词	音标	词性	释义	单词	音标	词性	释义
fortune	[ˈfɔ:tʃu:n]	*n.*	财富	splurge	[splɜ:dʒ]	*v.*	挥霍
mania	[ˈmeɪniə]	*n.*	狂热，热衷	investor	[ɪnˈvestə(r)]	*n.*	投资者
invoke	[ɪnˈvəʊk]	*v.*	唤起	account	[əˈkaʊnt]	*n.*	描述
buzzword	[ˈbʌzwɜ:d]	*n.*	流行语	cautionary	[ˈkɔ:ʃənəri]	*adj.*	警告的，告诫的
tale	[teɪl]	*n.*	故事，传说				

D段							
单词	音标	词性	释义	单词	音标	词性	释义
gaga	[ˈgɑ:gɑ:]	*adj.*	狂热的，着迷的	bloom	[blu:m]	*v.*	开花，绽放
enchant	[ɪnˈtʃɑ:nt]	*v.*	使陶醉，使入迷	bewitch	[bɪˈwɪtʃ]	*v.*	蛊惑；使着迷
ruler	[ˈru:lə(r)]	*n.*	统治者，管理者	passion	[ˈpæʃn]	*n.*	激情，热情
fertile	[ˈfɜ:taɪl]	*adj.*	肥沃的，富饶的				

E段							
单词	音标	词性	释义	单词	音标	词性	释义
embark on		*phr.*	从事，着手	resource	[rɪˈsɔ:s]	*n.*	自然资源；资源
commerce	[ˈkɒmɜ:s]	*n.*	贸易，商业	lucrative	[ˈlu:krətɪv]	*adj.*	获利多的，赚大钱的
voyage	[ˈvɔɪɪdʒ]	*n.*	航行，旅行	yield	[ji:ld]	*v.*	产生（收益、效益等）
profit	[ˈprɒfɪt]	*n.*	利润，盈利	display	[dɪˈspleɪ]	*v.*	展示，表现，显露
erect	[ɪˈrekt]	*v.*	搭建，建造；使竖立	estate	[ɪˈsteɪt]	*n.*	庄园，地产

F段							
单词	音标	词性	释义	单词	音标	词性	释义
comprehend	[ˌkɒmprɪˈhend]	*v.*	理解，领悟	exhibit	[ɪgˈzɪbɪt]	*v.*	展示，表现出
intense	[ɪnˈtens]	*adj.*	浓烈的	command	[kəˈmɑ:nd]	*v.*	值（高价）；掌控，控制
trader	[ˈtreɪdə(r)]	*n.*	交易者；商人	seek out (seek-sought-sought)		*phr.*	找出，搜出
speculator	[ˈspekjuleɪtə(r)]	*n.*	投机者				

G 段							
单词	音标	词性	释义	单词	音标	词性	释义
price	[praɪs]	*n.*	价格	wedge into		*phr.*	挤入，插入
mortgage	[ˈmɔːɡɪdʒ]	*v.*	抵押	change hands		*phr.*	转手
future	[ˈfjuːtʃə(r)]	*n.*	期货	conduct	[kənˈdʌkt]	*v.*	实施，进行
tavern	[ˈtævən]	*n.*	酒馆；客栈	peak	[piːk]	*n.*	巅峰，顶点
zenith	[ˈzenɪθ]	*n.*	顶峰；顶点	auction	[ˈɔːkʃn] [ˈɒkʃn]	*n.*	拍卖
H 段							
单词	音标	词性	释义	单词	音标	词性	释义
crash	[kræʃ]	*v.*	暴跌，破产	panic	[ˈpænɪk]	*n.*	恐慌，惊恐
fetch	[fetʃ]	*v.*	售得，卖得				
I 段							
单词	音标	词性	释义	单词	音标	词性	释义
differ	[ˈdɪfə(r)]	*v.*	不同于	aspect	[ˈæspekt]	*n.*	方面
establish	[ɪˈstæblɪʃ]	*v.*	建立，设立	speculation	[ˌspekjuˈleɪʃ(ə)n]	*n.*	投机，投机买卖
margin	[ˈmɑːdʒɪn]	*n.*	边缘	economic	[ˌiːkəˈnɒmɪk]	*adj.*	经济的，经济学的

题目精解

Questions 14-18

题型：段落信息配对题

Question 14

题干定位词 / 关键词	difference; bubble burst; tulip; high-tech shares
原文定位	I 段第一句 Tulip mania differed in one crucial aspect from the dot-com craze that grips our attention today: even at its height, the Amsterdam Stock Exchange, well-established in 1630, wouldn't touch tulips.
题目解析	题干：郁金香和高科技股票对泡沫破裂影响的区别。 根据关键词，可以定位到 I 段第一句，这里说郁金香热与如今吸引我们注意力的互联网热有一个关键的不同之处：即使在鼎盛时期，1630 年成立的阿姆斯特丹证券交易所也不会触碰郁金香，所以答案是 I。 本题的难点在于 bubble 这个词，dot-com bubble（互联网泡沫）是指一种经济现象，即 1995—2001 年互联网企业股价高速上升的现象，也就是文中的 dot-com craze。所以，本题题干的意思是郁金香带来的经济泡沫和高科技公司带来的经济泡沫之间的区别。
答案	I

Question 15

题干定位词 / 关键词	spread of tulip; before 17th century
原文定位	D 段全段
题目解析	题干：17 世纪之前郁金香的传播。 D 段说荷兰人不是第一个为郁金香而疯狂的人，早在第一朵郁金香在欧洲盛开之前，它就迷住了波斯人和奥斯曼帝国的统治者。但是在荷兰，人们对郁金香的热情达到了鼎盛。由此可知，D 段体现了郁金香的传播。
答案	D

Question 16

题干定位词 / 关键词	money offered for rare bulbs; in 17th century
原文定位	B 段第一句 Around 1624, the Amsterdam man who owned the only dozen specimens was offered 3,000 guilders for one bulb.
题目解析	题干：说明在 17 世纪人们为了罕见球茎出价。 本题有几个关键点：17 世纪，钱（在文中可能对应具体数额），罕见球茎。B 段第一句说，大约在 1624 年，一名拥有仅有的 12 个标本的阿姆斯特丹人被人出价以 3000 荷兰盾的价格购买一个球茎。这里 1624 年对应 17 世纪，the only dozen specimens 对应 rare bulb，3,000 guilders 对应 money，由此可知，B 段符合要求。
答案	B

Question 17

题干定位词 / 关键词	tulip was treated as money in Holland
原文定位	G 段第三句 In 1633, a farmhouse in Hoorn changed hands for three rare bulbs.
题目解析	题干：郁金香在荷兰被视为金钱。 本题比较难。首先分析题干，郁金香被视为金钱，指的是它可以用来买东西，所以可以以此为思路在文中寻找相关信息。G 段第三句说：1633 年，霍恩的一间农舍转手换了三个稀有球茎。也就是说，用三个郁金香球茎可以买一个农舍，即郁金香被视为金钱，可以用来交易。
答案	G

Question 18

题干定位词 / 关键词	comparison; between tulip and other plants
原文定位	F 段第二、三句 "It is impossible to comprehend the tulip mania without understanding just how different tulips were from every other flower known to horticulturists in the 17th century," says Dash. "The colors they exhibited were more intense and more concentrated than those of ordinary plants."
题目解析	题干：郁金香和其他植物的对比。 分析题干可知，答案句一定会出现"对比"和"其他植物"这类信息。F 段第二句引述达什的话"如果不了解郁金香与 17 世纪园艺学家所知的其他任何一种花卉有何不同，就不可能理解郁金香热。"这里 how different 对应 comparison，every other flower 对应 other plants。紧接着引述另一句话"它们所展示的颜色比普通植物更强烈、更集中。"这再一次体现了郁金香和其他植物的区别。
答案	F

Questions 19-23

题型：判断题

Question 19

题干定位词 / 关键词	1624; a man in Amsterdam
原文定位	B 段第一句 Around 1624, the Amsterdam man who owned the only dozen specimens was offered 3,000 guilders for one bulb.
题目解析	题干：1624 年，所有的郁金香收藏都属于阿姆斯特丹的一个人。 用 1624 定位到 B 段第一句，这里提到一个阿姆斯特丹人拥有仅有的 12 个标本（dozen=12），一个球茎被出价 3000 荷兰盾，也就是说所有郁金香都属于他，所以答案是 TRUE。
答案	TRUE

Question 20

题干定位词 / 关键词	first planted in Holland
原文定位	D 段第二句 Long before the first tulip bloomed in Europe—in Bavaria, it turns out, in 1559—the flower had enchanted the Persians and bewitched the rulers of the Ottoman Empire.
题目解析	题干：根据这篇文章，郁金香最初种植在荷兰。 根据 D 段第二句可知，在第一朵郁金香在欧洲开花之前（后来被证实是 1559 年，在巴伐利亚），这种花就曾让波斯人着迷，也让奥斯曼帝国的统治者着迷。由此可知，郁金香第一次开花是在巴伐利亚，并不是荷兰，所以答案是 FALSE。
答案	FALSE

Question 21

题干定位词 / 关键词	popularity; Holland; other countries; 17th century.
原文定位	D 段最后一句 It was in Holland, however, that the passion for tulips found its most fertile ground, for reasons that had little to do with horticulture.
题目解析	题干：在 17 世纪，郁金香在荷兰的受欢迎程度远远高于其他任何国家。 D 段最后一句指出，在荷兰，人们对郁金香的热情找到了最肥沃的土壤。也就是说，郁金香在荷兰是最受欢迎的，所以答案是 TRUE。
答案	TRUE

Question 22

题干定位词 / 关键词	Holland; the wealthiest country
原文定位	无
题目解析	题干：在 17 世纪，荷兰是世界上最富有的国家。 在原文无法定位，所以答案是 NOT GIVEN。
答案	NOT GIVEN

Question 23

题干定位词 / 关键词	1630; Amsterdam Stock Exchange
原文定位	I 段第一、二句 Tulip mania differed in one crucial aspect from the dot-com craze that grips our attention today: even at its height, the Amsterdam Stock Exchange, well-established in 1630, wouldn't touch tulips. "The speculation in tulip bulbs always existed at the margins of Dutch economic life," Dash writes.
题目解析	题干：从 1630 年起，阿姆斯特丹证券交易所开始规范郁金香交易市场。用 1630 和 Amesterdam Stock Exchange 定位到 I 段第一句，这里说即便是在鼎盛时期，1630 年建立的阿姆斯特丹证券交易所也不碰郁金香，对郁金香球茎的投机一直存在于荷兰经济生活的边缘。文中说的是证券交易所不碰郁金香，和题干的说法矛盾，所以答案是 FALSE。
答案	FALSE

Questions 24-26

题型：摘要填空题

Question 24

题干定位词 / 关键词	independence; Spain
原文定位	E 段第二句 Resources that had just a few years earlier gone toward fighting for independence from Spain now flowed into commerce.
题目解析	题干：在 17 世纪早期，荷兰专注于取得独立，通过 ____ 对抗西班牙。分析题干可知，by 在这里表示“通过……方式”，后面应该是名词或动词的 ing 形式。用 independence 和 Spain 定位到 E 段第二句：几年前用于争取从西班牙独立出来的资源现在流入了商业。这里提到了 fighting for independence from Spain（为了从西班牙独立而战），所以答案是 fighting。
答案	fighting

Question 25

题干定位词 / 关键词	spare resources
原文定位	E 段第二句 Resources that had just a few years earlier gone toward fighting for independence from Spain now flowed into commerce.
题目解析	题干：因此，空闲资源进入了 _____ 领域。 题干中的 consequently 表示结果，因此最好结合上一题分析。这里问荷兰从西班牙独立出来后，空闲资源用来干什么了，用 resources 定位到 E 段第二句：几年前用于争取从西班牙独立出来的资源现在流入了商业。由此可知，资源进入了 commerce（商业）领域。
答案	commerce

Question 26

题干定位词 / 关键词	traders; and speculator
原文定位	F 段第六句 These "florists", or professional tulip traders, sought out flower lovers and speculators alike.
题目解析	题干：被郁金香成功获利所吸引，交易员们不断寻找 _____ 和投机者以达成销售。 本题考查的是并列结构，答案应为和 speculator 并列的一个名词。定位到 F 段第六句：这些"花商"，或专业的郁金香商人，寻找花卉爱好者和投机者。这里和 speculators 并列的是 flower lovers，所以答案是 flower lovers。
答案	flower lovers

长难句分析

E 段：The Dutch population seemed torn by two contradictory impulses: a horror of living beyond one's means and the love of a long shot.

思路分析：这个句子的难点在于两个短语，live beyond one's means 指的是"入不敷出"，a long shot 指的是"不太会成功的尝试"（也可以指一种冒险）。

参考翻译：荷兰人似乎被两种相互矛盾的冲动拉扯着：一种是对入不敷出的恐惧，另一种是对冒险的热爱。

F 段：“It is impossible to comprehend the tulip mania without understanding just how different tulips were from every other flower known to horticulturists in the 17th century,” says Dash.

思路分析： 这是一个 it is + adj. to do sth. 的句型，并且这个句子里包含一个双重否定：impossible 和 without，在这里 without 翻译成“如果不”，所以句子的大致结构是“如果不了解……就无法理解郁金香热”，双重否定表示肯定，也就是“只有了解了……才能理解郁金香热”。另外，flower 后面的 known to horticulturists in the 17th century 是分词作定语修饰 flower。

参考翻译： 达什说：“如果不了解郁金香与 17 世纪园艺学家所知的其他任何一种花卉有何不同，就不可能理解郁金香热。”

参考译文

当郁金香泡沫破灭时

郁金香是春天盛开的多年生植物，由球茎生长而成。根据品种的不同，郁金香植株可以低至 4 英寸（10 厘米）或高达 28 英寸（71 厘米）。郁金香的大花通常在缺乏苞片的花葶或具花葶下茎上开放。大多数郁金香每根茎上只开一朵花，但也有少数品种的郁金香在花葶上开出多朵花（如土耳其郁金香）。这种艳丽的、通常是杯状或星形的郁金香花有三个花瓣和三个萼片，通常被统称为花被片，因为它们几乎完全相同。这六片花被片通常位于基部附近的内表面，颜色较深。郁金香花的颜色五花八门，除了纯蓝色（有几种名字中带有“蓝”字的郁金香有淡淡的紫罗兰色调）。

A 早在有人听说高通、CMGI、思科系统等在本轮牛市中暴涨的高科技股之前，就有了“永远的奥古斯都”。它比任何股票或债券都更平凡，也更崇高，它是一种异常美丽的郁金香，午夜蓝色的花瓣顶部有一条纯白的白边，并点缀着深红色的闪光。对于 17 世纪的荷兰居民来说，没有什么是像这样令人向往的。

B 大约在 1624 年，一位拥有仅有的 12 个标本的阿姆斯特丹人被人出价以 3000 荷兰盾的价格购买一个球茎。虽然没有准确的方法将其换算成今天的美钞，但这笔钱大致相当于一个富商的年收入。（几年后，伦勃朗的画作《守夜人》获得了该价格大约一半的收入。）然而，球茎的主人（他的名字已湮没在历史中）拒绝了这一提议。

C 谁更疯狂，是拒绝为一小笔财富出售球茎的郁金香爱好者，还是那个愿意挥霍的人。

这是看完英国记者迈克·达什的《郁金香热：世界上最受人追捧的花朵及其掀起的非凡热潮的故事》后，脑海中浮现的一个问题。近年来，由于投资者故意忘记了他们在《投资 101》中学到的一切，以增加对未经证实、无利可图的网络股的投资，郁金香热被频繁地提起。在这本简洁扼要、文笔巧妙的书中，达什讲述了这个流行语背后的真实历史，并为我们这个时代提供了一个警世故事。

D 荷兰人并不是第一个为郁金香而疯狂的人。早在欧洲第一朵郁金香开花之前（后来被证实是 1559 年，在巴伐利亚），这种花就曾让波斯人着迷，也让奥斯曼帝国的统治者着迷。然而，正是在荷兰，人们对郁金香的热情找到了最肥沃的土壤，而原因与园艺无关。

E 17 世纪初的荷兰正迎来它的黄金时代。几年前用于争取从西班牙独立出来的资源现在流入了商业。阿姆斯特丹商人处于利润丰厚的东印度群岛贸易的中心，在那里，一次航行可以产生 400% 的利润。他们通过建造被花园环绕的大庄园来展示他们的成功。荷兰人似乎被两种相互矛盾的冲动拉扯着：一种是对入不敷出的恐惧，另一种是对冒险的热爱。

F 郁金香登场了。达什说："如果不了解郁金香与 17 世纪园艺学家所知的其他任何一种花卉有何不同，就不可能理解郁金香热。""它们所展示的颜色比普通植物更强烈、更集中。"尽管稀有球茎的价格很离奇，但普通郁金香是论磅出售的。然而，1630 年左右，一种新型的郁金香爱好者出现了，他们被丰厚利润的传说所吸引。这些"花商"，或专业的郁金香商人，寻找花卉爱好者和投机者。但是，当郁金香买家迅速增长时，球茎的供应却没有增长。郁金香是供应紧张的同谋者：从种子长成一株郁金香需要 7 年时间。虽然球茎每年可以产生两到三个克隆体，或"侧球"，但母球茎只能维持几年。

G 随着越来越多的投机者挤入市场，郁金香球茎价格在整个 17 世纪 30 年代稳步上涨。织工和农民不惜一切代价通过抵押来筹集资金开始交易。1633 年，霍恩的一间农舍转手换了三个稀有球茎。到了 1636 年，任何郁金香——即使是最近被认为是垃圾的球茎——都可以被卖掉，价格通常为数百荷兰盾。当时还出现了郁金香球茎的期货市场，郁金香商人在数百家荷兰酒馆开展业务。郁金香热在 1636—1637 年的冬天达到了顶峰，当时一些球茎在一天内转手十次。那年冬天，高潮提前到来，出现在一场为七个孤儿举办的拍卖会上，他们唯一的资产是父亲留下的 70 朵优质郁金香。其中，一株即将分裂成两半的 Violetten Admirael van Enkhuizen（恩克赫伊曾的紫色海军上将）稀有球茎，以 5200 荷兰盾的价格创造了历史记录。这 70 朵花总共卖了近 5.3 万荷兰盾。

H 不久之后，郁金香市场彻底崩塌，令人叹为观止。事情始于哈勒姆一个例行的球茎拍卖会，第一次出现了“更傻的傻瓜”(指追涨杀跌者)不愿出现并支付的情况。没过几天，恐慌情绪就蔓延到了全国。尽管贸易商努力提振需求，郁金香市场还是蒸发了。几周前还能卖到 5000 荷兰盾的郁金香，现在只能卖到原来的百分之一。郁金香热并非十全十美。达什在郁金香从亚洲到荷兰的迁徙上花了太多时间。但他用启发性、通俗易懂的描述解释了这一令人难以置信的金融愚蠢行为。

I 郁金香热与如今吸引我们注意力的互联网热有一个关键的不同之处：即使在鼎盛时期，1630 年成立的阿姆斯特丹证券交易所也不会触碰郁金香。“对郁金香球茎的投机一直存在于荷兰经济生活的边缘，”达什写道。市场崩塌后，各方达成了妥协，允许大多数商人以其债务的一小部分偿还债务。这对荷兰经济的整体影响可以忽略不计。当华尔街当前的痴迷最终走到尽头时，我们还会说同样的话吗？

READING PASSAGE 3

Termite Mounds

文章结构

体裁	说明文
题材	生物和环境
主题	白蚁丘的构造、功能、研究方法及研究意义
段落概括	A 段：白蚁虽是害虫，但也有有用的一面。 B 段：描述白蚁丘的构造。 C 段：讲解白蚁丘的功能。 D 段：描述白蚁的消化系统。 E 段：白蚁体内平衡功能的转移。 F 段：一种研究白蚁丘的方法。 G 段：研究白蚁丘的模型对未来建筑的价值。

重点词汇

A 段							
单词	音标	词性	释义	单词	音标	词性	释义
termite	[ˈtɜːmaɪt]	*n.*	白蚁	destructive	[dɪˈstrʌktɪv]	*adj.*	破坏性的，毁灭性的
insect	[ˈɪnsekt]	*n.*	昆虫	damage	[ˈdæmɪdʒ]	*n.*	损害，伤害
devastating	[ˈdevəsteɪtɪŋ]	*adj.*	毁灭性的，极具破坏力的	scale	[skeɪl]	*n.*	等级；规模，范围
B 段							
单词	音标	词性	释义	单词	音标	词性	释义
mound	[maʊnd]	*n.*	土堆，石堆	impressive	[ɪmˈpresɪv]	*adj.*	给人印象深刻的
cavity	[ˈkævəti]	*n.*	洞，腔	harsh	[hɑːʃ]	*adj.*	（环境）恶劣的，艰苦的
lattice	[ˈlætɪs]	*n.*	格状结构	blood vessel		*phr.*	血管

C 段							
单词	音标	词性	释义	单词	音标	词性	释义
system	[ˈsɪstəm]	*n.*	系统	capture	[ˈkæptʃə(r)]	*v.*	俘获，捕获
expel	[ɪkˈspel]	*v.*	排出（空气、水、气体等）	spent	[spent]	*adj.*	用过已废的
respiratory	[rəˈspɪrətri] [ˈrespərətri]	*adj.*	呼吸的	suffocate	[ˈsʌfəkeɪt]	*v.*	（使）窒息而死，（使）闷死
continuous	[kənˈtɪnjuəs]	*adj.*	连续不断的，持续的	provision	[prəˈvɪʒn]	*n.*	提供，供应
regulate	[ˈreɡjuleɪt]	*v.*	管控，调节	cellar	[ˈselə(r)]	*n.*	地下室，地窖
D 段							
单词	音标	词性	释义	单词	音标	词性	释义
evolve	[ɪˈvɒlv]	*v.*	进化，演化；逐步发展	outsource	[ˈaʊtsɔːs]	*v.*	外包
digestive	[daɪˈdʒestɪv]	*adj.*	消化的	digestible	[daɪˈdʒestəbl]	*adj.*	易消化的
fungus	[ˈfʌŋɡəs]	*n.*	真菌	thrive	[θraɪv]	*v.*	茁壮成长
internal	[ɪnˈtɜːnl]	*adj.*	内部的，体内的	generate	[ˈdʒenəreɪt]	*v.*	产生，引起
E 段							
单词	音标	词性	释义	单词	音标	词性	释义
label	[ˈleɪbl]	*v.*	贴标签	organism	[ˈɔːɡənɪzəm]	*n.*	生物，有机体
come to light		*phr.*	真相大白	unique	[juˈniːk]	*adj.*	独一无二的，独特的
feature	[ˈfiːtʃə(r)]	*n.*	特点，特征	ultimately	[ˈʌltɪmətli]	*adv.*	最终，最后
redefine	[ˌriːdɪˈfaɪn]	*v.*	重新定义				
F 段							
单词	音标	词性	释义	单词	音标	词性	释义
reveal	[rɪˈviːl]	*v.*	揭示，透露	structure	[ˈstrʌktʃə(r)]	*n.*	结构，构造
paste	[peɪst]	*n.*	面糊，糊状物	sequentially	[sɪˈkwenʃəli]	*adv.*	循序地，连续地
scan	[skæn]	*v.*	扫描	three-dimensional		*phr.*	三维的，立体的

G 段							
单词	音标	词性	释义	单词	音标	词性	释义
model	[ˈmɒdl]	*n.*	模型，模式	external	[ɪkˈstɜːnl]	*adj.*	外部的，外面的
condition	[kənˈdɪʃn]	*n.*	条件，环境	draw on		*phr.*	利用
invaluable	[ɪnˈvæljuəbl]	*adj.*	极有用的，极宝贵的	architectural	[ˌɑːkɪˈtektʃərəl]	*adj.*	建筑学的，建筑方面的
approach	[əˈprəʊtʃ]	*v.*	靠近，临近	fuel	[ˈfjuːəl]	*n.*	燃料，燃烧剂
arid	[ˈærɪd]	*adj.*	（土地或气候）干燥的，干旱的	habitat	[ˈhæbɪtæt]	*n.*	（动植物的）生活环境，栖息地
hostile	[ˈhɒstaɪl]	*adj.*	艰苦的				

题目精解

Questions 27-33

题型：标题题

小标题	译文
i. Methods used to investigate termite mound formation	研究白蚁丘形成的方法
ii. Challenging our assumptions about the nature of life	挑战我们对生命本质的设想
iii. Reconsidering the termite's reputation	重新考虑白蚁的名声
iv. Principal functions of the termite mound	白蚁丘的主要功能
v. Distribution of termite mounds in sub-Saharan Africa	撒哈拉以南非洲白蚁丘的分布
vi. Some potential benefits of understanding termite architecture	了解白蚁建筑的一些潜在好处
vii. The astonishing physical dimensions of the termite mound	白蚁丘惊人的外形尺寸
viii. Termite mounds under threat from global climate change	白蚁丘受到全球气候变化的威胁
ix. Mutually beneficial relationship	互惠关系

Question 27

题干定位词 / 关键词	reconsidering; reputation
原文定位	A 段第一、二句 To most of us, termites are destructive insects which can cause damage on a devastating scale. But according to Dr. Rupert Soar of Loughborough University's School of Mechanical and Manufacturing Engineering, these pests may serve a useful purpose for us after all.
题目解析	A 段第一句说我们多数人都认为白蚁是害虫，后面紧接着用 But 转折，说根据 Dr. Rupert 的研究，它们对我们可能是有用的。也就是说，白蚁以前名声不好，现在有了变化，发现了它好的一面，所以我们要"重新考虑白蚁的名声"了，对应 iii。 在分析段落主旨时，一定要注意段落中出现的转折词，比较高频的转折词有 however，but，yet。
答案	iii

Question 28

题干定位词 / 关键词	astonishing physical dimensions
原文定位	B 段第一句 Termite mounds are impressive for their size alone; typically they are three metres high, and some as tall as eight metres by found.
题目解析	B 段第一句提到白蚁丘的尺寸令人印象深刻，这里 size 对应 physical dimensions，impressive 对应 astonishing。接着往下阅读，第二句说白蚁丘能够延伸到地下，第三句介绍巢穴的位置，第四句介绍白蚁丘复杂的网状结构，这些均在讲述白蚁丘的 physical dimensions（外形尺寸）。本题需特别注意 physical 一词，它的常见意思有"物理的，身体的，外形的"，这里的意思是"外形的"。
答案	vii

Question 29

题干定位词 / 关键词	functions
原文定位	C 段
题目解析	C 段第一句说这个复杂的隧道系统（也就是白蚁丘）可以从外部吸入空气，捕捉风能，使其穿过土丘。接着第二句用 It also serves to（用来做……；起……作用）句式介绍白蚁丘的功能。再往下阅读，第四句开头说 The mound also automatically regulates moisture（白蚁丘还能自动调节湿度），这里依然在讲功能。考生要特别注意第二、四句里 also 这个词的用法，它说明前后文在内容上是一致的，即都在讲功能。
答案	iv

Question 30

题干定位词 / 关键词	mutually beneficial relationship
原文定位	D 段
题目解析	D 段第一句很明显是主旨句，说白蚁会把一些生物功能外包（outsource）出去，后面具体讲解如何外包。第二句说它们消化过程的一部分是由一种真菌完成的，而这些真菌是白蚁在土丘里“种植”的。重点是第四句，该句说白蚁用轻微咀嚼过的木浆喂养真菌，真菌将木浆分解成可消化的含糖食物，为昆虫提供能量，以及用于建筑的纤维素。显然，这是一种互惠关系（mutually beneficial relationship）。
答案	ix

Question 31

题干定位词 / 关键词	challenging our assumption; the nature of life
原文定位	E 段
题目解析	E 段第一句主要解释 homeostasis（内稳态）的概念。第二句说白蚁将自我平衡功能从它们的身体转移到它们生活的蚁穴中。重点是最后一句，该句说随着关于白蚁丘独特之处的信息越来越多，我们最终可能需要重新定义对“活”有机体的理解，也就是说这个发现挑战了我们对“活”的有机体的认知，对应 ii。
答案	ii

Question 32

题干定位词 / 关键词	methods; investigate; formation
原文定位	F 段
题目解析	F 段第一句说为了揭示土丘的结构，索尔的团队首先向土丘填充并覆盖了熟石膏。第二句说研究人员将熟石膏雕刻成半毫米厚的薄片，并按顺序拍摄。第三句说一旦将这些照片进行扫描，计算机技术就能重建土丘的三维图像。最后一句说这些模型使团队能够以前所未有的详细程度绘制白蚁的巢穴结构。这一段明显是在介绍研究白蚁丘构造的具体方法和步骤，所以选 i。 在阅读过程中，考生应格外注意一些表示时间顺序的词，如 begin, then, sequentially, once 等。
答案	i

Question 33

题干定位词 / 关键词	potential benefits; understanding termite architecture
原文定位	G 段
题目解析	G 段第一句说索尔希望这些模型能解释白蚁丘是如何创造一个自我调节的生活环境的，它能在不依赖任何外部能源的情况下对不断变化的内部和外部条件做出反应。重点在第二句，该句说这些发现将为未来的建筑设计提供宝贵的启示，为自给自足、环境友好和运行成本低廉的建筑提供灵感。这些都是“潜在好处”（potential benefits），对应 vi。
答案	vi

Questions 34-37

题型：图表填空题

Question 34

题干定位词 / 关键词	network of
原文定位	B 段最后一句 The mound itself is formed of an intricate lattice of tunnels, which split into smaller and smaller tunnels, much like a person’s blood vessels.
题目解析	题干：_____ 的网络有助于为白蚁提供恒定的 _____ 供应，并保持有限的温度范围。 对于图表填空题，考生一定要先分析图表，由图可以判断出这组填空题是关于白蚁丘的构造的，对应文章 B 段部分。出题位置确定之后，再来看第 34 题的题干，本题的重点在于 network（网络；网状系统）这个词，要在文中找到与它对应的内容。带着定位词在 B 段扫读，直到最后一句：土丘本身由错综复杂的隧道格子组成，这些隧道分裂成越来越小的隧道，很像人的血管。这里有一个词 lattice, 它的意思是“格状结构”，正好对应 network，所以答案就是 tunnels。如果不认识 lattice 这个单词 , 后面还提到 much like a person’s blood vessles（很像人的血管），由于人的血管也是网状的，据此也可以判断答案。
答案	tunnels

Question 35

题干定位词 / 关键词	a constant; supply; a limited temperature range
原文定位	C 段第二句 It also serves to expel spent respiratory gases from the nest to prevent the termites from suffocating, so ensuring them a continuous provision of fresh, breathable air.
题目解析	题干：_____ 的网络有助于为白蚁提供恒定的 _____ 供应，并保持有限的温度范围。 分析题干可知，空格处应填恒定供应的某种东西，答案大概率是一个名词。用定位词定位到 C 段第二句，该句的后半句说确保白蚁能持续获得新鲜、可呼吸的空气供应，这里 continuous（持续的）对应 constant，provision（供应）对应 supply，所以答案就是 air。
答案	air

Question 36

题干定位词 / 关键词	cellar; control of
原文定位	C 段倒数第二句 The mound also automatically regulates moisture in the air, by means of its underground ‘cellar’, and evaporation from the top of the mound.
题目解析	题干：地窖以帮助控制土丘中 _____ 的水平。 用 cellar 和 control 定位到 C 段倒数第二句，原文说通过地下“地窖”和顶部的蒸发，土丘还能自动调节空气的湿度。这里 regulates 和 control 对应，所以答案就是 moisture。
答案	moisture

Question 37

题干定位词 / 关键词	top of the mound
原文定位	C 段倒数第二句 The mound also automatically regulates moisture in the air, by means of its underground ‘cellar’, and evaporation from the top of the mound.
题目解析	题干：土丘顶部允许 _____。 用 top of the mound 定位到 C 段倒数第二句的后半句，这里提到土丘顶部的蒸发（evaporation），也就是说顶部是允许蒸发的，所以答案是 evaporation。
答案	evaporation

Questions 38-40

题型：判断题

Question 38

题干定位词 / 关键词	refuse material; internally
原文定位	D 段最后一句 And, although the termites must generate waste, none ever leaves the structure, indicating that there is also some kind of internal waste-recycling system.
题目解析	题干：白蚁丘似乎在内部处理垃圾。 用 refuse material 和 internally 定位到 D 段最后一句，该句说尽管白蚁肯定会产生粪便，但却没有白蚁会离开这个巢穴，这表明其内部也存在某种废物回收系统。由此可知，答案是 YES。
答案	YES

Question 39

题干定位词 / 关键词	a single photograph; computer
原文定位	F 段第二句 The researchers then carves the plaster of Paris into half-millimatre-thick slices, and photograph them sequentially.
题目解析	题干：索尔的重建工作包括将一张完整土丘的照片扫描到计算机中。 用 photograph 定位到 F 段第二句：然后，研究人员将熟石膏雕刻成半毫米厚的薄片，并按顺序拍摄。本题的重点在于分析句子的后半句，原文说 photograph them sequentially（将它们按顺序拍摄），这表明不只是一张照片，所以答案是 NO。
答案	NO

Question 40

题干定位词 / 关键词	new information, termite architecture; help; future energy crises
原文定位	G 段最后两句 “As we approach a world of climate change, we need temperatures to rise”, he explains, “there will not be enough fuel to drive air conditioners around the world”. It is hoped, says Soar, “that the findings will provide clues that aid the ultimate development of new kinds of human habitats, suitable for a variety of arid, hostile environments not only on the earth but maybe one day on the moon and beyond.”
题目解析	题干：关于白蚁结构的新信息可以帮助人们应对未来的能源危机。 根据定位词定位到 G 段最后两句，最后两句引述索尔的话“我们面临一个气候变化的世界，我们需要温度上升，但没有足够的燃料来驱动全球各地的空调。”“人们希望这些发现能为帮助人类最终开发出新型的人类栖息地提供线索，这些栖息地不仅适合地球上各种干旱、恶劣的环境，也许有一天也适合月球甚至更远的地方。” 这里虽然提到没有足够的燃料，但是文中说的是这些信息可以帮助我们开发新的栖息地，而没有提到是否能解决能源危机，所以答案是 NOT GIVEN。
答案	NOT GIVEN

长难句分析

F 段：To reveal the structure of the mounds, Soar's team begins by filling and covering their plaster of Paris, a chalky white paste based on the mineral gypsum, which becomes rock-solid when dry.

思路分析：可能很多考生不知道 plaster of Paris 的意思，故对整个句子的意思比较困惑。但是逗号后面紧接着用同位语对其进行了解释，是一种基于矿物石膏的白色膏体（a chalky white paste based on the mineral gypsum），后面 which 引导的定语从句依然用于修饰 plaster of Paris，which 作主语，指代 plaster of Paris。

参考翻译：为了揭示土丘的结构，索尔的团队首先向土丘填充并覆盖了他们的熟石膏，这是一种基于矿物石膏的白色膏体，干燥后会变得坚如磐石。

G 段：Soar hopes that the models will explain how termite mounds create a self-regulating living environment which manages to respond to changing internal and external conditions without drawing on any outside source of power.

思路分析：这个句子中有一个 which 引导的定语从句，修饰前面的 a self-regulating living environment，还要注意后面的 without，在这里表示一种条件，即“在不……的情况下”。

参考翻译：索尔希望这些模型能够解释白蚁丘是如何创造一个自我调节的生活环境的，在不依赖任何外部能源的情况下，这个环境能对不断变化的内部和外部条件做出反应。

参考译文

白蚁丘

在撒哈拉以南非洲地区，由昆虫建造的巨大泥塔能成为未来我们的节能建筑的关键吗？

A 对我们大多数人来说，白蚁是一种破坏性的昆虫，可以造成毁灭性的破坏。但拉夫堡大学机械与制造工程学院的鲁珀特·索尔博士表示，这些害虫可能对我们还是有用处的。他的由英国和美国的工程师和生物学家组成的多学科团队已经开始调查白蚁在撒哈拉以南非洲纳米比亚建造的巨大土丘，这是迄今为止对这些结构进行的最广泛研究的一部分。

B 白蚁丘仅就其规模而言就令人印象深刻；已发现的一般都有 3 米高，有的高达 8 米。它们还能深入地下，在那里昆虫“挖掘”它们的建筑材料，仔细筛选它们要用的每一粒沙子。白蚁的巢穴被安置在土堆的中央洞穴中，免受外界恶劣环境的影响。土丘本身由错综复杂的隧道格子组成，这些隧道分裂成越来越小的隧道，很像人的血管。

C 这个复杂的隧道系统可以从外部吸入空气，捕捉风能，使其穿过土丘。同时，它还能将用过的呼吸气体排出巢穴，防止白蚁窒息，从而确保白蚁能持续获得新鲜、可呼吸的空气供应。这种设计非常精细，所以尽管从白天的酷热到最冷的夜晚气温低于零度，温差高达 50℃，它的温度却保持在恒定的 3℃以内。通过地下“地窖”和顶部的蒸发，土丘还能自动调节空气的湿度。在撒哈拉以南非洲最热的地区，一些蚁群甚至在 20 米高的地方安装了“烟囱”，以控制湿度。

D 此外，白蚁还进化出了一种方式将它们的一些生物功能外包出去了。它们消化过程的一部分是由一种真菌完成的，这种真菌是白蚁在土丘里“种植”的。这种真菌在地球上其他地方都找不到，它们在土丘中恒定而最佳的环境中茁壮成长。白蚁用轻微咀嚼过的木浆喂养这些真菌，真菌将木浆分解成可消化的含糖食物，为昆虫提供能量，以及用于建筑的纤维素。而且，尽管白蚁肯定会产生粪便，但却没有白蚁会离开这个巢穴，这表明其内部也存在某种废物回收系统。

E 科学家们对这些土丘感到非常兴奋，他们给它们贴上了“超级有机体”的标签，因为用索尔的话来说，“它们在我们感知到的温度边缘舞动以保持凉快，或者如果太冷了，就需要茁壮成长：这被称为内稳态。白蚁所做的就是将自我平衡功能从它们的身体转移到它们生活的蚁穴中。随着关于白蚁丘独特之处的信息越来越多，我们最终可能需要重新定义对‘活’有机体的理解。”

F 为了揭示土丘的结构，索尔的团队首先向土丘填充并覆盖了他们的熟石膏，这是一种基于矿物石膏的白色膏体，干燥后会变得坚如磐石。然后，研究人员将熟石膏雕刻成半毫米厚的薄片，并按顺序拍摄。一旦这些照片被数字扫描，计算机技术就能够重建这些土丘的复杂三维图像。这些模型使研究小组能够以前所未有的详细程度绘制白蚁的巢穴结构。

G 索尔希望这些模型能够解释白蚁丘是如何创造一个自我调节的生活环境的，在不依赖任何外部能源的情况下，这个环境能对不断变化的内部和外部条件做出反应。如果他们能做到这一点，这些发现将为未来的建筑设计提供宝贵的启示，为自给自足、环境友好和运行成本低廉的建筑提供灵感。他解释说：“我们面临一个气候变化的世界，我们需要温度上升，但没有足够的燃料来驱动全球各地的空调。”索尔说，“人们希望这些发现能为帮助人类最终开发出新型的人类栖息地提供线索，这些栖息地不仅适合地球上各种干旱、恶劣的环境，也许有一天也适合月球甚至更远的地方。”

TEST 3 解析

READING PASSAGE 1

Koalas

文章结构

体裁	说明文
题材	动物类
主题	考拉的生活习性、生存现状、面临的威胁及相关保护措施
段落概括	A 段：考拉生活在一个安全的环境中。 B 段：考拉在澳大利亚的数量变化。 C 段：考拉数量骤减的原因（桉树、疾病、车祸、偷猎等）。 D 段：考拉生存面临的其他威胁（丛林大火、生育率低）。 E 段：考拉最新面临的问题（动物园利用它们拍照挣钱）。 F 段：考拉有专门的消化系统来消化桉树叶。 G 段：考拉不具有攻击性。 H 段：考拉非常脆弱，易死于疾病。 I 段：拥抱考拉的危害以及政府发起的禁止措施。

重点词汇

A 段							
单词	音标	词性	释义	单词	音标	词性	释义
occasional	[əˈkeɪʒənl]	*adj.*	偶尔的，不经常的	prey	[preɪ]	*n.*	猎物，捕获物
enemy	[ˈenəmi]	*n.*	敌人	arboreal	[ɑːˈbɔːriəl]	*adj.*	栖息在树上的
couch potato		*phr.*	极为懒惰的人				
B 段							
单词	音标	词性	释义	单词	音标	词性	释义
flourish	[ˈflʌrɪʃ]	*v.*	繁荣，昌盛	species	[ˈspiːʃiːz]	*n.*	（动植物的）种，物种
aborigine	[ˌæbəˈrɪdʒəni]	*n.*	土著	co-exist	[ˌkəʊɪgˈzɪst]	*v.*	共存

C段							
单词	音标	词性	释义	单词	音标	词性	释义
scattered	[ˈskætəd]	*adj.*	分散的，零散的	eucalyptus	[ˌjuːkəˈlɪptəs]	*n.*	桉树，桉属植物
parasite	[ˈpærəsaɪt]	*n.*	寄生植物（或动物），寄生虫	poacher	[ˈpəʊtʃə(r)]	*n.*	偷猎者，侵入者
ironically	[aɪˈrɒnɪkli]	*adv.*	讽刺地	wildlife sanctuary		*phr.*	野生动物保护区
D段							
单词	音标	词性	释义	单词	音标	词性	释义
rage	[reɪdʒ]	*v.*	（火灾、疾病）迅速蔓延，快速扩散	shelter	[ˈʃeltə(r)]	*n.*	居所，住处，庇护所
paw	[pɔː]	*n.*	（动物的）爪子	ember	[ˈembə(r)]	*n.*	余火，余烬
zoologist	[zuˈɒlədʒɪst]	*n.*	动物学家	burgeoning	[ˈbɜːdʒənɪŋ]	*adj.*	迅速发展的，快速生长的
survival	[səˈvaɪvl]	*n.*	存活，幸存	reproductive rate		*phr.*	繁殖率
lifespan	[ˈlaɪfspæn]	*n.*	（人或动物的）寿命				
E段							
单词	音标	词性	释义	单词	音标	词性	释义
insidious	[ɪnˈsɪdiəs]	*adj.*	潜伏的	hug	[hʌg]	*v.*	拥抱
bundle	[ˈbʌndl]	*n.*	婴儿	cruel	[ˈkruːəl]	*adj.*	残酷的，残忍的
delicate	[ˈdelɪkət]	*adj.*	柔和的，脆弱的	disposition	[ˌdɪspəˈzɪʃn]	*n.*	性情，性格
precariously	[prɪˈkeəriəsli]	*adv.*	不安全地；不牢靠地				
F段							
单词	音标	词性	释义	单词	音标	词性	释义
foliage	[ˈfəʊliɪdʒ]	*n.*	（植物的）枝叶，叶子	toxic	[ˈtɒksɪk]	*adj.*	有毒的
digest	[daɪˈdʒest]	*v.*	消化	bacteria	[bækˈtɪəriə]	*n.*	细菌
fibre	[ˈfaɪbə(r)]	*n.*	（食物的）纤维素	properly	[ˈprɒpəli]	*adv.*	正确地，适当地

G段							
单词	音标	词性	释义	单词	音标	词性	释义
rip	[rɪp]	v.	（使）撕裂	claw	[klɔː]	n.	（动物的）爪，爪子
aggressive	[əˈgresɪv]	adj.	好斗的	grip	[grɪp]	v.	（尤指通过摩擦力）牢牢地附着
H段							
单词	音标	词性	释义	单词	音标	词性	释义
breeding	[ˈbriːdɪŋ]	n.	（动物的）饲养	succumb	[səˈkʌm]	v.	死于（某疾病）
infection	[ɪnˈfekʃn]	n.	传染病	stoic	[ˈstəʊɪk]	adj.	坚忍的
marsupial	[mɑːˈsuːpiəl]	adj.	有袋的				
I段							
单词	音标	词性	释义	单词	音标	词性	释义
ambassador	[æmˈbæsədə(r)]	n.	大使	cuddling	[ˈkʌdlɪŋ]	n.	拥抱，搂抱
scream	[skriːm]	v.	呼吁，抗议	campaign	[kæmˈpeɪn]	v.	领导（参加）运动
publicity	[pʌbˈlɪsəti]	n.	（媒体的）关注，报道				

题目精解

Questions 1-5

题型：单选题

Question 1

题干定位词 / 关键词	reason; declined; killed
原文定位	C段第四、五句 Koalas have been killed by parasites, Chlamydia epidemics and a tumour-causing retro-virus. And every year 11000 are killed by cars, ironically most of them in wildlife sanctuaries, and thousands are killed by poachers.
题目解析	题干：考拉数量下降的主要原因不包括什么引起的死亡？ A：偷猎者 B：生病 C：生了很多宝宝但存活率低 D：路上的车祸 根据declined可能首先会定位到B段，但是在B段里，选项中的关键词均未提及，所以往下阅读C段，可以发现这一段在讲考拉数量骤减的原因，同时出现了killed，poachers等关键词，据此可以确定定位正确。C段第四、五句中提到考拉被杀死的原因有选项A、选项B和选项D（原文为killed by cars），用排除法可确定答案为选项C。此外，D段最后一句提到了考拉的繁殖，原文的意思是考拉的繁殖率低，与选项C矛盾，由此也可确定答案为选项C。
答案	C

Question 2

题干定位词 / 关键词	fully digest; food
原文定位	F 段第三句到最后 To handle this cocktail, koalas have a specialized digestive system. Cellulose-digesting bacteria in the caecum break down fibre, while a specially adapted gut and liver process the toxins. To digest their food properly, koalas must sit still for 21 hours every day.
题目解析	题干：什么东西可以帮助考拉完全消化它们的食物？ A：叶子中的有毒物质 B：可以分解纤维的器官 C：保持一段时间不活动 D：吃桉树（叶子） 由题干中的 digest 可以定位到 F 段第三句，往下阅读，直到本段最后一句提到为了适当地消化食物，考拉每天必须静坐 21 个小时，由此可以确定答案为选项 C。properly 对应 fully，sit still 对应 remaining inactive，21 hours 对应 a period。 F 段第二句提到树叶中含有毒素（precursors of toxic cyanides），但是并未提到树叶中的有毒物质能帮助消化，所以排除选项 A。 F 段第四句提到盲肠中的纤维素消化细菌能帮助分解纤维，且仅仅分解纤维，但不处理毒素（Cellulose-digesting bacteria in the caecum break down fibre, while a specially adapted gut and liver process the toxins），由此可知盲肠无法帮助考拉完全消化食物，故排除选项 B。 桉树叶是考拉的食物（Koalas only eat the foliage of certain species of eucalyptus trees），并不是帮助考拉消化食物的方式，故选项 D 也可以排除。
答案	C

Question 3

题干定位词 / 关键词	dangerous situation
原文定位	G 段第二句到最后 Although they are capable of ripping open a man's arm with their needle-sharp claws, or giving a nasty nip, they simply wouldn't. If you upset a koala, it may blink or swallow, or hiccup. But attack? No way! Koalas are just not aggressive. They use their claws to grip the hard smooth bark of eucalyptus trees.

题目解析	题干：遇到危险情况时考拉会做什么？ A：表现出被冒犯的迹象 B：猛烈地反击 C：用尖爪将人撕开 D：用爪子抓树皮 做完第 2 题后继续往下阅读至 G 段，G 段主要讲考拉不具有攻击性。G 段第二句至结尾指出，虽然考拉能用针尖的爪子撕开人的胳膊，或者狠狠地咬上一口，但它们不会这么做。如果人们惹到考拉了，考拉可能会眨眼、吞咽或打嗝，但是却不会攻击人类。它们的爪子是用来抓住桉树坚硬光滑的树皮的。由此可知，眨眼、吞咽、打嗝是考拉遇到危险情况的迹象，故选选项 A。 选项 B 和选项 C 与原文表述不符，虽然考拉具备一定的反击能力，但是它们却不会这么做。 选项 D 是考拉爪子的用途，并不是它们遇到危险情况的表现，故也排除。
答案	A

Question 4

题干定位词 / 关键词	Australian zoos, exploit
原文定位	E 段第三句 Australian zoos and wildlife parks have taken advantage of their uncomplaining attitudes, and charge visitors to be photographed hugging the furry bundles.
题目解析	题干：澳大利亚的动物园是如何利用考拉的？ A：鼓励人们将考拉当宠物养 B：允许游客拥抱考拉 C：把它们放在树上作为象征 D：发起考拉运动 文中提到 Australia zoos 的地方有 E 段第三句和 I 段。E 段第三句表明澳大利亚的动物园和野生动物园利用考拉毫无怨言的态度，让游客抱着这些毛茸茸的小家伙拍照，并收取费用，对应选项 B，其中 exploit 对应 take advantages of。 C 段提及考拉数量下降的原因之一是被非法当作宠物（Some are also taken illegally as pets），与动物园无关，故排除选项 A。 I 段提及考拉是澳大利亚的动物大使（the marsupial has become the Animal Ambassador of the nation），以及考拉喜欢把驯兽师的胳膊当成树（use his or her arm as a tree），与选项 C 无关。 选项 D 与原文不符，发起考拉运动的主体是澳大利亚动物和海洋公园协会（the Association of Fauna and Marine parks, an Australian conservation society is campaigning to ban koala cuddling），而不是动物园。
答案	B

Question 5

题干定位词 / 关键词	government, protect
原文定位	I 段倒数第三句 Policy on koala handling is determined by state government authorities.
题目解析	题干：政府将做什么来使考拉免于濒临灭绝？ A：出台保护考拉的指导方针 B：关闭一些动物园 C：鼓励人们抵制拜访动物园 D：劝说公众学习更多知识 通过 government 定位到 I 段倒数第三句，该句表明关于抚摸考拉的政策是由州政府当局决定的，对应选项 A。 选项 B、选项 C 和选项 D 在原文中均未提及。
答案	A

Questions 6-12

题型：判断题

Question 6

题干定位词 / 关键词	new coming human settlers
原文定位	B 段第二句到最后 Now they seem to be in decline, but exact numbers are not available as the species would not seem to be "under threat". Their problem, however, has been man, more specifically, the white man. Koala and aborigine had co-existed peacefully for centuries.
题目解析	题干：新来的人类给考拉造成危险。 通过题干中的 human settlers 定位到 B 段第三句中的 white man。浏览前后文可知，考拉和土著居民和平地共处了几个世纪，但是现在它们的数量开始下降，问题就在于它们受到了白人（非土著居民）的威胁，文中的 white man 即为题干中的 new coming human settlers，题干与原文表述一致，故正确。
答案	YES

Question 7

题干定位词 / 关键词	be seen; most of the places; Australia.
原文定位	C 段第一句 Today koalas are found only in scattered pockets of southeast Australia, where they seem to be at risk on several fronts.
题目解析	题干：在澳大利亚的大部分地方仍然可以看到考拉。 通过 be seen 和 Australia 定位到 C 段第一句，该句表示考拉如今只在澳大利亚东南部的一些零散地区被发现，在那里它们似乎受到了几方面的威胁，这与题干表述相矛盾，故错误。
答案	NO

Question 8

题干定位词 / 关键词	eucalyptus trees; recover; fire
原文定位	D 段倒数第二句 The koalas will be aided by the eucalyptus, which grows quickly and is already burgeoning forth after the fires.
题目解析	题干：大火过后，桉树需要十年时间才能恢复。 通过 fire 和 eucalyptus trees 定位到 D 段倒数第二句，该句表示桉树生长迅速，火灾后已经开始萌芽了，这与题干表述不符，故错误。
答案	NO

Question 9

题干定位词 / 关键词	fight; food; scarce
原文定位	无
题目解析	题干：当食物稀缺时，考拉之间会相互斗争。 文中与食物短缺相关的信息只在 C 段有所提及，但是并没有提及考拉间会斗争，所以答案为 NOT GIVEN。
答案	NOT GIVEN

Question 10

题干定位词 / 关键词	not easy to notice; ill
原文定位	H 段第五句 A sudden loss of weight is usually the only warning keepers have that their charge is ill.
题目解析	题干：不容易注意到考拉生病。 通过 ill 可定位到 H 段第五句，该句表明体重突然下降通常是饲养员得到的唯一警告，表明考拉生病了，这与题干的表述一致，the only warning 对应题干中的 not easy to notice，故答案为正确。
答案	YES

Question 11

题干定位词 / 关键词	infected; disease; cuddling
原文定位	无
题目解析	题干：通过拥抱，考拉很容易感染人类的一些传染病。 原文中与拥抱考拉相关的内容出现在 E 段与 I 段，但是这两段均未提到拥抱考拉会使其感染疾病，与疾病相关的内容出现在 H 段，但与人类的拥抱无关，故答案为 NOT GIVEN。
答案	NOT GIVEN

Question 12

题干定位词 / 关键词	arm; embraced
原文定位	I 段第四句 Secondly, most people have no idea of how to handle the animals; they like to cling on to their handler, all in their own good time and use his or her arm as a tree.
题目解析	题干：被拥抱时考拉喜欢抱住人的胳膊。 通过 arm 定位到 G 段和 I 段。G 段提及它们能用针尖的爪子撕开人的胳膊，与本题无关。I 段第四句表示高兴时它们喜欢抓住驯兽师不放，把驯兽师的胳膊当树用，这与题干表述一致，故答案为正确。
答案	YES

Question 13

题型：单选题

Question 13

题干定位词 / 关键词	written by
原文定位	无
题目解析	题干：你觉得这篇文章是谁写的？ A：为杂志撰稿的记者 B：伦敦动物园的饲养员 C：刚从澳大利亚回来的游客 D：研究考拉以制定法律的政府官员 这篇文章讲述了考拉的历史、生活环境、数量变化及其原因、生活习性及保护措施，很像为杂志撰稿的记者所写的，故答案为选项 A。 饲养员没有动机去撰写澳大利亚考拉的情况，故排除选项 B。 游客可能会倾向于描述自己这次出行的经历与趣闻，故排除选项 C。 I 段提到对考拉的保护措施，但是没有迹象表明想要制定法律，故排除选项 D。
答案	A

长难句分析

D 段：So the main problem to their survival is their slow reproductive rate—they produce only one baby a year over a reproductive lifespan of about nine years.

思路分析：本句的结构为 the main problem is their slow reproduction rate，to their survival 作 problem 的后置定语，表示“它们生存的主要问题”。破折号后面的句子是对 their slow reproductive rate 的具体说明，其主要结构为 they produce only one baby a year，后面的 over...nine years 作状语，表示“在大约 9 年的繁殖寿命中”。

参考翻译：因此，它们生存的主要问题是它们的繁殖率低——在大约 9 年的繁殖寿命中，它们每年只能生一个宝宝。

H 段：They are also very sensitive, and the slightest upset can prevent them from breeding, cause them to go off their food, and succumb to gut infections.

思路分析：整个句子由第一个“and”连接的两个子句组成，第一个子句为 they are also very sensitive，第二个子句的主语是 the slightest upset，情态动词 can 后并列了三个动作，分别是 prevent them from breeding、cause them to go off their food 和 succumb to gut infections。go off 表示“失去兴趣”，succumb 表示“死于（某种疾病）”。

参考翻译：它们也非常敏感，稍有不安就会阻止它们繁殖，导致它们厌食，并死于肠道感染。

参考译文

考拉

A 考拉的生活简直太好了。除了幼崽偶尔会被猛禽抓走，考拉没有天敌。在一个理想的世界里，树栖沙发土豆[①] 的生活是完全安全的，也是令人满意的。

B 就在 200 年前，考拉在澳大利亚遍地开花。现在它们的数量似乎在减少，但确切的数字尚不可知，因为这个物种似乎并没有“受到威胁”。然而，它们的问题在于人类，更确切地说，是白人。考拉和土著人和平共处了几个世纪。

C 如今，考拉只在澳大利亚东南部的一些零散地区被发现，在那里它们似乎受到了几方面的威胁。考拉唯一的食物来源——桉树，数量减少了。在过去的 200 年里，澳大利亚三分之一的桉树林消失了。考拉也被寄生虫、衣原体流行病和一种致肿瘤逆转录病毒杀死。而且每年还有 11000 只考拉死于车祸，讽刺的是，其中大多数都是死于野生动物保护区，还有数千只死于偷猎者。有些还被非法当作宠物带走。这些动物通常很快就会死亡，但它们很容易被取代。

D 丛林大火构成了另一个威胁。最近新南威尔士州肆虐的可怕大火杀死了 100 到 1000 只考拉。许多被带到避难所的考拉被灼热的余灰烧伤了爪子。但动物学家表示，该物种应该会恢复。桉树将帮助考拉种群的恢复，桉树生长迅速，而且火灾后已经开始萌芽了。因此，它们生存的主要问题是它们的繁殖率低——在大约 9 年的繁殖寿命中，它们每年只能生一个宝宝。

E 这个物种面临的最新问题可能更加隐晦。毛茸茸的灰色皮毛，暗琥珀色的眼睛和纽扣鼻子，考拉简直就是可爱的化身。澳大利亚的动物园和野生动物园利用它们毫无怨言的态度，让游客抱着这些毛茸茸的小家伙拍照，并收取费用。但人们可能没有意识到这有多残忍。由于考拉的性格娇弱，不断的抚摸会把它本已不稳定的生理平衡推向崩溃的边缘。

---

①：指懒得出门的人

F 考拉只吃某些种类的桉树的叶子，每天 600 克到 1250 克。这种坚韧的叶子富含纤维素、单宁酸、芳香油和有毒氰化物的前体细胞。为了对付这种混合物，考拉有专门的消化系统。盲肠中的纤维素消化细菌负责分解纤维，而专门进化的肠道和肝脏则负责处理毒素。为了适当地消化食物，考拉每天必须静坐 21 个小时。

G 考拉是天真无邪的化身。虽然它们能用针尖的爪子撕开人的胳膊，或者狠狠地咬上一口，但它们不会这样做。如果你惹到考拉了，它可能会眨眼、吞咽或打嗝。但攻击呢？绝对不会！考拉没有攻击性。它们的爪子是用来抓住桉树坚硬光滑的树皮的。

H 它们也非常敏感，稍有不安就会阻止它们繁殖，导致它们厌食，并死于肠道感染。考拉是一种坚忍的动物，直到临死前都要摆出一副坚强的面孔。今天它们可能看起来很健康，明天可能就死了。圈养的考拉每天必须称体重，以检查它们是否进食正常。体重突然下降通常是饲养员得到的唯一警告，表明考拉生病了。伦敦动物园只允许两名饲养员和一名兽医管理考拉，因为这些动物只喜欢和它们熟悉的人在一起。动物园拒绝了带考拉去见女王的请求，因为这会给这一有袋动物带来痛苦。遗憾的是，伦敦动物园已经没有考拉了。两年前，这只雌性考拉死于逆转录病毒引起的癌症。当雌性考拉进入发情期时，它们会变得更加活跃，并开始减轻体重，但大约 16 天后，发情期结束，体重又开始反弹。但伦敦的考拉却没有。手术显示它长了数百个豌豆大小的肿瘤。

I 澳大利亚几乎每个动物园都有考拉——这种有袋动物已经成为国家的动物大使，但在澳大利亚以外的任何地方都不允许公众触摸考拉。拥抱考拉违反了所有爱护考拉的规则。第一，有些动物园允许考拉在陌生人之间传递，很多小朋友都爱用力抱。第二，大多数人根本不知道该怎么抚摸这些动物，在高兴的时候，它们喜欢紧紧抓住自己的驯兽师，把驯兽师的胳膊当树用。出于这样的原因，澳大利亚动物和海洋公园协会（一个澳大利亚保护协会）发起了一项运动，禁止拥抱考拉。关于抚摸考拉的政策是由州政府当局决定的，大部分是由澳大利亚自然保护局制定的，目的是制定国家指导方针。在一波宣传之后，一些动物园和野生动物园已经停止与考拉拍照了。

READING PASSAGE 2

Is Graffiti Art or Crime

文章结构

体裁	说明文
题材	艺术类
主题	讨论涂鸦是艺术还是犯罪
段落概括	A 段：关于“涂鸦”的介绍。 B 段：涂鸦应该尽快清除的原因。 C 段：清除涂鸦需要考虑的问题。 D 段：清除涂鸦的两种方法以及操作注意事项。 E 段：解决反复出现涂鸦问题的多种预防策略。 F 段：使用防涂鸦涂层可以避免反复清除涂鸦对物体表面造成的损坏。 G 段：使用防涂鸦涂层的好处。

重点词汇

A 段							
单词	音标	词性	释义	单词	音标	词性	释义
graffiti	[grəˈfi:ti]	*n.*	涂鸦	derive	[dɪˈraɪv]	*v.*	起源于
scratching	[ˈskrætʃɪŋ]	*n.*	划伤	phenomenon	[fəˈnɒmɪnən]	*n.*	现象
archaeological	[ˌɑ:kiəˈlɒdʒɪkl]	*adj.*	考古学的	pervasive	[pəˈveɪsɪv]	*adj.*	遍布的
B 段							
单词	音标	词性	释义	单词	音标	词性	释义
priority	[praɪˈɒrəti]	*n.*	优先事项，最重要的事	emulation	[ˌemjuˈleɪʃn]	*n.*	仿效，模仿
surface	[ˈsɜ:fɪs]	*n.*	表面	racist	[ˈreɪsɪst]	*n.*	种族主义者
vandalism	[ˈvændəlɪzəm]	*n.*	故意破坏（或损坏）财产的行为	deterioration	[dɪˌtɪəriəˈreɪʃn]	*n.*	恶化

C 段							
单词	音标	词性	释义	单词	音标	词性	释义
eyesore	[ˈaɪsɔ:(r)]	*n.*	眼中钉	proposal	[prəˈpəʊzl]	*n.*	提议，建议
robust	[rəʊˈbʌst]	*adj.*	（物体）结实的，坚固的	utilitarian	[ˌju:tɪlɪˈteəriən]	*n.*	功利主义；实用主义
culprit	[ˈkʌlprɪt]	*n.*	罪犯，过失者	prosecution	[ˌprɒsɪˈkju:ʃn]	*n.*	起诉，诉讼
D 段							
单词	音标	词性	释义	单词	音标	词性	释义
dissolve	[dɪˈzɒlv]	*v.*	（使）溶解	solvent	[ˈsɒlvənt]	*n.*	溶剂
hazardous	[ˈhæzədəs]	*adj.*	危险的，有害的	cocktail	[ˈkɒkteɪl]	*n.*	混合物
comply	[kəmˈplaɪ]	*v.*	遵从，服从	legislation	[ˌledʒɪsˈleɪʃn]	*n.*	法规，法律
operative	[ˈɒpərətɪv]	*n.*	技工，工人	substrate	[ˈsʌbstreɪt]	*n.*	基层，底面
E 段							
单词	音标	词性	释义	单词	音标	词性	释义
preventive	[prɪˈventɪv]	*adj.*	预防（性）的	surveillance	[sɜ:ˈveɪləns]	*n.*	监视，监察
prominently	[ˈprɒmɪnəntli]	*adv.*	显著地	patrol	[pəˈtrəʊl]	*n.*	巡逻，巡查
deterrent	[dɪˈterənt]	*n.*	威慑，遏制	recurring	[rɪˈkɜ:rɪŋ]	*adj.*	反复出现，再次发生
vulnerable	[ˈvʌlnərəbl]	*adj.*	脆弱的，易受攻击的				
F 段							
单词	音标	词性	释义	单词	音标	词性	释义
proposition	[ˌprɒpəˈzɪʃn]	*n.*	主张，观点	coating	[ˈkəʊtɪŋ]	*n.*	涂层
isolate	[ˈaɪsəleɪt]	*v.*	孤立，分离				
G 段							
单词	音标	词性	释义	单词	音标	词性	释义
low-pressure	[ˌləʊ ˈpreʃə(r)]	*adj.*	低压的	barrier	[ˈbæriə(r)]	*n.*	障碍，壁垒

题目精解

Questions 14-19

题型：段落信息配对题

Question 14

题干定位词 / 关键词	chemically cleaning; damage
原文定位	D 段第三句 Chemical preparations are based on dissolving the media; these solvents can range from water to potentially hazardous chemical "cocktails".
题目解析	题干：为什么用化学方式清除涂鸦会造成损害？ 由题干中的 chemically cleaning 定位到 D 段第三句：化学制剂以溶解介质为基础；这些溶剂可以是水，也可以是有潜在危险的化学"混合物"。由原文的表述可知，用来清除涂鸦的化学制剂有可能本身就是有害的（hazardous），所以会造成损害。
答案	D

Question 15

题干定位词 / 关键词	benefit; precautionary strategy; gentle removal
原文定位	G 段第一句 Removal of graffiti from a surface that has been treated in this way is much easier, usually using low-pressure water which reduces the possibility of damage.
题目解析	题干：关于温和地清除（涂鸦）的预防措施的好处。 由题干中的 precautionary strategy 首先定位到 E 段，E 段首次提到对于涂鸦的预防措施，但是这里只介绍了三种防范方式，并未提及其好处，也没有提及"温和地清除"，所以要继续往下阅读。F 段提到了一种较温和的清除方式——防涂鸦涂层，但是也没有提到好处。直到 G 段第一句指出，这种涂层能够使清除涂鸦变得更容易，减少建筑物被破坏的可能性，这里才提及了好处，由此可以得出答案。
答案	G

Question 16

题干定位词 / 关键词	damaging; accumulative impact; community
原文定位	B 段第三句到最后 The first is to prevent "copy-cat" emulation which can occur rapidly once a clean surface is defaced. It may also be of a racist or otherwise offensive nature and many companies and councils have a policy of removing this type of graffiti within an hour or two of it being reported. Also, as paints, glues and inks dry out over time they can become increasingly difficult to remove and are usually best dealt with as soon as possible after the incident. Graffiti can also lead to more serious forms of vandalism and, ultimately, the deterioration of an area, contributing to social decline.
题目解析	题干：涂鸦对社区的破坏性和累积性影响。 由题干中的 damaging 和 impact 可以定位到 B 段，其中提到的"模仿行为迅速发生""带有种族主义或其他冒犯性质""随着时间的推移更难去除"，以及最后的"社会的衰落"，都能体现涂鸦带来的破坏性、累积性影响，所以选 B 段。
答案	B

Question 17

题干定位词 / 关键词	preventive measures
原文定位	E 段整段
题目解析	题干：对用来处理涂鸦的不同预防措施的需求。 由题干中的preventive measures定位到E段，该段第一句就是段落主旨句，句中的 preventive strategies 是对题干关键词的同义替换。该段提到了"监控""巡逻""物理屏障"三种预防涂鸦的方式。
答案	E

Question 18

题干定位词 / 关键词	legal proposal; owner of building
原文定位	C 段第二句到最后 In the event of graffiti incidents, it is important that the owners of buildings or other structures and their consultants are aware of the approach they should take in dealing with the problem. The police should be informed as there may be other related attacks occurring locally. An incidence pattern can identify possible culprits, as can stylised signatures or nicknames, known as "tags", which may already be familiar to local police. Photographs are useful to record graffiti incidents and may assist the police in bringing a prosecution. Such images are also required for insurance claims and can be helpful in cleaning operatives, allowing them to see the problem area before arriving on site.
题目解析	题干：给楼房业主的应对涂鸦的法律建议。 由题干中的 owner of building 可定位到 C 段第二句：在发生涂鸦事件时，重要的是楼房或其他建筑物的业主及其顾问应了解他们在处理这一问题时应采取的方法。通过该句及后面的内容可知，这一段的主要内容是向楼房或建筑物业主提供如何面对涂鸦事件的建议，而且从"警方"（police）、"诉讼"（prosecution）等处可以看出，这些建议与法律相关。
答案	C

Question 19

题干定位词 / 关键词	reasons; removing graffiti; soon
原文定位	B 段前两句 It is usually considered a priority to remove graffiti as quickly as possible after it appears. This is for several reasons.
题目解析	题干：尽快清除涂鸦的原因。 根据题干中的 removing graffiti 和 reasons 可原词定位到 B 段第一、二句：通常认为，在涂鸦出现后当务之急是尽快清除它。这出于几个原因考虑。as soon as 在原文中对应 as quickly as。由此可知，这一段将围绕这一主题句展开叙述尽快清除涂鸦的原因。
答案	B

Questions 20-23

题型：多选题

解析：多选题考查的是考生在文中寻找细节信息的能力，此类题型顺序性不明显，需要通过题干或选项中的某些特殊信息来确定出题段落。通常情况下，出题句是文章中的 1 ~ 2 个句子。

Questions 20-21

题干定位词 / 关键词	removal
原文定位	D 段整段
题目解析	题干：关于清除涂鸦，以下哪两个说法是正确的？ A：混合物清除比水清除更安全 B：在大规模清除前先在一小块地方试用 C：化学处理是最贵的清除涂鸦的方式 D：化学方法和机械方法都有风险 E：机械清除比化学处理更适用 根据定位词 removal 定位到 D 段第一句：清除涂鸦的方法多种多样。由此可知，D 段是围绕这一主题句展开论述的。 B 选项对应 D 段最后一句：If there is any doubt regarding this, then small trial areas should be undertaken to assess the impact of more extensive treatment（如果对基材的承受能力有任何疑问，那么应该进行小范围的试验，以评估此清除涂鸦方式带来的更广泛的影响）。small trail areas 和 extensive treatment 分别对应选项 B 中的 small patch trail 和 large scale of removing。 D 段介绍完化学和机械清除方式后，开始叙述操作中的注意事项，从侧面表明这些清除方式可能给操作者、路人以及建筑物本身带来的危害，与选项 D 表述一致。 选项 A、选项 C 和选项 E 均未在文中提及。
答案	B D

Questions 22-23

题干定位词 / 关键词	preventive measures; effectively
原文定位	E 段
题目解析	题干：文章提到了哪两种有效应对涂鸦的预防措施？ A：在城市社区组织更多反涂鸦运动 B：增加警察道路巡逻 C：修建使用防水材料的新建筑 D：安装更多可视化摄像头 E：提供带有化学涂层的全新表面 通过 preventive measures 可以定位到 E 段第一句，这里提到 a variety of preventive strategies（多种预防措施）可以用来解决在特定地点反复出现的涂鸦问题。 选项 B 对应 E 段第六句 Security patrols will also act as a deterrent to prevent recurring attacks，由此可知安全巡逻可以起到威慑作用，防止涂鸦事件再次发生。 选项 D 对应 E 段第四、五句 Surveillance systems such as closed-circuit television may also help. In cities and towns around the country, prominently placed cameras have been shown to reduce anti-social behavior of all types including graffiti，由此可知，闭路电视等监控系统也可能有所帮助，在全国各地的城镇安装摄像头，可以减少包括涂鸦在内的各种反社会行为。prominently placed cameras 对应选项 D 中的 more visible security cameras。 选项 A、选项 C 和选项 E 均未在文中提及。
答案	B D

Questions 24-27

题型：句子填空题

解析：句子填空题属于顺序题，即题目顺序与原文顺序一致，解答这类题时需根据空格前后的内容判断答案的词性，再回原文定位，然后根据原文大意及字数要求作答即可。句子填空题的答案多为原文原词，考生无须更改其词性及形式，照抄原文即可。

Question 24

题干定位词 / 关键词	ancient; significance; of life
原文定位	A 段倒数第二句 In such circumstances it has acquired invaluable historical and archaeological significance, providing a social history of life and events at that time.
题目解析	题干：古代的涂鸦意义重大，详细地记录了当时的 ____ 生活。 本题通过语法知识可判断空格处应填入与 life 相关的名词。通过 ancient graffiti 可知题干在描述涂鸦的历史，据此定位到 A 段。然后通过并列结构前的 significance 定位到 A 段倒数第二句：在这样的情况下，它就具有了宝贵的历史和考古意义，提供了一部当时的生活和事件的社会史。后半句关键词 of life 原词重现，因此可以轻松锁定所填内容为 social history。
答案	social history

Question 25

题干定位词 / 关键词	police; signatures; familiar with
原文定位	C 段第三、四句 The police should be informed as there may be other related attacks occurring locally. An incidence pattern can identify possible culprits, as can stylised signatures or nicknames, known as "tags", which may already be familiar to local police.
题目解析	题干：通过他们熟悉的被称为 _____ 的签名，警察可以识别新的涂鸦事件。 通过 police 定位到 C 段第三句：他们应该通知警方，因为当地可能会发生其他相关的袭击事件。继续往下阅读，第四句：事件发生模式可以识别出可能的罪犯，也可以识别风格化的签名或昵称，它们被称为"标签"，当地警察可能对此已经很熟悉了，其中 identify 替换 recognize，incidence pattern 替换 committed incidents，signatures 原词重现，known as 替换 called，familiar 原词重现，因此能够得出答案为引号中的 tags。
答案	tags

Question 26

题干定位词 / 关键词	operatives; rules; put on
原文定位	D 段第六句 Operatives should follow product guidelines in terms of application and removal, and wear the appropriate protective equipment.
题目解析	题干：操作者在操作时应该遵守相关规则，穿上适当的 _____。 根据主语 operatives、动词 put on 可以推测，空格处应填能够穿戴的物品。通过 operatives 定位到 D 段第六句：操作人员应遵从产品使用和清除指南，并穿戴适当的防护设备。往前读一句（D 段第五句）会找到 comply with（遵守）原词，其中 health and safety legislation 替换 rules。在第六句中，wear 替换 put on，appropriate 替换 suitable，因此可得出答案为 protective equipment。
答案	protective equipment

Question 27

题干定位词 / 关键词	removal of graffiti from; convenient
原文定位	G 段第一句 Removal of graffiti from a surface that has been treated in this way is much easier, usually using low-pressure water which reduces the possibility of damage.
题目解析	题干：使用 _____ 可以方便地清除一种新的涂层表面的涂鸦。 通过语法知识可判断空格处应该填一个和方便地清除涂鸦的方式相关的名词。通过关键词定位到 G 段第一句：清除用这种方法处理过的表面上的涂鸦要容易得多，通常使用低压水，减少损坏的可能性。在该句中，removal of graffiti from a surface 原词重现，easier 替换 convenient，using 后面即为正确答案 low-pressure water。
答案	low-pressure water

长难句分析

C 段：Although graffiti may be regarded as an eyesore, any proposal to remove it from sensitive historic surfaces should be carefully considered: techniques designed for more robust or utilitarian surfaces may result in considerable damage.

思路分析：本句开头是一个although引导的让步状语从句，句子的主体结构为any proposal should be carefully considered。to remove it from sensitive historic surfaces为主语any proposal的后置定语，表明这个提议的内容。冒号后面的部分是为了解释这些提议要仔细斟酌的原因，这部分的主体结构为techniques may result in considerable damage，designed for... surfaces为分词定语，修饰techniques。

参考翻译：尽管涂鸦可能被认为有碍观瞻，但是任何将其从敏感的历史建筑物表面清除的建议都应仔细考虑：为更坚固或更实用的表面而设计的（清除涂鸦）技术都可能导致相当大的破坏。

B 段：Also, as paints, glues and inks dry out over time they can become increasingly difficult to remove and are usually best dealt with as soon as possible after the incident.

思路分析：本句中的as paints, glues and inks dry out over time为as引导的原因状语从句，意思是"这些涂鸦材料会随着时间推移而变干"。后面的主句为and连接的两个并列句子，共用一个主语they（这里表示涂鸦），即they can become ... remove和they are usually best dealt with ... incident。因为they（涂鸦）与动词处理（deal with）为被动关系，所以中间加上be动词are构成被动语态。

参考翻译：此外，随着时间的推移，油漆、胶水和墨水会变干，这使得它们越来越难去除，所以通常最好在事情发生后尽快处理。

参考译文

涂鸦是艺术还是犯罪

A "涂鸦"一词来源于意大利语"graffito"，意思是"抓伤"，可以被定义为物体、建筑结构和自然地貌上不请自来的标记或书写。涂鸦并不是一个新现象：在世界各地的古代建筑上都可以找到涂鸦的例子，在某些情况下，早于希腊人和罗马人。在这样的情况下，它就具有了宝贵的历史和考古意义，提供了一部当时的生活和事件的社会史。因为其廉价且快速的标记手段，涂鸦现在已经成为一个普遍存在的问题。

B　通常认为，在涂鸦出现后当务之急是尽快清除它。这出于几个原因考虑。首先是为了防止“山寨”模仿，一旦干净的表面被损坏，这种模仿行为就会迅速发生。涂鸦也可能带有种族主义或其他冒犯性质，许多公司和地方议会都有这样的政策，要求在举报后的一两个小时内清除这类涂鸦。此外，随着时间的推移，油漆、胶水和墨水会变干，这使得它们越来越难去除，所以通常最好在事情发生后尽快处理。涂鸦也会导致更加严重的破坏行为，并最终导致一个地区的恶化，造成社会的衰落。

C　尽管涂鸦可能被认为有碍观瞻，但是任何将其从敏感的历史建筑物表面清除的建议都应仔细考虑：为更坚固或更实用的表面而设计的（清除涂鸦）技术都可能导致相当大的破坏。在发生涂鸦事件时，重要的是楼房或其他建筑物的业主及其顾问应了解他们在处理这一问题时应采取的方法。他们应该通知警方，因为当地可能会发生其他相关的袭击事件。事件发生模式可以识别出可能的罪犯，风格化的签名或昵称也可以，它们被称为“标签”，当地警察可能对此已经很熟悉了。照片对于记录涂鸦事件很有帮助，可能有助于警方提起诉讼。保险理赔也需要这样的图像，对清洁人员也有帮助，让他们在到达现场之前就能看到问题区域。

D　清除涂鸦的方法多种多样。这些方法大体上可分为化学方式和机械方式。化学制剂以溶解介质为基础；这些溶剂可以是水，也可以是有潜在危险的化学“混合物”。机械方法，如钢丝刷和喷砂清理，试图将介质从表面擦掉或切碎。操作时应注意遵守健康和安全法规，以保护路人和任何进行清洁的人。操作人员应遵从产品使用和清除指南，并穿戴适当的防护设备。必须采取措施确保水流、空中雾、滴漏和飞溅不会威胁到未受保护的公众。在审视涂鸦事件时，重要的是评估基材承受指定处理措施的能力。如果对此有任何疑问，那么应该进行小范围的试验，以评估更广泛的处理措施所带来的影响。

E　可以采取多种预防措施来解决在特定地点反复出现的涂鸦问题。因为没有两个地点是完全相同的，所以没有一套保护措施能适用于所有情况。每个地点都必须单独考察。闭路电视等监控系统也可能有所帮助。在全国各地的城镇，放置在显眼位置的摄像头已被证明可以减少包括涂鸦在内的所有类型的反社会行为。安全巡逻也将起到威慑作用，以防止袭击再次发生。然而，对于大多数情况来说，这样做的成本可能太高了。可以引入墙、栏杆、门或大门等物理屏障，以阻止未经许可的人进入易受攻击的地点。然而，必须考虑到这些措施对被保护建筑的影响。在最坏的情况下，这些措施对环境质量的破坏几乎与它们想阻止的涂鸦一样。在另一些情况下，它们可能只是为涂鸦提供了一个新的表面。

F 与清除涂鸦相关的最重要的问题之一是需要将其从反复受到攻击的表面上清除。在这种情况下，即使是使用最温和的方法反复清除涂鸦，最终也会对表面材料造成损害。在某些情况下，上面提到的预防策略可能不起作用，或者在特定的地点行不通。防涂鸦涂料通常是用刷子或喷雾来涂抹的，留下一层薄薄的贴面，这样基本上可以将涂鸦与表面隔离开来。

G 清除用这种方法处理过的表面上的涂鸦要容易得多，通常使用低压水，减少损坏的可能性。根据所选择的屏障类型，可能需要在每次清除涂鸦后重新涂上涂层。

READING PASSAGE 3

Asian Space Satellite Technology

文章结构

体裁	说明文
题材	科技类
主题	亚洲太空科技的发展
段落概括	A 段：火箭的历史以及今天中国火箭技术的发展。 B 段：过去十年亚洲太空技术的发展。 C 段：竞争驱动航天创新。 D 段：当前亚洲太空技术的发展。 E 段：亚洲各个国家遥感技术的发展。 F 段：低成本卫星带来的竞争优势。 G 段：其他因素对科技发展的影响。

重点词汇

A 段							
单词	音标	词性	释义	单词	音标	词性	释义
progress	[prəˈgres]	*v.*	进步，进展	repel	[rɪˈpel]	*v.*	击退，驱逐
invader	[ɪnˈveɪdə(r)]	*n.*	侵略者	stand in stark contrast to sth.		*phr.*	和……形成鲜明对比

B 段							
单词	音标	词性	释义	单词	音标	词性	释义
decade	[ˈdekeɪd]	*n.*	十年	growth	[grəʊθ]	*n.*	成长，生长；增长，发展
utilization	[ˌjuːtəlaɪˈzeɪʃn]	*n.*	利用，使用	satellite	[ˈsætəlaɪt]	*n.*	人造卫星
expansion	[ɪkˈspænʃn]	*n.*	扩大，扩张	commentator	[ˈkɒmənteɪtə(r)]	*n.*	现场解说员，评论员
predict	[prɪˈdɪkt]	*v.*	预言，预计	eager	[ˈiːgə(r)]	*adj.*	热切的，渴望的
embrace	[ɪmˈbreɪs]	*v.*	拥抱，欣然接受				

C 段							
单词	音标	词性	释义	单词	音标	词性	释义
innovative	[ˈɪnəveɪtɪv]	*adj.*	革新的，新颖的	explore	[ɪkˈsplɔː(r)]	*v.*	探讨，探究，探索
revolutionary	[ˌrevəˈluːʃənəri]	*adj.*	革命的；突破性的	effect	[ɪˈfekt]	*n.*	作用，影响
telemedicine	[ˈtelɪˌmedɪsɪn]	*n.*	远程医疗，远距离治病	agricultural	[ˌæɡrɪˈkʌltʃərəl]	*adj.*	农业的，与农业有关的
influence	[ˈɪnfluəns]	*n.*	影响，作用	competitive	[kəmˈpetətɪv]	*adj.*	竞争的，好胜的
commercial	[kəˈmɜːʃl]	*adj.*	商业的，商务的；商业化的	sector	[ˈsektə(r)]	*n.*	区域，部分；部门
industrial	[ɪnˈdʌstriəl]	*adj.*	工业的	financial	[faɪˈnænʃl]	*adj.*	财政的，金融的
evident	[ˈevɪdənt]	*adj.*	清楚的，显然的	trend	[trend]	*n.*	趋势，动态

D 段							
单词	音标	词性	释义	单词	音标	词性	释义
comprehensive	[ˌkɒmprɪˈhensɪv]	*adj.*	综合性的，全面的	capability	[ˌkeɪpəˈbɪləti]	*n.*	能力，才能
infrastructure	[ˈɪnfrəstrʌktʃə(r)]	*n.*	基础设施，基础建设	self-sufficient	[ˌself səˈfɪʃnt]	*adj.*	自给自足的
manufacturing	[ˌmænjuˈfæktʃərɪŋ]	*n.*	制造，制造业	border	[ˈbɔːdə(r)]	*v.*	接壤，毗邻
indigenous	[ɪnˈdɪdʒənəs]	*adj.*	本土的				

E 段							
单词	音标	词性	释义	单词	音标	词性	释义
suffer from		*phr.*	忍受，遭受	flood	[ˈflʌd]	*n.*	洪水
deforestation	[ˌdiːˌfɒrɪˈsteɪʃn]	*n.*	毁林，滥伐森林	instrument	[ˈɪnstrəmənt]	*n.*	器械，仪器
photograph	[ˈfəʊtəɡrɑːf]	*n.*	照片，相片	disaster	[dɪˈzɑːstə(r)]	*n.*	灾难，灾害
prevention	[prɪˈvenʃn]	*n.*	预防，防止	monitor	[ˈmɒnɪtə(r)]	*v.*	监视；监听
facility	[fəˈsɪləti]	*n.*	设施，设备	learning curve		*phr.*	学习曲线

F段							
单词	音标	词性	释义	单词	音标	词性	释义
fundamental	[ˌfʌndəˈmentl]	*adj.*	根本的，基本的	emergence	[ɪˈmɜːdʒəns]	*n.*	出现，显现
adoption	[əˈdɒpʃn]	*n.*	采用，接受	establish	[ɪˈstæblɪʃ]	*v.*	建立，设立；证实，确定
shorten	[ˈʃɔːtn]	*v.*	缩短	military	[ˈmɪlətri]	*adj.*	军事的，军队的
component	[kəmˈpəʊnənt]	*n.*	组成部分				
G段							
单词	音标	词性	释义	单词	音标	词性	释义
law	[lɔː]	*n.*	定律	physics	[ˈfɪzɪks]	*n.*	物理学，物理现象
principle	[ˈprɪnsəpl]	*n.*	准则；定律	political	[pəˈlɪtɪkl]	*adj.*	政治（上）的
boundary	[ˈbaʊndri]	*n.*	边界，界限	immutability	[ɪˌmjuːtəˈbɪləti]	*n.*	永恒性；不变性
acquisition	[ˌækwɪˈzɪʃn]	*n.*	获得，习得	expertise	[ˌekspɜːˈtiːz]	*n.*	专长，专门技能（知识）

题目精解

Questions 28-32

题型：标题题

小标题	翻译
i. Western countries provide essential assistance	西方国家提供了必要的援助
ii. Unbalanced development for an essential space technology	一项重要的航天技术的不平衡发展
iii. Innovative application compelled by competition	竞争催生的创新应用
iv. An ancient invention which is related to the future	一项与未来有关的古老发明
v. Military purpose of satellites	卫星的军事用途
vi. Rockets for application in ancient China	中国古代的火箭应用
vii. Space development in Asia in the past	亚洲过去的太空发展
viii. Non-technology factors count	非技术因素也算数
ix. Competitive edge gained by more economically feasible satellites	在经济上更可行的卫星获得的竞争优势
x. Current space technology development in Asia	亚洲空间技术发展现状

Question 28

题干定位词 / 关键词	ancient invention; future
原文定位	A 段
题目解析	A 段第一句表明自公元前 500 年左右中国首次使用“火箭”并在公元 1232 年的宋朝开封之战中击退了蒙古入侵者以来，火箭技术取得了长足的进步。该句提到了古老的发明（fire arrows）与未来（rocket technology）的关系。后面的句子说这些古代的火箭与中国现在的“长征”运载火箭形成了鲜明的对比，也说明了古老发明和未来的关系。
答案	iv

Question 29

题干定位词 / 关键词	space development; past
原文定位	B 段
题目解析	B 段第一句表明在过去十年中，亚洲的空间活动在空基服务的利用以及卫星和发射装置的生产方面都有了显著增长，这与 vii 选项所述内容一致，growth 对应 development，in the last decade 对应 in the past。
答案	vii

Question 30

题干定位词 / 关键词	innovative application, competition
原文定位	C 段
题目解析	C 段第一句提到 new and innovative uses for satellites（卫星的创新性用途），与 iii 选项中的 innovative application 相对应。第二句提到竞争激烈的商业航天部门、低成本微型卫星的出现以及工业和金融市场的全球化在很大程度上影响了亚洲的航天，这些都是 iii 选项中 competition 的体现，文中的 is very much influenced by 对应 compelled。
答案	iii

Question 31

题干定位词 / 关键词	unbalanced development; space technology
原文定位	E 段
题目解析	E 段前半部分说明了遥感（remote sensing）技术在东南亚地区发展迅速的原因，后半部分介绍了多个国家遥感技术的发展情况，有的国家处于领先地位，有的则稍显落后。“遥感”对应选项 ii 中的 an essential space technology，各国的发展情况则体现了 unbalanced（不平衡）的特点。
答案	ii

Question 32

题干定位词 / 关键词	competitive edge; economically feasible
原文定位	F 段
题目解析	由 F 段第一句 In recent years there have been fundamental changes in the way satellites are designed and built to drastically reduce costs（近年来，为了大幅降低成本，卫星的设计和制造方式发生了根本性的变化）可知，该段主要讲述卫星制造的变化与成本的降低。第二句举了一个小卫星（small satellite）的例子，后面所说的亚洲国家迅速采用（quick adoption）、缩短学习曲线（shorten their learning curve）均对应选项 ix 的内容。
答案	ix

Questions 33-36

题型：句子配对题

解析：句子配对题的解题方法与选择题类似，都是用题干所给信息进行定位，建议考生进行定位之前把选项中的关键词先画出来，定位到原文后，对句子进行精读并理解，最后从选项表中选择一个与原文表达最为接近的选项。

Question 33

题干定位词 / 关键词	remote-photographic technology; environmental problems
原文定位	E 段第三句 Remote sensing satellites equipped with instruments to take photographs of the ground at different wavelengths provide essential information for natural resource accounting, environmental management, disaster prevention and monitoring, land-use mapping, and sustainable development planning.
题目解析	题干：远程摄影技术为什么被用来解决环境问题？ 由题干中的 remote-photographic technology 和 environmental problems 可以定位到 E 段。E 段第一、二句说明遥感（remote sensing）技术在东南亚地区发展迅速是因为这些地区长期遭受大规模环境问题，如 storms and flooding（风暴和洪水），forest fires and deforestation（森林火灾和森林砍伐）以及 crop failures（作物歉收）；第三句表明远程摄影技术对解决这类问题的有效性，即“配备有仪器的遥感卫星可以拍摄不同波长的地面照片，为自然资源核算、环境管理、灾害预防和监测、土地使用制图以及可持续发展规划提供必要的信息”，所以本题答案为选项 F“因为诸如发生在东南亚的丛林大火之类的灾难”。
答案	F

Question 34

题干定位词 / 关键词	medicine area
原文定位	C 段第一句 New and innovative uses for satellites are constantly being explored with potential revolutionary effects, such as in the field of health and telemedicine, distance education, crime prevention (piracy on the high sea), food and agricultural planning and production (rice crop monitoring).
题目解析	题干：卫星技术为什么被用于医疗领域？ 由题干中的 medicine area 可定位到 C 段第一句：人们正在探索卫星的创新性用途，这些用途正在产生潜在的革命性影响，如在保健和远程医疗、远程教育、犯罪预防（公海海盗活动）、粮食和农业规划及生产（水稻作物监测）等领域。这里提到 telemedicine（远程医疗），也就是说卫星技术运用的目的之一是用于远程治疗疾病，进而可以理解为给一些 unapprochable areas（无法到达的地方）进行医疗。另外，因为 telemedicine 是作为前半句的例子出现的，所以需要仔细研究前半句想表达的意思。前半句说人们正在探索卫星的创新性用途，这些用途正在产生潜在的革命性影响，由此可知，将卫星技术运用到医疗领域是为了开拓创新，探索一些还未触及的领域，这也对应选项 B 中的 unapproachable areas，所以本题答案为选项 B“因为有一些无法触及的领域”。
答案	B

Question 35

题干定位词 / 关键词	Asian; satellite technology; limited for development
原文定位	G 段第一至四句 The laws of physics are the same in Tokyo as in Toulouse, and the principles of electronics and mechanics know no political or cultural boundaries. However, no such immutability applies to engineering practices and management; they are very much influenced by education, culture, and history. These factors, in turn, have an effect on costs, lead times, product designs and, eventually, international sales. Many Asian nations are sending their engineers to be trained in the West.
题目解析	题干：亚洲国家的卫星技术为什么发展受限？ 本题定位较难，虽然文章中多处提到“社会因素”，但是都没有提到“亚洲国家的卫星技术发展受限”，直到 G 段第一至四句指出，电子和机械的原理是没有政治和文化边界的（political or cultural boundaries）。然而，这种不变性并不适用于工程实践和管理，它们受教育、文化和历史的影响很大。这些因素会影响卫星的成本、交付时间、产品设计，并最终影响国际销售。许多亚洲国家正在派遣他们的工程师到西方接受培训。这说明亚洲国家在工程实践和管理上的发展受到了一些社会因素的影响，与选项 D 的内容一致。
答案	D

Question 36

题干定位词 / 关键词	agricultural area
原文定位	C 段第一句 New and innovative uses for satellites are constantly being explored with potential revolutionary effects, such as in the field of health and telemedicine, distance education, crime prevention (piracy on the high sea), food and agricultural planning and production (rice crop monitoring).
题目解析	题干：卫星技术为什么被部署到农业领域？ 根据 agricultural 可以定位到 C 段第一句：人们正在探索卫星的创新性用途，这些用途正在产生潜在的革命性影响，如在保健和远程医疗、远程教育、犯罪预防（公海海盗活动）、粮食和农业规划及生产（水稻作物监测）等领域。第二个括号里的内容说明卫星技术是通过对水稻作物进行监测来帮助粮食和农业规划及生产的，对应选项 A “因为它帮助管理作物”。
答案	A

Questions 37-40

题型：判断题

Question 37

题干定位词 / 关键词	ancient China; military purpose; 500 years
原文定位	A 段第一句 Rocket technology has progressed considerably since the days of "fire arrows" (bamboo poles filled with gunpowder) first used in China around 500 BC, and, during the Sung Dynasty, to repel Mongol invaders at the battle of Kaifeng (Kai-fung fu) in AD 1232.
题目解析	题干：早在 500 年前，古代中国已经将火箭用于军事用途。 通过题干中的 ancient China 和 500 years 定位到 A 段。A 段第一句表明公元前 500 年左右中国首次使用火箭，而首次将其运用在军事领域是在公元 1232 年，与题干所述不符。
答案	FALSE

Question 38

题干定位词 / 关键词	literacy
原文定位	无
题目解析	题干：太空技术提高了亚洲的文化素养。 文章中多次提到亚洲和太空技术，但是并没有任何一处表明"太空技术提高了亚洲的文化素养"，题干内容属于无中生有。
答案	NOT GIVEN

Question 39

题干定位词 / 关键词	photos; natural catastrophes prevention; surveillance
原文定位	E 段第三句 Remote sensing satellites equipped with instruments to take photographs of the ground at different wavelengths provide essential information for natural resource accounting, environmental management, disaster prevention and monitoring, land-use mapping, and sustainable development planning.
题目解析	题干：通过具有一定技术的卫星拍摄的图片可以帮助预防和监测自然灾害。 通过 photos、natural catastrophes 和 surveillance 可以定位到 E 段。E 段第三句表明配备有仪器的遥感卫星可以拍摄不同波长的地面照片，为自然资源核算、环境管理、灾害预防和监测、土地使用制图以及可持续发展规划提供必要的信息，题干中的 photos taken 对应 take photographs，natural catastrophes prevention and surveillance 对应 disaster prevention and monitoring，所以答案为 TRUE。
答案	TRUE

Question 40

题干定位词 / 关键词	commercial competition; technology development
原文定位	C 段第二句 Space in Asia is very much influenced by the competitive commercial space sector, the emergence of low cost mini-satellites, and the globalization of industrial and financial markets.
题目解析	题干：商业竞争是亚洲技术发展的一个推动因素。 通过 commercial competition 定位到 C 段。C 段第二句提到竞争激烈的商业航天部门、低成本微型卫星的出现以及工业和金融市场的全球化在很大程度上影响了亚洲的航天，这与题干表述一致，所以答案为 TRUE。
答案	TRUE

长难句分析

E 段：Remote sensing satellites equipped with instruments to take photographs of the ground at different wavelengths provide essential information for natural resource accounting, environmental management, disaster prevention and monitoring, land-use mapping, and sustainable development planning.

思路分析：对于长难句，首先要明确句子的主语和谓语，这个句子的主语是 remote sensing satellites，接着找谓语，在 equipped with 和 provide 中，谓语肯定是 provide，因为动词原形无法做其他修饰成分，那么主语和谓语动词中间的部分就是修饰成分，即分词作定语，意思是什么样的 remote sensing satellites 提供了必要的信息，后面的介词短语 for... 引出对象。

参考翻译：配备有仪器的遥感卫星可以拍摄不同波长的地面照片，为自然资源核算、环境管理、灾害预防和监测、土地使用制图以及可持续发展规划提供必要的信息。

G 段：The laws of physics are the same in Tokyo as in Toulouse, and the principles of electronics and mechanics know no political or cultural boundaries.

思路分析：这个句子的难点在单词上，要注意 laws 和 principles 在句中是“定律”和“原理”的意思。

参考翻译：物理定律在东京和图卢兹是一样的，电子和机械的原理也是没有政治和文化边界的。

参考译文

亚洲空间卫星技术

太空时代始于 1957 年俄罗斯人造卫星斯普特尼克（Sputnik）的发射，并随着美俄登月竞赛而进一步发展。这场竞争的特点是技术先进、预算庞大。在这个过程中，有惊人的成功，有一些失败，也有很多衍生产品。欧洲、日本、中国、印度迅速加入这些超级大国的太空俱乐部。随着成本相对较低的高性能微型卫星和发射器的出现，亚洲小国获得本土太空能力成为可能。然而，如何、以何种方式、出于何种目的来实现这些能力呢？

A 自公元前 500 年左右中国首次使用“火箭”（装满火药的竹竿）并在公元 1232 年的宋朝开封之战中击退了蒙古入侵者以来，火箭技术已经取得了长足的进步。这些古代的火箭与今天的中国运载火箭“长征”形成了鲜明的对比。

B 在过去十年中，亚洲的空间活动在空基服务的利用以及卫星和发射装置的生产方面都有了显著增长。这种快速扩张使许多评论员和分析人士预测，亚洲（国家）将成为世界太空强国。太空时代在世界范围内产生了巨大的影响，直接发展的空间技术影响着电信、气象预报、地球资源和环境监测以及减灾（洪水、森林火灾和石油泄漏）。亚洲国家尤其热衷于接受这样的发展。

C 人们正在探索卫星的创新性用途，这些用途正在产生潜在的革命性影响，如在保健和远程医疗、远程教育、犯罪预防（公海海盗活动）、粮食和农业规划及生产（水稻作物监测）等领域。竞争激烈的商业航天部门、低成本微型卫星的出现以及工业和金融市场的全球化在很大程度上影响了亚洲的航天。面对这些趋势，目前尚不清楚亚洲航天在未来几十年将如何发展。然而，在确定其对该区域可能产生的后果时，了解和评估影响亚洲太空活动和发展的因素和力量十分重要。

D 目前，日本、中国和印度这三个亚洲国家拥有全面的端到端太空能力，并拥有完善的太空基础设施：太空技术、卫星制造、火箭和太空港。韩国在卫星设计和制造方面已经自给自足，目前正试图加入他们的行列，计划开发一个发射场和一个太空港。此外，东南亚国家以及与印度次大陆接壤的国家（尼泊尔、巴基斯坦和孟加拉国）已经有了或正在开始发展本国的太空计划。东南亚国家联盟（简称东盟 ）在不同程度上接受了使用外国技术的太空应用，并且在过去 5 年左右的时间里，其太空活动一直在扩大。在电信（移动和固定服务）、互联网和遥感应用的驱动下，东南亚预计将成为商业空间产品和应用的最大和增长最快的市场。在这项技术的发展过程中，经济、政治、文化、历史等诸多非技术因素相互作用并发挥着重要作用，进而影响亚洲科技。

E 亚洲，特别是东南亚，遭受着一长串反复出现的大规模环境问题，包括风暴和洪水、森林火灾和森林砍伐以及作物歉收。因此，该地区最受关注的太空应用是遥感。配备有仪器的遥感卫星可以拍摄不同波长的地面照片，为自然资源核算、环境管理、灾害预防和监测、土地使用制图以及可持续发展规划提供必要的信息。这些应用的进展迅速且令人印象深刻。与日本、中国、印度不同，东盟成员国没有自己的遥感卫星，但大多数成员国都拥有接收、处理、解读美国和欧洲卫星数据的设施。特别是泰国、马来西亚和新加坡拥有世界一流的遥感处理设施和研究项目。东盟计划开发（和发射）自己的卫星，特别是遥感卫星。鉴于太空活动所涉及的技术挑战和高风险，要获得成功，需要经历一个非常漫长和昂贵的学习曲线。日本的卫星制造是基于美国和欧洲所采用的年代久远且传统的国防和军事采购方法的。

F 近年来，为了大幅降低成本，卫星的设计和制造方式发生了根本性的变化。“小卫星”的出现，以及亚洲国家迅速采用它们作为开发低成本卫星技术和迅速建立太空能力的一种方式，使这些国家有可能将其学习曲线缩短十年或更长时间。全球技术转让机制的增加，以及利用现成的商业技术取代昂贵的航天和军用标准部件，很可能促成一个具有高度竞争力的亚洲卫星制造工业。

G 物理定律在东京和图卢兹是一样的，电子和机械的原理也是没有政治和文化边界的。然而，这种不变性并不适用于工程实践和管理，它们受教育、文化和历史的影响很大。这些因素反过来又会影响成本、交付时间、产品设计，并最终影响国际销售。许多亚洲国家正在派遣他们的工程师到西方接受培训，这些经验丰富的工程师再回到不断发展的亚洲航天工业中工作。这种专业技术的获取，再加上世界闻名的日本制造和管理技术，是否会应用于建造世界级的卫星并降低成本呢?

TEST 4 解析

READING PASSAGE 1

Multitasking Debate:
Can you do them at the same time?

文章结构

体裁	说明文
题材	社科类
主题	关于多任务处理的实验、限制因素分析及一些研究结果
段落概括	A 段：人们可能无法真正进行多任务处理。 B 段：一项实验：大脑是否有症结妨碍多任务处理。 C 段：两项任务间隔时间越长，延迟时间越短。 D 段：影响多任务处理的第一个限制因素：注意瞬脱。 E 段：影响多任务处理的第二个限制因素：短期视觉记忆。 F 段：影响多任务处理的第三个限制因素：选择对刺激的反应。 G 段：另一项实验：经过足够的练习，一些人可以同时完成两项任务。 H 段：练习有时可以消除干扰效应。 I 段：随着年龄的增长，人们的多任务处理能力会下降。 J 段：老年人可以从练习中受益。

重点词汇

A 段							
单词	音标	词性	释义	单词	音标	词性	释义
multitasking	[ˌmʌltiˈtɑːskɪŋ]	*n.*	多任务处理	bottleneck	[ˈbɒtlnek]	*n.*	瓶颈
underperform	[ˌʌndəpəˈfɔːm]	*v.*	表现不佳	parallel	[ˈpærəlel]	*adj.*	平行的，并行的

B 段							
单词	音标	词性	释义	单词	音标	词性	释义
psychologist	[saɪˈkɒlədʒɪst]	*n.*	心理学家	sticking point		*phr.*	症结，关键点
demonstrate	[ˈdemənstreɪt]	*v.*	证明	devise	[dɪˈvaɪz]	*v.*	设计，发明
peak	[piːk]	*n.*	巅峰，顶点	elicit	[ɪˈlɪsɪt]	*v.*	引出；得到
C 段							
单词	音标	词性	释义	单词	音标	词性	释义
flummoxed	[ˈflʌməkst]	*adj.*	困惑的	postpone	[pəˈspəʊn]	*v.*	推迟，延缓
simultaneously	[ˌsɪmlˈteɪniəsli]	*adv.*	同时地	interval	[ˈɪntəvl]	*n.*	间隔，间隙
D 段							
单词	音标	词性	释义	单词	音标	词性	释义
blink	[blɪŋk]	*n.*	片刻的犹豫	crucial	[ˈkruːʃl]	*adj.*	至关重要的
register	[ˈredʒɪstə(r)]	*v.*	注意到，受到注意；显示	cortex	[ˈkɔːteks]	*n.*	皮层，（尤指）大脑皮层
E 段							
单词	音标	词性	释义	单词	音标	词性	释义
short-term	[ˌʃɔːt ˈtɜːm]	*adj.*	短期的	estimate	[ˈestɪmət]	*v.*	估计，判断
identical	[aɪˈdentɪkl]	*adj.*	完全相同的	dearth	[dɜːθ]	*n.*	缺乏
F 段							
stimulus	[ˈstɪmjələs]	*n.*	刺激（物），促进因素	delay	[dɪˈleɪ]	*v.*	推迟，耽误
G 段							
单词	音标	词性	释义	单词	音标	词性	释义
dual-task	[ˈdjuːəl tɑːsk]	*n.*	双重任务	interference	[ˌɪntəˈfɪərəns]	*n.*	干涉，干预
prioritise	[praɪˈɒrətaɪz]	*v.*	按优先顺序处理	optimist	[ˈɒptɪmɪst]	*n.*	乐观主义者，乐天派
cognitive	[ˈkɒgnətɪv]	*adj.*	认知的	competently	[ˈkɒmpɪtəntli]	*adv.*	胜任地；适合地
coordinate	[kəʊˈɔːdɪneɪt]	*v.*	协调，配合	discretion	[dɪˈskreʃn]	*n.*	自行决定权，判断力
H 段							
单词	音标	词性	释义	单词	音标	词性	释义
erase	[ɪˈreɪz]	*v.*	抹去，擦掉	speculate	[ˈspekjuleɪt]	*v.*	猜测，推测
execute	[ˈeksɪkjuːt]	*v.*	执行，实施	subconscious	[ˌsʌbˈkɒnʃəs]	*adj.*	下意识的，潜意识的
I 段							
单词	音标	词性	释义	单词	音标	词性	释义
precipitous	[prɪˈsɪpɪtəs]	*adj.*	险峻的	scene	[siːn]	*n.*	场面；景色

J 段							
单词	音标	词性	释义	单词	音标	词性	释义
scan	[skæn]	*n.*	扫描检查	sobering	[ˈsəʊbərɪŋ]	*adj.*	清醒的
almighty	[ɔːlˈmaɪti]	*adj.*	全能的	crippling	[ˈkrɪplɪŋ]	*adj.*	造成严重后果的

题目精解

Questions 1-5

题型：段落信息配对题

Question 1

题干定位词 / 关键词	theory; delay; selecting one reaction
原文定位	F 段第二、三句 Selecting a response to one of these things will delay by some tenths of a second your ability to respond to the other. This is called the "response selection bottleneck" theory, first proposed in 1952.
题目解析	题干：一个解释选择一个反应时延迟发生的理论。 通过关键词可以定位到 F 段第二、三句：选择对其中一件事情进行响应会将对另一件事情做出响应的时间延迟十分之一秒。这就是 1952 年首次提出的"反应选择瓶颈"理论。这与题干表述一致，delay 原词重现，selecting one reaction 对应 selecting a response to one of these things，theory 即"response selection bottleneck"理论。
答案	F

Question 2

题干定位词 / 关键词	different age group
原文定位	I 段第二、三句 According to Art Kramer at the University of Illinois at Urbana- Champaign, who studies how ageing affects our cognitive abilities, we peak in our 20s. Though the decline is slow through our 30s and on into our 50s, it is there; and after 55, it becomes more precipitous.
题目解析	题干：不同年龄的人对重要事情的反应有所不同。 通过 different age group 定位到 I 段第二、三句，这两句主要阐述衰老会影响我们的认知能力，我们的认知能力在 20 多岁时达到顶峰，虽然在 30 多岁到 50 多岁之间下降缓慢，但在 55 岁以后会急剧下降。由此可知，不同年龄段对于事情的认知和反应是不同的。
答案	I

Question 3

题干定位词 / 关键词	visual and audio; simultaneously
原文定位	C 段第一、二句 The trouble comes when Marios shows the volunteers an image, and then almost immediately plays them a sound. Now they're flummoxed.
题目解析	题干：视觉和听觉元素同时出现时会产生冲突。 通过 visual and audio 可定位到 B、C 两段。B 段提到图像和声音，但是并没有说两者同时呈现，直到读到 C 段第一、二句：当马鲁瓦给志愿者们展示了一幅图像，然后几乎立刻给他们播放一种声音时，问题就来了。现在他们很困惑。image 对应 visual，sound 对应 audio，flummoxed 对应 conflicts。
答案	C

Question 4

题干定位词 / 关键词	experiment; critical part in brain
原文定位	B 段第一、二句 The problem, according to René Marois, a psychologist at Vanderbilt University in Nashville, Tennessee, is that there's a sticking point in the brain. To demonstrate this, Marois devised an experiment to locate it.
题目解析	题干：一个用来证明大脑中进行多任务处理的关键部分的实验。 通过 critical part in brain 定位到 B 段第一、二句：田纳西州纳什维尔范德比尔特大学的心理学家勒内·马鲁瓦认为，问题在于大脑中有一个症结。为了证明这一点，马鲁瓦设计了一个实验来定位它。这与题干表述一致。experiment 原词重现，devised 对应 designed，a sticking point in the brain 对应 critical part in brain。
答案	B

Question 5

题干定位词 / 关键词	optimistic side
原文定位	G 段倒数第二句 His experiments have shown that with enough practice - at least 2000 tries - some people can execute two tasks simultaneously as competently as if they were doing them one after the other.
题目解析	题干：一个支持多任务并行的积极一面的观点。 A 段至 F 段都在说我们可能难以实现多任务并行，直到 G 段才开始出现反驳观点。G 段倒数第二句指出，只要有足够的练习，至少尝试 2000 次，一些人就能同时执行两项任务，效果就像他们做完一项任务再做另一项一样。由此可知，多任务处理是有可能实现的，即为一种积极的观点。
答案	G

Questions 6-8

题型：单选题

Question 6

题干定位词 / 关键词	correct; experiment; René Marois
原文定位	B 段第四句 Different coloured circles require presses from different fingers.
题目解析	题干：关于勒内 · 马鲁瓦的实验，以下说法中正确的是哪个？ A：参与者在单独的听力任务上表现很差 B：志愿者根据不同颜色按下不同按键 C：参与者需要对不同颜色的物体使用不同的手指 D：当图片和声音一起出现时表现更好 根据关键词定位到 B 段。B 段第四句表明不同颜色的圆圈需要用不同的手指按压，与选项 C 表述一致。 B 段倒数第一至四句表明志愿者在单独听到声音时的反应很及时，是没有问题的（Then they learn to listen to different recordings and respond by making a specific sound. For instance, when they hear a bird chirp, they have to say "ba"; an electronic sound should elicit a "ko", and so on. Again, no problem. A normal person can do that in about half a second, with almost no effort），所以排除选项 A。 与选项 B 相关的内容出现在 B 段第二至四句（To demonstrate this, Marois devised an experiment to locate it. Volunteers watch a screen and when a particular image appears, a red circle, say, they have to press a key with their index finger. Different coloured circles require presses from different fingers），文中说的是用不同手指按压同一个按键，所以排除选项 B。 C 段第一、二句表明在图像和声音一起出现时，志愿者们表现不佳（The trouble comes when Marios shows the volunteers an image, and then almost immediately plays them a sound. Now they're flummoxed），所以选项 D 也被排除。
答案	C

TEST 4 解析

Question 7

题干定位词 / 关键词	correct; first limitation; Marois's experiment
原文定位	D 段第二至四句 The first is in simply identifying what we're looking at. This can take a few tenths of a second, during which time we are not able to see and recognize a second item. This limitation is known as the "attentional blink" : experiments have shown that if you're watching out for a particular event and a second one shows up unexpectedly any time within this crucial window of concentration, it may register in your visual cortex but you will be unable to act upon it.
题目解析	题干：关于马鲁瓦实验的第一个限制，以下说法中正确的是哪个？ A："注意瞬脱"需要 10 秒钟 B：如果我们集中注意力在一个物体上，当另一个物体出现时，就会出现滞后 C：我们对第二个物体的反应总是有困难的 D：通过一些措施，可以避免第一个限制 通过 first limitation 定位到 D 段。D 段第二、三句提及我们识别正在看的东西需要十分之几秒的时间，在这段时间内，我们无法看到和识别第二个物品，这一限制被称为"注意瞬脱"，与选项 B 相符。 选项 A 与 D 段第三句 This can take a few tenths of a second（这可能需要十分之几秒的时间）不符，故排除。 选项 C 与 D 段倒数第二句 Interestingly, if you don't expect the first event, you have no trouble responding to the second（有趣的是，如果你没有预料到第一个事件，那么你回应第二个事件就没有问题）不符，故排除。 文中并未提及有任何方法能够避免"注意瞬脱"，所以选项 D 也不对。
答案	B

TEST 4 解析

Question 8

题干定位词 / 关键词	NOT correct; Meyer's experiments
原文定位	G 段
题目解析	题干：关于梅耶的实验和观点，以下说法中不正确的是哪个？ A：只需要失败几次后人们就能进行双重任务处理 B：练习可以克服双重任务的干扰 C：梅耶与马鲁瓦的意见相左 D：有一个处理器决定是否推迟另一项任务 通过人名定位到 G 段。根据 G 段倒数第二句中的 with enough practice—at least 2000 tries—some people can execute two tasks simultaneously（只要有足够的练习，至少尝试 2000 次，一些人就能同时执行两项任务）可知，选项 A 表述不正确，选项 B 表述正确。由于本题要求选错误选项，故选项 A 为本题答案。 G 段第一句 But David Meyer...doesn't buy the bottleneck idea 表明 Meyer 不相信瓶颈的观点，与选项 C 表述相符。 选项 D 与 G 段最后一句 He suggests that there is a central cognitive processor that coordinates all this and, what's more, he thinks it uses discretion: sometimes it chooses to delay one task while completing another（他认为有一个中央认知处理器来协调这一切，更重要的是，他认为它使用了自由裁量权：有时它会选择在完成一项任务的同时推迟另一项任务）表述相符。
答案	A

Questions 9-13

题型：判断题

Question 9

题干定位词 / 关键词	longer gap; shorter delay
原文定位	C 段最后一句 The largest dual-task delays occur when the two tasks are presented simultaneously; delays progressively shorten as the interval between presenting the tasks lengthens.
题目解析	题干：两个任务呈现的时间间隔越长，对第二个任务的延迟就越短。 通过 gap 定位到 C 段（gap 对应 interval）。C 段最后一句表明：当两项任务同时呈现时，出现最大程度的双任务延迟；随着任务呈现间隔的延长，延迟逐渐缩短。这与题干表述一致，故答案为 YES。
答案	YES

Question 10

题干定位词 / 关键词	human memory; similar images
原文定位	E 段第一至四句 A second limitation is our short-term visual memory. It's estimated that we can keep track of about four items at a time, fewer if they are complex. This capacity shortage is thought to explain, in part, our astonishing inability to detect even huge changes in scenes that are otherwise identical, so-called "change blindness". Show people pairs of near-identical photos—say, aircraft engines in one picture have disappeared in the other—and they will fail to spot the differences.
题目解析	题干：人类的记忆能力不足，导致人们在看到两幅相似的图像时，有时会忽略其中的差异。 通过 human memory 定位到 E 段。E 段前两句说明第二个限制是我们的短期视觉记忆，并给出了具体说明。第三、四句表明短期视觉记忆能力可以在某种程度上解释为什么我们无法检测到在其他方面完全相同的场景中的巨大变化，与题干表述相符。this capacity shortage 指代 incapable in human memory，inability to detect 对应 miss the differences，identical 对应 similar。
答案	YES

Question 11

题干定位词 / 关键词	different opinion; bottleneck effect
原文定位	G 段第一句 But David Meyer, a psychologist at the University of Michigan, Ann Arbor, doesn't buy the bottleneck idea.
题目解析	题干：马鲁瓦对训练可以消除瓶颈效应的说法持不同意见。 通过 different opinion 定位到 G 段。由 G 段第一句可知，梅耶对瓶颈理论持不同观点，不是马鲁瓦，主语错误。
答案	NO

Question 12

题干定位词 / 关键词	Art Kramer; correlation; genders
原文定位	无
题目解析	题干：阿特 · 克雷默证明了多任务并行与性别之间的关联。 通过阿特 · 克雷默定位到 I 段，由于 I 段只提到多任务处理能力与年龄的关系，并未提及是否与性别有关，故答案为 NOT GIVEN。
答案	NOT GIVEN

Question 13

题干定位词 / 关键词	author; effect of practice; variation
原文定位	J 段第四句 While it's clear that practice can often make a difference, especially as we age, the basic facts remain sobering.
题目解析	题干：作者不相信练习的效果会带来任何变化。 由于本题问的是作者的想法，所以可以考虑在结尾段找答案。J 段第四句前半句表明练习会产生影响，与题干所述相悖。
答案	NO

长难句分析

E 段：This capacity shortage is thought to explain, in part, our astonishing inability to detect even huge changes in scenes that are otherwise identical, so-called "change blindness".

思路分析：这个句子的主句为 This capacity shortage is thought to explain our inability，in part 为插入语，阅读时可暂时忽略，to detect even huge changes in scenes 为 inability 的具体说明，that are otherwise identical 为定语从句，修饰 scenes，so-called 为形容词，表示"所谓的"，修饰 inability。

参考翻译：这种存储容量不足被认为可以部分解释为什么我们无法检测到在其他方面完全相同的场景中的巨大变化，即所谓的"变化盲视"。

G 段：His experiments have shown that with enough practice—at least 2000 tries—some people can execute two tasks simultaneously as competently as if they were doing them one after the other.

思路分析：这个句子的主句为 show 引导的宾语从句，that 后的内容为从句，解释实验揭示的内容。at least 2000 tries 为对 enough practice 的补充，说明"足够的练习"的次数大致是多少次。as competently... after the other 形容两项任务同时完成的程度。

参考翻译：他的实验表明，只要有足够的练习，至少尝试 2000 次，一些人就能同时执行两项任务，效果就像他们做完一项任务再做另一项一样。

参考译文

关于多任务处理的争论：你能同时处理多项任务吗？

A 开车时打电话并不是我们在多任务处理方面比想象中更糟糕的唯一情况。新的研究发现了我们大脑中的一个瓶颈，有人说，这意味着我们根本无法真正地进行多任务处理。如果实验结果反映了现实生活中的表现，那么那些认为自己在同时处理多项任务的人可能只是在所有方面表现不佳，或者充其量，除了一项任务，其他并行任务都表现不佳。练习可能会改善你的表现，但你永远不会像一次专注于一项任务时那样出色。

B 田纳西州纳什维尔范德比尔特大学的心理学家勒内 · 马鲁瓦认为，问题在于大脑中有一个症结。为了证明这一点，马鲁瓦设计了一个实验来定位它。志愿者观看屏幕，当某个特定的图像出现时，比如一个红色的圆圈，他们必须用食指按下一个键。不同颜色的圆圈需要用不同手指按压。一般的反应时间约为半秒，志愿者们很快就达到了他们的最佳表现。然后，他们学着听不同的录音，并通过发出特定的声音做出反应。例如，当他们听到鸟叫时，必须说“ba”，听到电子声音时要发出“ko”，以此类推。同样，这也没问题。一个正常人可以在大约半秒钟内完成这项工作，几乎不需要任何努力。

C 当马鲁瓦给志愿者们展示了一幅图像，然后几乎立刻给他们播放一种声音时，问题就来了。现在他们很困惑。他说：“如果你同时展示一幅图像和播放一种声音，一项任务就会被推迟。”事实上，如果第二项任务是在半秒左右（第一项任务处理和反应需要的时间）的时间内被引入的，那么它将被简单地延迟到第一项任务完成。当两项任务同时呈现时，出现最大程度的双任务延迟；随着任务呈现间隔的延长，延迟逐渐缩短。

D 马鲁瓦说我们至少在三个方面似乎陷入了困境。第一个是简单地识别我们正在看的东西。这可能需要十分之几秒的时间，在这段时间内，我们无法看到和识别第二个物品。这一限制被称为“注意瞬脱”：实验表明，如果你在关注某一特定事件时，第二个事件在这个关键的集中窗口内随时意外出现，它可能会在你的视觉皮层中出现，但你将无法对此采取行动。有趣的是，如果你没有预料到第一个事件，那么你回应第二个事件就没有问题。究竟是什么原因导致了注意力的瞬脱，这仍然是一个值得争论的问题。

E 第二个限制是我们的短期视觉记忆。据估计，我们可以一次跟踪大约四个项目，如果它们很复杂，则更少。这种存储容量不足被认为可以部分解释为什么我们无法检测到在其他方面完全相同的场景中的巨大变化，即所谓的“变化盲视”。向人们展示几组几乎相同的照片，比如一张照片中的飞机引擎在另一张照片上消失了，他们无法发现差异。然而，人们对什么是真正的限制要素再一次出现了分歧。这是因为存储容量不足，还是因为观众的关注程度不够？

F 第三个限制是选择对刺激的反应，例如，当你看到路上有孩子时会刹车，或者当你的母亲在电话里告诉你她想离开你的父亲时做出回复，这些都需要脑力。选择对其中一件事情进行响应会将对另一件事情做出响应的时间延迟十分之一秒。这就是1952年首次提出的“反应选择瓶颈”理论。

G 但是密歇根大学安娜堡分校的心理学家大卫·梅耶并不相信瓶颈的观点。他认为双重任务干扰只是大脑用来优先处理多个活动的策略的证据。梅耶被同龄人称为乐观主义者。他写过一些论文，有一篇叫《双重任务表现中近乎完美的时间分享：解开中心认知瓶颈》。他的实验表明，只要有足够的练习，至少尝试 2000 次，一些人就能同时执行两项任务，效果就像他们做完一项任务再做另一项一样。他认为有一个中央认知处理器来协调这一切，更重要的是，他认为它使用了自由裁量权：有时它会选择在完成一项任务的同时推迟另一项任务。

H 马鲁瓦同意练习有时可以消除干扰效应。他发现，当志愿者连续两周每天练习一小时时，他们在同时处理两项任务方面有了巨大的进步。他与梅耶的分歧在于大脑正在做什么来实现这一点。马鲁瓦推测，练习可能会让我们有机会找到一些不那么拥挤的路径来执行任务，就像我们找一条可靠的小路来避免主路的拥挤一样，使我们有效地对任务做出潜意识的反应。毕竟，我们大多数人每天都会下意识地同时处理多任务，比如：一边走路一边说话，一边吃饭一边看书，一边看电视一边叠衣服。

I 一般来说，随着年龄的增长，我们同时处理多项任务的能力就会变差，这并不奇怪。伊利诺伊大学厄巴纳—香槟分校的阿特 · 克雷默研究了衰老如何影响我们的认知能力，他认为，我们的这种能力在 20 多岁时达到顶峰。虽然在 30 多岁时这种能力的下降速度很慢并且会持续到 50 多岁，但这种下降确实存在且在 55 岁之后会急剧下降。在一项研究中，他和他的同事们让年轻人和老年人在进行对话的同时进行模拟驾驶任务。他发现，年轻的司机往往会忽略背景变化，而年长的司机却没有注意到与任务高度相关的事情。同样，年长的受试者比年轻的驾驶员更难关注场景中更重要的部分。

J 不过，对于 55 岁以上的人来说，也不都是坏消息。克雷默还发现，老年人可以从练习中受益。他们不仅学会了如何表现得更优秀，而且大脑扫描显示，这种改善的根本原因是大脑活动方式的改变。显然，练习往往会产生影响，尤其是随着我们年龄的增长，但一些基本事实仍然令人警醒。马鲁瓦说：“我们印象里大脑是复杂的，无所不能的，但我们有非常卑微和严重的局限性。”他说在我们历史的大部分时间里，我们可能从来都不需要一次做一件以上的事情，所以我们还没有进化到能够做到这一点。不过，也许我们将来会这样做。也许有一天，我们回顾像黛比和阿伦这样的人，会认为他们是新一代真正的多任务者祖先。

READING PASSAGE 2

The Cacao: A Sweet History

文章结构

体裁	说明文
题材	植物类
主题	巧克力的起源与发展史
段落概括	第一章：巧克力曾经被高度珍视。 第二章第一段：玛雅人在两千年前学会种植可可树并制成可可饮料。 第二章第二段：可可和巧克力是玛雅文化的重要组成部分。 第二章第三段：巧克力在阿兹特克文化中也有特殊作用。 第三章：巧克力在欧洲逐渐传播、流行。 第四章：可可树的种植条件及种类。 第五章第一段：可可种子在工厂加工变成巧克力的过程。 第五章第二段：巧克力制作是一项大生意。

重点词汇

第一章							
单词	音标	词性	释义	单词	音标	词性	释义
treasure	[ˈtreʒə(r)]	*v.*	珍惜，珍视	tropical	[ˈtrɒpɪkl]	*adj.*	热带的，热带地区的
encompass	[ɪnˈkʌmpəs]	*v.*	包含，包括				
第二章第一段							
seed	[si:d]	*n.*	种子，籽	crush	[krʌʃ]	*v.*	捣碎，碾成粉末
unsweetened	[ˌʌnˈswi:tnd]	*adj.*	未加糖的；不甜的	foam	[fəʊm]	*n.*	泡沫，气泡
第二章第二段							
ceremony	[ˈserəməni]	*n.*	仪式，典礼	union	[ˈju:niən]	*n.*	联合，结合
第二章第三段							
royal	[ˈrɔɪəl]	*adj.*	皇家的	religious	[rɪˈlɪdʒəs]	*adj.*	宗教的
sacred	[ˈseɪkrɪd]	*adj.*	神圣的				

第三章							
empire	[ˈempaɪə(r)]	*n.*	帝国	colony	[ˈkɒləni]	*n.*	殖民地
第四章							
shady	[ˈʃeɪdi]	*adj.*	阴凉的，背阴的	pod	[pɒd]	*n.*	豆荚
harvest	[ˈhɑːvɪst]	*v./n.*	收割；收获，成果	threaten	[ˈθretn]	*v.*	威胁，恐吓
activist	[ˈæktɪvɪst]	*n.*	积极分子，活动家				
第五章第一段							
sort	[sɔːt]	*v.*	整理，把……分类，拣选	nib	[nɪb]	*n.*	种子粒
liquor	[ˈlɪkə(r)]	*n.*	液，汁	finely	[ˈfaɪnli]	*adv.*	微小地，细微地
mold	[məʊld]	*n.*	模具				
第五章第二段							
specialty	[ˈspeʃəlti]	*n.*	特色食品，特产，专卖店	costly	[ˈkɒstli]	*adj.*	昂贵的，代价大的

题目精解

Questions 14-18

题型：段落信息配对题

Question 14

题干定位词 / 关键词	part of cacao trees; produce chocolate
原文定位	Chapter D 第五、六句 After about five years, cacao trees start producing large fruits called pods, which grow near the trunk of the tree. The seeds inside the pods are harvested to make chocolate.
题目解析	题干：用来制作巧克力的可可树的部分。 全篇多处提到可可树，但是只有 Chapter D 具体介绍了巧克力是用可可树的哪一部分制作的。Chapter D 第五、六句表示：大约五年后，可可树开始结出被称为豆荚的大型果实，这些果实生长在树干附近。豆荚里的种子被收集起来用于制作巧克力。由此可知，对应 Chapter D。
答案	D

Question 15

题干定位词 / 关键词	average chocolate consumption; US
原文定位	Chapter E 第二段第五句 Each year, Americans eat an average of more than five kilograms of chocolate per person.
题目解析	题干：美国人每年人均的巧克力消费量。 根据关键词定位到 Chapter E 的第二段。Chapter E 第二段第五句表明：每年，美国人平均每人会吃掉 5 公斤以上的巧克力。这与题干表述相对应。each year 替换 per year，Americans 替换 people in the US，eat 即表示 consumption。
答案	E

Question 16

题干定位词 / 关键词	risks; farmers
原文定位	Chapter D 倒数第三至六句 Cacao trees grown on farms are much more easily threatened by diseases and insects than wild trees. Growing cacao is very hard work for farmers. They sell their harvest on a futures market. This means that economic conditions beyond their control can affect the amount of money they will earn.
题目解析	题干：农民们在可可业务上面临的风险。 通过 farmers 定位到 Chapter D。Chapter D 倒数第三至六句提及种植可可树的农民面临的风险有可可树会染上疾病、来自昆虫的威胁、收入不稳定等，与题干中的 risks 相对应。
答案	D

Question 17

题干定位词 / 关键词	sweetened chocolate drink; appeared
原文定位	Chapter C 第七句 The wealthy people of Spain first enjoyed a sweetened version of chocolate drink.
题目解析	题干：加糖的巧克力饮料首次出现的地方。 通过 sweetened 定位到 Chapter C 第七句，该句表明：西班牙的富人首先享用了一种加糖的巧克力饮料。这与题干表述相对应，这个地方即为西班牙。
答案	C

Question 18

题干定位词 / 关键词	ancient American civilizations
原文定位	Chapter B 第一段第二句 The Maya took cacao trees from the rainforests and grew them in their gardens.
题目解析	题干：古代美洲文明是怎么得到可可的。 通过 ancient American civilizations（对应文中的 Maya people of Central America）定位到 Chapter B。第二句提及玛雅人将雨林中的可可树种植在自己的花园里，这表明了玛雅人获取可可的途径，与题干表述相对应。
答案	B

Questions 19-23

题型：判断题

Question 19

题干定位词 / 关键词	ceremonies; restricted; Maya royal families
原文定位	Chapter B 第二段第三、四句 Ruling families drank chocolate at special ceremonies. And, even poorer members of the society could enjoy the drink once in a while.
题目解析	题干：只有玛雅的皇室可以在仪式上使用可可和巧克力。 通过 ceremonies 和 Maya 定位到 Chapter B 第二段第三句，该句提到统治阶层的家庭会在特殊仪式上喝巧克力，但接着后一句又说即使是社会上的穷人也可以偶尔喝上一杯，可见在仪式上喝巧克力是没有限制的，这与题干表述相矛盾。
答案	FALSE

Question 20

题干定位词 / 关键词	Hernando Cortes; invested
原文定位	Chapter C 第二句 But it was the Spanish explorer Hernando Cortes who understood that chocolate could be a valuable investment.
题目解析	题干：西班牙探险家埃尔南多 · 科尔特斯投资了巧克力和巧克力饮料。 通过 Hernando Cortes 定位到 Chapter C 的第二句，该句表明：但是是西班牙探险家埃尔南多 · 科尔特斯明白了巧克力可能是一项有价值的投资。该句没有提及他是否投资了巧克力和巧克力饮料，对此没有相关信息。
答案	NOT GIVEN

Question 21

题干定位词 / 关键词	forastero tree
原文定位	Chapter D 第八句 Most of the world's chocolate is made from the seed of the forastero tree.
题目解析	题干：弗拉斯特罗树生产最好的巧克力。 通过 forastero tree 定位到 Chapter D 第八句，该句提到世界上大部分的巧克力都是用弗拉斯特罗树的种子制成的，但是并没有说这种树的种子是否能生产出最好的巧克力，对此没有相关信息。
答案	NOT GIVEN

Question 22

题干定位词 / 关键词	got rid of; chocolate process
原文定位	Chapter E 第一段第一至三句 To become chocolate, cacao seeds go through a long production process in a factory. Workers must sort, clean and cook the seeds. Then they break off the covering of the seeds so that only the inside fruit, or nibs, remain.
题目解析	题干：在巧克力加工过程中可可的一些部分被丢掉了。 通过 chocolate process 定位到 Chapter E 的第一段第一句，该句提到要变成巧克力，可可种子要在工厂里经历漫长的生产过程，第三句又说工人们剥去种子的外壳，只留下里面的果实，也就是种子粒。由此可知，在制作过程中，可可种子的外壳被丢掉了，这与题干表述一致。
答案	TRUE

Question 23

题干定位词 / 关键词	welcomed more
原文定位	Chapter E 第二段第三句 Chocolate is especially popular in Europe and the United States.
题目解析	题干：巧克力在某些国家或大陆比世界上其他地方更受欢迎。 Chapter E 第二段第三句提到巧克力在欧洲和美国特别受欢迎，这与题干表述一致。
答案	TRUE

Questions 24-27

题型：流程图填空题

解析：流程图填空题和一般填空题的做题方法一样，首先要注意所填单词字数限制，其次在审题的时候要注意分析空格处所填词的词性，预判词义，以及把握这个词和空格前后词的逻辑关系。需要特别注意的是，流程图填空题一定要特别关注指示性的箭头或者短语，如 stage one，stage two 等。

Question 24

题干定位词 / 关键词	chocolate making; sorting; cleaning; cooking
原文定位	Chapter E 第一段第三句 Then they break off the covering of the seeds so that only the inside fruit, or nibs, remain.
题目解析	题干：将可可种子分类、清洗、烹煮、去掉它们的 _____。 本题是关于 chocolate making 的流程的，可以定位到 Chapter E。Chapter E 第一段第一句说可可种子在变成巧克力前会在工厂里经历一个漫长的生产过程；第二句提到了几个关键的动词 sort，clean，cook；第三句说剥去种子的外壳，只留下里面的果实，也就是种子粒。由此可知，空格处应填 covering（外壳）。
答案	covering

Question 25

题干定位词 / 关键词	crushing
原文定位	Chapter E 第一段第四句 Workers crush the nibs into a soft substance called chocolate liquor.
题目解析	题干：碾压后得到 _____。 通过 crushing 可以定位到 Chapter E 的第一段第四句，该句说工人们将种子粒碾压成一种被叫作巧克力浆的软状物质，所以在碾压后形成的是 chocolate liquor（巧克力浆）。
答案	chocolate liquor

TEST 4 解析

Question 26

题干定位词 / 关键词	sugar; milk
原文定位	Chapter E 第一段倒数第三句 Chocolate makers have their own special recipes in which they combine chocolate liquor with exact amounts of sugar, milk and cocoa fat.
题目解析	题干：加入糖、牛奶和 _____。 通过 sugar 和 milk 可以定位到 Chapter E 第一段倒数第三句，该句表明：巧克力制造商有自己的特殊配方，他们将巧克力浆与精确量的糖、牛奶和可可脂混合在一起。题干要求填写除糖和牛奶之外添加的物质，即为 cocoa fat（可可脂）。
答案	cocoa fat

Question 27

题干定位词 / 关键词	crumb mixture; a shape
原文定位	Chapter E 第一段倒数第一句 The mixture then goes through two more processes before it is shaped into a mold form.
题目解析	题干：将碎屑混合物充分研磨，然后在 _____ 中成型。 通过 crumb mixture 定位到 Chapter E 第一段倒数第二句，该句没有答案，继续往下看，最后一句提到在成型为模具之前，混合物还要经过两道工序。题干问在什么中成型，答案自然就是 mold（模具）了。
答案	mold (form)

长难句分析

E 段：Chocolate makers have their own special recipes in which they combine chocolate liquor with exact amounts of sugar, milk and cocoa fat.

思路分析：这个句子的主干为 Chocolate makers have special recipes，in which（相当于 where）后为定语从句，解释这个独特的配方的具体内容，combine...with... 表示“把……与……相结合”，with 后连接三个与 chocolate liquor 混合的物质，即 exact amounts of sugar、milk 和 cocoa fat。

参考翻译：巧克力制造商有自己的特殊配方，他们将巧克力浆与精确量的糖、牛奶和可可脂混合在一起。

D 段 : After about five years, cacao trees start producing large fruits called pods, which grow near the trunk of the tree.

思路分析： 这个句子的主干为 cacao trees start producing large fruits，after about five years 为句子的时间状语，called pods 作 large fruits 的后置定语，用于补充说明，which 后为定语从句，修饰 pods，说明 pods 生长的地点。

参考翻译： 大约五年后，可可树开始结出被称为豆荚的大型果实，这些果实生长在树干附近。

参考译文

可可的甜蜜历史

A 第一章

如今，大多数人认为巧克力是一种很甜的食物或饮品，可以在世界各地的商店里轻易找到。巧克力曾经被高度珍视，这可能会让你感到惊讶。可可树的美味秘密是 2000 年前在美洲热带雨林中被发现的。巧克力从一种中美洲本地饮料发展成为全球性甜食的故事涵盖了许多文化，跨越了许多大洲。

B 第二章

历史学家认为，中美洲的玛雅人大约在 2000 年前首次学会了种植可可树。玛雅人从雨林中收集可可树，并种植在自家花园里。他们将可可豆煮熟，然后把它们碾成软糊状。他们将这些糊状物与水和香料混合，制成无糖的可可饮料。玛雅人在两个容器之间来回倒入这种饮料，使液体出现一层气泡或泡沫。

可可和巧克力是玛雅文化的重要组成部分。玛雅建筑和艺术品上经常出现可可树的图像。统治阶层的家庭会在特殊仪式上喝巧克力。而且，即使是社会上比较贫穷的成员也可以偶尔喝上一杯。历史学家认为，可可豆也被用于结婚仪式，作为夫妻结合的标志。

如今墨西哥的阿兹特克文化也很珍视巧克力。但是，可可树不能在阿兹特克人居住的地区生长。所以，他们通过交易得到可可。他们甚至将可可豆作为一种货币来交税。巧克力在玛雅和阿兹特克王室及宗教活动中也发挥了特殊作用。牧师们在神圣的仪式上向神灵献上可可豆和祭品，并供应巧克力饮料。只有阿兹特克社会的富人才能喝得起巧克力，因为可可非常珍贵。据说阿兹特克统治者蒙特祖马每天要喝 50 杯巧克力。一些专家认为，“巧克力”这个词来自阿兹特克语的“xocolatl”，在纳瓦特尔语中，这个词的意思是“苦水”。其他人认为，“巧克力”一词是由玛雅语和纳瓦特尔语组合而成的。

C 第三章

1502 年，探险家克里斯托弗 · 哥伦布前往中美洲后，将可可种子带到了西班牙。但是是西班牙探险家埃尔南多 · 科尔特斯明白了巧克力可能是一项有价值的投资。1519 年，科尔特斯抵达今天的墨西哥。他相信这种巧克力饮料会受到西班牙人的欢迎。西班牙士兵击败阿兹特克帝国后，他们得以俘获可可的供应并将其送回家。西班牙后来开始在美洲殖民地种植可可，以满足对巧克力的大量需求。西班牙的富人首先享用了一种加糖的巧克力饮料。后来，这种饮料开始在整个欧洲流行。英国人、荷兰人和法国人开始在自己的殖民地种植可可树。直到 18 世纪，巧克力仍然是一种只有富人才能喝得起的饮料。在工业革命时期，新技术降低了巧克力的生产成本。

D 第四章

在非洲、中美洲和南美洲的许多国家，农民种植可可树。这些树生长在地球赤道附近的雨林的阴凉处。但这些树其实很难种植。它们需要精确的水量、温度、土壤和保护。大约五年后，可可树开始结出被称为豆荚的大型果实，这些果实生长在树干附近。豆荚里的种子被收集起来用于制作巧克力。可可树有好几个种类。世界上大部分的巧克力都是由弗拉斯特罗树的种子制成的。但农民也可以种植克里奥洛或特立尼达可可树。农场种植的可可树比野生可可树更容易受到疾病和昆虫的威胁。种植可可对农民来说是非常辛苦的工作。他们在期货市场上出售收成。这意味着不受他们控制的经济状况会影响他们的收入。今天，巧克力行业的官员、积极分子和科学家正在与农民合作。他们正在努力确保可可的种植方式对农民公平、对环境安全。

E 第五章

为了变成巧克力，可可种子要在工厂里经历漫长的生产过程。工人们必须对种子进行分类、清洗和烹饪。然后他们剥去种子的外壳，只留下里面的果实，也就是种子粒。工人们将这些种子粒碾压成一种被叫作巧克力浆的软状物质。巧克力浆被分离成可可固体和一种被叫作可可脂的脂肪。巧克力制造商有自己的特殊配方，他们将巧克力浆与精确量的糖、牛奶和可可脂混合在一起。他们将这种“碎屑”混合物充分碾碎，使其变得顺滑。然后，在成型为模具之前，混合物还要经过两道工序。

巧克力制作是一项大生意。全球每年可可作物的市场价值超过 50 亿美元。巧克力在欧洲和美国特别受欢迎。例如，2005 年，美国购买了价值 14 亿美元的可可制品。每年，美国人平均每人会吃掉 5 公斤以上的巧克力。出售昂贵巧克力的专卖店也很受欢迎。很多（专卖店）给巧克力爱好者提供了品尝世界各地种植的巧克力的机会。

READING PASSAGE 3

Australia's Lost Giants

文章结构

体裁	说明文
题材	动物类
主题	对澳大利亚不复存在的巨型动物的研究及推测
段落概括	A 段：一位化石猎人在南澳大利亚发现古老的巨型动物群骨头。 B 段：古生态学家针对巨型动物的消失提出假说，认为是人类造成的。 C 段：澳大利亚大型动物灭绝的原因推测。 D 段：关于巨型动物是否和人类共存的争论。 E 段：在另一著名的埋骨地发现了已知最大的有袋类动物。 F 段：科学家们只能从有限的数据（如岩画）中对过去进行推测。

重点词汇

A 段							
单词	音标	词性	释义	单词	音标	词性	释义
fossil	[ˈfɒsl]	*n.*	化石	cave	[keɪv]	*n.*	洞穴，山洞
chamber	[ˈtʃeɪmbə(r)]	*n.*	洞穴	litter	[ˈlɪtə(r)]	*v.*	使（某事物）充满；散乱覆盖
trapped	[træpt]	*adj.*	受困的，受限制的	megafauna	[ˈmegəˌfɔːnə]	*n.*	巨型动物
B 段							
单词	音标	词性	释义	单词	音标	词性	释义
disappearance	[ˌdɪsəˈpɪərəns]	*n.*	消亡，灭绝	mammoth	[ˈmæməθ]	*n.*	猛犸，毛象
sloth	[sləʊθ]	*n.*	树懒	paleoecologist	[ˌpæliəʊiˈkɒlədʒɪst]	*n.*	古生态学家
havoc	[ˈhævək]	*n.*	灾难，混乱	annihilate	[əˈnaɪəleɪt]	*v.*	歼灭；战胜
bison	[ˈbaɪsn]	*n.*	北美野牛；欧洲野牛				

C段							
单词	音标	词性	释义	单词	音标	词性	释义
baffling	[ˈbæflɪŋ]	*adj.*	令人困惑的	deforestation	[ˌdiːˌfɒrɪˈsteɪʃn]	*n.*	毁林，滥伐森林
dramatic	[drəˈmætɪk]	*adj.*	巨大而突然的，急剧的	dominant	[ˈdɒmɪnənt]	*adj.*	占支配地位的，占优势的
invasion	[ɪnˈveɪʒn]	*n.*	侵略，入侵	prone	[prəʊn]	*adj.*	有做……倾向的，易于……的
controversial	[ˌkɒntrəˈvɜːʃl]	*adj.*	有争议的	aborigine	[ˌæbəˈrɪdʒəni]	*n.*	土著；土著居民
D段							
单词	音标	词性	释义	单词	音标	词性	释义
pivot	[ˈpɪvət]	*v.*	围绕（主旨），以……为核心	sediment	[ˈsedɪmənt]	*n.*	沉淀物
circumstantial	[ˌsɜːkəmˈstænʃl]	*adj.*	偶然的	vocal	[ˈvəʊkl]	*adj.*	直言不讳的，大声表达的
overlap	[ˌəʊvəˈlæp]	*n.*	（物体或范围）重叠部分	redeposit	[ˌriːdɪˈpɒzɪt]	*v.*	再沉积
E段							
单词	音标	词性	释义	单词	音标	词性	释义
marsupial	[mɑːˈsuːpiəl]	*adj.*	有袋的	pouch	[paʊtʃ]	*n.*	（袋鼠、考拉等的）育儿袋
protrusion	[prəˈtruːʒn]	*n.*	突出；突出物	haul	[hɔːl]	*v.*	（用力）拖，拉
chaotic	[keɪˈɒtɪk]	*adj.*	混乱的，无秩序的				
F段							
单词	音标	词性	释义	单词	音标	词性	释义
haphazardly	[hæpˈhæzədli]	*adv.*	偶然地，随意地	disintegrate	[dɪsˈɪntɪgreɪt]	*v.*	崩溃，瓦解
erode	[ɪˈrəʊd]	*v.*	侵蚀，腐蚀	conceal	[kənˈsiːl]	*v.*	隐匿，隐藏

题目精解

Questions 28-32

题型：段落信息配对题

Question 28

题干定位词 / 关键词	naturally occurring events; hard to trace
原文定位	F 段第一、二句 Unfortunately, the Earth preserves its history haphazardly. Bones disintegrate, the land erodes, the climate changes, forests come and go, rivers change their course—and history, if not destroyed, is steadily concealed.
题目解析	题干：对自然发生的、使过去难以追溯的事件的描述。 通过 naturally occurring events 可以定位到 F 段第一、二句：不幸的是，地球随意地保存着它的历史。骨骼分解，土地侵蚀，气候变化，森林重生，河流改道，历史即使没有被摧毁，也会被逐步地掩盖。其中提及的骨骼分解、土地侵蚀等都是 naturally occurring events 的具体体现，“会被逐步地掩盖”意味着难以追踪（hard to trace）。
答案	F

Question 29

题干定位词 / 关键词	discovery; died out
原文定位	E 段第一句和倒数第三句 Another famous boneyard in the same region is a place called Wellington Caves, where Diprotodon, the largest known marsupial—an animal which carries its young in a pouch like kangaroos and koalas—was first discovered. Owen recognized that the Wellington cave bones belonged to an extinct marsupial.
题目解析	题干：关于一种已经灭绝的特殊动物的发现的叙述。 通过 E 段第一句和倒数第三句可知，在威灵顿洞穴发现了一种已知的最大的有袋动物。欧文认出这个骨头属于一种已灭绝的有袋动物。was first discovered 对应 discovery，extinct 对应 died out。
答案	E

Question 30

题干定位词 / 关键词	reason; died; in the same small area
原文定位	A 段第四句 It took Wells a moment to realize what he was looking at: the bones of thousands of creatures that must have fallen through holes in the ground above and become trapped.
题目解析	题干：各种各样的动物都死在同一个小区域的原因。 A 段第四句说成千上万头生物的骨头肯定是从地上的洞里掉下来的，然后被困在了这里。由此可知，原因是地上有洞，动物们不小心跌落了下来。
答案	A

Question 31

题干定位词 / 关键词	uncover; inappropriate
原文定位	E 段倒数第二句 Later, between 1909 and 1915 sediments in Mammoth Cave that contained fossils were hauled out and examined in a chaotic manner that no scientist today would approve.
题目解析	题干：暗示一个揭开化石秘密的程序是不恰当的。 E 段倒数第二句表明：后来，在 1909 年至 1915 年间，猛犸象洞穴中含有化石的沉积物被运出，以一种混乱的方式进行检查，这种检查方式现今没有科学家会认可。其中 uncover 替换 hauled out，inappropriate 替换 no scientist today would approve。
答案	E

Question 32

题干定位词 / 关键词	examples; did not die out; hunting
原文定位	B 段最后两句 But this period of extinction wasn't comprehensive. North America kept its deer, black bears and a small type of bison, and South America kept its jaguars and llamas.
题目解析	题干：没有因为狩猎而灭绝的动物的例子。 B 段倒数第三句提到人类消灭动物，但最后两句又说这一时期的灭绝并不是全面的灭绝。北美地区的鹿、黑熊和一种小型野牛，南美地区的美洲虎和美洲驼，均存活了下来。鹿、黑熊等都是没有因为人类狩猎而灭绝的动物的例子。
答案	B

Questions 33-36

题型：多选题

Questions 33-34

题干定位词 / 关键词	possible reasons; extinction
原文定位	C 段第三、四句 Indeed, Australia has been drying out for over a million years, and the megafauna were faced with a continent where vegetation began to disappear. Australian paleontologist Tim Flannery suggests that people, who arrived on the continent around 50,000 years ago, used fire to hunt, which led to deforestation
题目解析	题干：文中提到的澳大利亚巨型动物灭绝的可能原因是哪两个？ A：人类活动 B：疾病 C：失去栖息地 D：温度下降 E：新物种的引入 关于澳大利亚巨型动物灭绝的原因的内容在 C 段出现。C 段第三句提到澳大利亚已经干旱了 100 多万年，巨型动物面临着一个植被开始消失的大陆，对应选项 C。 C 段第四句提到澳大利亚古生物学家蒂姆 · 弗兰纳里的观点，他认为大约在 5 万年前抵达这块大陆的人开始用火狩猎，这导致了森林砍伐，对应选项 A。 选项 B、选项 D 和选项 E 都不是澳大利亚巨型动物灭绝的原因。
答案	A C

Questions 35-36

题干定位词 / 关键词	proof; humans having contact; found
原文定位	E 段最后一句和 F 段第四、五句 Still, one bone in particular has drawn extensive attention: a femur with a cut in it, possibly left there by a sharp tool. Australia's first people expressed themselves in rock art. Paleontologist Peter Murray has studied a rock painting in far northern Australia that shows what looks very much like a megafauna marsupial known as Palorchestes.
题目解析	题干：作者提到的关于人类与澳大利亚巨型动物有联系的可能的证据是哪两个？ A：由人造物体造成的骨损伤 B：早期武器附近的骨头 C：用来抓捕动物的人造洞口 D：巨型动物物种的保存图像 E：篝火旁的动物残骸 E 段最后一句提到一块股骨上面有一个切口，这可能是利器留下的。利器是人制造的，因此对应选项 A。 F 段第四句提到澳大利亚最早的人类在岩画中表达自己，第五句提到古生物学家彼得 · 默里研究了澳大利亚北部的一幅岩画，画中的对象很像一种被称为“袋貘”的巨型有袋动物。这体现了人和澳大利亚巨型动物的关联，对应选项 D。 选项 B 和选项 C 在原文中均没有提及。选项 E 与原文描述不符，原文说的是在美洲发现了这些证据，但在澳大利亚却没有（Such kill sites have been found in the Americas but not in Australia）。
答案	A D

Questions 37-40

题型：判断题

Question 37

题干定位词 / 关键词	dinosaurs
原文定位	A 段倒数第二句 Given how much ink has been spilled on the extinction of the dinosaurs, it's a wonder that even more hasn't been devoted to megafauna.
题目解析	题干：灭绝的巨型动物应该比恐龙的灭绝受到更多的关注。 通过 dinosaurs 定位到 A 段倒数第二句：鉴于在恐龙灭绝问题上已经有了太多的笔墨，令人惊讶的是，并没有关于大型动物的更多研究。由此可知，作者认为巨型动物的灭绝应该比恐龙的灭绝受到更多的关注，与题干表述一致。
答案	YES

Question 38

题干定位词 / 关键词	"blitzkrieg" hypothesis
原文定位	B 段第二句 In the 1960s, paleoecologist Paul Martin developed what became known as the blitzkrieg hypothesis.
题目解析	题干：保罗 · 马丁关于美洲"闪电战"的假说有一些问题。 通过 ' blitzkrieg' hypothesis 定位到 B 段第二句：20 世纪 60 年代，古生态学家保罗 · 马丁提出了被称为"闪电战"的假说。该段只说明了这一理论的内容，并未说明这一理论是否存在问题。
答案	NOT GIVEN

Question 39

题干定位词 / 关键词	Aborigines; protest; Flannery's book
原文定位	C 段第六句至段末 In Flannery's 1994 book called *The Future Eaters*, he sets out his thesis that human beings are a new kind of animal on the planet, and are in general, one prone to ruining ecosystems. Flannery's book was proved highly controversial. Some viewed it as critical of the Aborigines, who pride themselves on living in harmony with nature. The more basic problem with Flannery's thesis is that there is no direct evidence that they killed any Australian megafauna. It would be helpful if someone uncovered a Diprotodon skeleton with a spear point embedded in a rib—or perhaps Thylacoleo bones next to the charcoal of a human campfire. Such kill sites have been found in the Americas but not in Australia.
题目解析	题干：原住民应该寻找一种更有效的方法对抗弗兰纳里的书。 通过 Flannery's book 可定位到 C 段第六句：在弗兰纳里于 1994 年出版的《未来食者》一书中，他阐述了自己的观点，即人类是地球上的一种新动物，而且一般来说，人类很容易破坏生态系统。由于 C 段相关内容只说明了这本书的部分内容和对原住民的观点，并未提及原住民抗议，故无相关信息。
答案	NOT GIVEN

Question 40

题干定位词 / 关键词	sufficient evidence; Tim Flannery's ideas
原文定位	C 段倒数第三句 The more basic problem with Flannery's thesis is that there is no direct evidence that they killed any Australian megafauna.
题目解析	题干：有足够的证据支撑蒂姆 · 弗兰纳里关于巨型动物灭绝的观点。 C 段倒数第三句提及弗兰纳里的观点的问题是没有直接证据表明人类杀死了任何澳大利亚巨型动物，由此可知，弗兰纳里的观点证据不足，这与题干表述相矛盾。
答案	NO

长难句分析

E 段：Another famous boneyard in the same region is a place called Wellington Caves, where Diprotodon, the largest known marsupial—an animal which carries its young in a pouch like kangaroos and koalas—was first discovered.

思路分析：Another famous boneyard...Wellington Caves 为主句部分，后面是 where 引导的定语从句，修饰 Wellington Caves，说明它的特点。从句的主体部分为 Diprotodon was first discovered，the largest known marsupial 是对 Diprotodon 的补充说明，an animal which carries its young in a pouch like kangaroos and koalas 为插入语，用来解释说明什么是 marsupial。插入语中 which 引导的定语从句修饰 animal。

参考翻译：同一地区另一个著名的埋骨地是一个叫威灵顿洞穴的地方，在那里首次发现了已知最大的有袋类动物双门齿兽，这种动物像袋鼠和考拉一样将其幼崽装在袋子里。

E 段：Later, between 1909 and 1915 sediments in Mammoth Cave that contained fossils were hauled out and examined in a chaotic manner that no scientist today would approve.

思路分析：这个句子的主体部分为 sediments in Mammoth Cave were hauled out and examined。Later, between 1909 and 1915 为句子的时间状语，that contained fossils 为修饰 Mammoth Cave 的定语从句。in a chaotic manner 说明这个沉积物（sediments）是如何被检测（examined）的，that no scientist today would approve 为修饰 chaotic manner 的定语从句，用于说明这种检测方式的特点。

参考翻译：后来，在 1909 年至 1915 年间，猛犸象洞穴中含有化石的沉积物被运出，以一种混乱的方式进行检查，这种检查方式现今没有科学家会认可。

参考译文

澳大利亚失落的巨兽

曾经生活在澳大利亚这个广袤的大陆上的巨型动物群发生了什么？

A 1969 年，一位名叫罗德 · 威尔斯的化石猎人来到了南澳大利亚的纳拉科特，探索当时被称为“维多利亚洞穴”的地方。威尔斯艰难地穿过狭窄的通道，最终进入一个巨大的洞穴。它的红土地上散落着一些奇怪的物体。威尔斯花了一点时间才意识到自己眼前的是什么：成千上万头生物的骨头，它们一定是从地上的洞里掉下来的，然后被困在了这里。有一些最古老的骨头是属于哺乳动物的，这些哺乳动物比今天在澳大利亚发现的任何动物都要大得多。它们是古老的澳大利亚巨型动物群——更新世时期的巨型动物。在整个大陆的动物尸骨堆放地，科学家们发现了巨蛇、不会飞的巨大鸟类和七英尺高的袋鼠等动物的化石。鉴于在恐龙灭绝问题上已经有了太多的笔墨，令人惊讶的是，并没有关于大型动物的更多研究。史前人类从未向霸王龙投掷长矛，但确实猎杀了猛犸象和乳齿象。

B 美洲巨型动物群——猛犸象、剑齿猫、巨型树懒等的消失发生在人类到来后不久，距今约 13000 年。20 世纪 60 年代，古生态学家保罗 · 马丁提出了被称为“闪电战”的假说。马丁说，现代人类在美洲扩张时制造了巨大的破坏，挥舞着长矛消灭了那些从未面对过有如此技术的捕食者的动物。但这一时期的灭绝并不是全面的灭绝。鹿、黑熊和一种小型野牛在北美地区存活了下来，而美洲虎和美洲驼在南美地区存活了下来。

C 澳大利亚大型动物的遭遇令人困惑。多年来，科学家们将物种灭绝归咎于气候变化。事实上，澳大利亚已经干旱了 100 多万年，巨型动物面临着一个植被开始消失的大陆。澳大利亚古生物学家蒂姆 · 弗兰纳里认为，大约在 5 万年前来到这块大陆的人们用火狩猎，导致了森林砍伐。大约在 46000 年前的某个地方，澳大利亚的主要陆地生物发生了巨大的变化，在一种会使用工具、高度智能的捕食者入侵不久后，变化更明显。在弗兰纳里于 1994 年出版的《未来食者》一书中，他阐述了自己的观点，即人类是地球上的一种新动物，而且一般来说，人类很容易破坏生态系统。弗兰纳里的书被证明极具争议。一些人认为这是对原住民的批评，他们以与自然和谐相处而自豪。关于弗兰纳里的观点，更基本的问题是没有直接证据表明人类杀死了任何澳大利亚巨型动物。如果有人发现了一具肋骨被矛尖刺入的双门齿兽骨骼，或者在人类篝火的木炭旁发现了袋狮的骨头，这将提供有利证据。在美洲发现了这种杀戮地点，但在澳大利亚却没有。

D 关于巨型动物的争论在很大程度上取决于对古老骨骼及埋藏这些骨骼的沉积物进行年代测定的技术。如果科学家们能够证明巨型动物很快灭绝，而且这种灭绝发生在人类到来后的几百年甚至几千年内，那么这是一个强有力的证据，即使是一个纯粹的间接证据（一件事是另一件事的直接结果）。碰巧，有一个地方可能有这样的证据：新南威尔士州的 Cuddie Springs。今天，对该遗址最敢发声的人是考古学家朱迪斯·菲尔德。1991 年，她在石器旁边发现了巨型动物骨骼——这是一个引人注目的发现。她说，有两层化石显示了这种关联，一层大约有 3 万年历史，另一层有 3.5 万年历史。如果这个年代测定是准确的，那就意味着人类和巨型动物在澳大利亚共存了大约 2 万年。菲尔德说：“Cuddie Springs 展示的是人类和大型动物群之间存在着广泛的重叠。”她的批评者认为这是胡说。他们说，这些化石已经被从原来的位置移走，并重新沉积在较新的沉积物中。

E 同一地区另一个著名的埋骨地是一个叫威灵顿洞穴的地方，在那里首次发现了已知最大的有袋类动物双门齿兽，这种动物像袋鼠和考拉一样将其幼崽装在袋子里。科学家迈克 · 奥杰说："这是澳大利亚古生物学中的一个圣地。"原因如下：1830 年，一位名叫乔治 · 兰金的当地官员用绳子绑在洞穴壁的凸出物上，将自己吊进了洞穴。这个凸出物后来被证实是一块骨头。一位名叫托马斯 · 米切尔的测量员于当年晚些时候抵达，对该地区的洞穴进行了勘探，并将化石运送给英国古生物学家理查德 · 欧文，后者后来因揭露恐龙的存在而闻名。欧文认出威灵顿洞穴的骨头属于一种已灭绝的有袋动物。后来，在 1909 年至 1915 年间，猛犸象洞穴中含有化石的沉积物被运出，以一种混乱的方式进行检查，这种检查方式现今没有科学家会认可。尽管如此，有一块骨头特别引起了广泛的关注：这是一块股骨，上面有一个切口，可能是利器留下的。

F 不幸的是，地球随意地保存着它的历史。骨骼分解，土地侵蚀，气候变化，森林重生，河流改道，历史即使没有被摧毁，也会被逐步地掩盖。必然地，这些叙述都是根据有限的数据构建的。澳大利亚最早的人类在岩画中表达自己。古生物学家彼得 · 默里研究了澳大利亚北部的一幅岩画，画中的对象非常像一种巨型有袋动物，被称为"袋貘"。在西澳大利亚的另一处遗址上，似乎画着一个猎人和一只有袋类狮子或一只塔斯马尼亚虎——这里要做一个主要的区别，因为有袋类狮子灭绝了，而体型小得多的塔斯马尼亚虎存活到了更近的历史时期。但正如穆雷所说："每一步都涉及解释。数据本身并不能说明一切。"

TEST 5 解析

READING PASSAGE 1

Animal Minds: Parrot Alex

文章结构

体裁	说明文
题材	生物与环境
主题	一个以鹦鹉亚历克斯为对象的关于动物思维的实验
段落概括	A 段：佩珀伯格做了一件非常大胆的事情：教一只灰鹦鹉模仿英语发音。 B 段：动物能思考的说法一直存在很大争议，这也是佩珀伯格进行实验的初衷。 C 段：大量研究证实很多物种具有较高的心智能力。 D 段：持续 30 年的实验以及亚历克斯被选择的原因。 E 段：科学家们认为黑猩猩是更好的研究对象，但佩珀伯格坚持训练鹦鹉，并卓有成效。 F 段：亚历克斯模仿英文进步大，有助于人类了解鸟类的认知。 G 段：亚历克斯的表现彰显了他的思想。 H 段：亚历克斯的行为为动物具有思想提供更多证据。

重点词汇

A 段							
单词	音标	词性	释义	单词	音标	词性	释义
graduate	[ˈgrædʒuət]	*n.*	毕业生；大学毕业生	bold	[bəʊld]	*adj.*	大胆的
automaton	[ɔːˈtɒmətən]	*n.*	自动机；小机器人	reproduce	[ˌriːprəˈdjuːs]	*v.*	复制；再现
creature	[ˈkriːtʃə(r)]	*n.*	生物	lab	[læb]	*n.*	实验室

B 段							
单词	音标	词性	释义	单词	音标	词性	释义
dialogue	[ˈdaɪəlɒg]	*n.*	对话	incapable	[ɪnˈkeɪpəbl]	*adj.*	无能力的，不能的
stimuli	[ˈstɪmjʊlaɪ]	*n.*	刺激（物）；促进因素	lack	[læk]	*v.*	缺乏，缺少
controversial	[ˌkɒntrəˈvɜːʃl]	*adj.*	引起争论的，有争议的	instinct	[ˈɪnstɪŋkt]	*n.*	本能；天性；直觉
C 段							
单词	音标	词性	释义	单词	音标	词性	释义
self-awareness	[ˌself əˈweənəs]	*n.*	自我意识；自觉	imitate	[ˈɪmɪteɪt]	*v.*	仿效；模仿
ingenious	[ɪnˈdʒiːniəs]	*adj.*	精巧的；新颖独特的	species	[ˈspiːʃiːz]	*n.*	种，物种
distinctive	[dɪˈstɪŋktɪv]	*adj.*	独特的，特别的	variety	[vəˈraɪəti]	*n.*	种类，品种
D 段							
单词	音标	词性	释义	单词	音标	词性	释义
assistant	[əˈsɪstənt]	*n.*	助理，助手	flock	[flɒk]	*n.*	（鸟或羊等动物）群
dominate	[ˈdɒmɪneɪt]	*v.*	支配，控制	tolerate	[ˈtɒləreɪt]	*v.*	忍受，容许，允许
futile	[ˈfjuːtaɪl]	*adj.*	徒劳的，无效的				
E 段							
单词	音标	词性	释义	单词	音标	词性	释义
subject	[ˈsʌbdʒɪkt]	*n.*	接受试验者	tutelage	[ˈtjuːtəlɪdʒ]	*n.*	监护；指导
vocal tract		*phr.*	声道	symbol	[ˈsɪmbl]	*n.*	象征；符号
F 段							
单词	音标	词性	释义	单词	音标	词性	释义
observe	[əbˈzɜːv]	*v.*	观察，注意到	behavior	[bɪˈheɪvjə(r)]	*n.*	行为，表现
repetitious	[ˌrepəˈtɪʃəs]	*adj.*	重复的	rap	[ræp]	*v.*	敲打
avian	[ˈeɪviən]	*adj.*	鸟（类）的	cognition	[kɒgˈnɪʃn]	*n.*	认知；感知

G 段							
单词	音标	词性	释义	单词	音标	词性	释义
approximation	[əˌprɒksɪˈmeɪʃn]	*n.*	近似值	demonstrate	[ˈdemənstreɪt]	*v.*	证明，说明
retrieve	[rɪˈtriːv]	*v.*	取回	hesitation	[ˌhezɪˈteɪʃn]	*n.*	犹豫，疑虑
digitized	[ˈdɪdʒɪtaɪzd]	*adj.*	数字化的	ventriloquist	[venˈtrɪləkwɪst]	*n.*	腹语术表演者

H 段							
单词	音标	词性	释义	单词	音标	词性	释义
distinguish	[dɪˈstɪŋgwɪʃ]	*v.*	区分，辨别	material	[məˈtɪəriəl]	*n.*	材料，原料
arithmetic	[əˈrɪθmətɪk]	*n.*	算数，计算	interrupt	[ˌɪntəˈrʌpt]	*v.*	打断，打扰
obstinate	[ˈɒbstɪnət]	*adj.*	固执的，执拗的	moody	[ˈmuːdi]	*adj.*	喜怒无常的

题目精解

Questions 1-6

题型：判断题

Question 1

题干定位词 / 关键词	firstly; Alex; vocabulary
原文定位	A 段倒数第二句 She brought a one-year-old African gray parrot she named Alex into her lab to teach him to reproduce the sounds of the English language.
题目解析	题干：亚历克斯一开始就掌握了很多词汇。 原文提到亚力克斯被教模仿英语的发音。但“亚力克斯一开始就掌握了很多词汇”这一说法在文章中并未体现，因此答案为 NOT GIVEN。
答案	NOT GIVEN

Question 2

题干定位词 / 关键词	at the beginning; Alex; humans
原文定位	D 段第四句 Alex dominated his fellow parrots, acted huffy at times around Peeperberg, tolerated the other female humans, and fell to pieces over a male assistant who dropped by for a visit.
题目解析	题干：在研究之初，亚历克斯面对人类感到害怕。 D 段第四句提到亚历克斯统领着他的鹦鹉同伴，有时在佩珀伯格身边表现得怒气冲冲，他可以容忍其他女性人类，但会因为一个来访的男性助理而崩溃。本题非常容易出错，考生需要注意原文虽然提到了亚历克斯在实验中对人类的态度，但是并没有任何内容表明在研究之初亚历克斯对人类的态度如何，因此本题的答案为 NOT GIVEN。
答案	NOT GIVEN

Question 3

题干定位词 / 关键词	many scientists; ability of thinking
原文定位	B 段第一句 When Pepperberg began her dialogue with Alex, who died last September at the age of 31, many scientists believed animals were incapable of any thought.
题目解析	题干：以前，许多科学家认识到动物具有思考的能力。 B 段第一句提到，对话开始前，很多科学家认为动物是没有任何思考能力的，题干与原文说法相悖，因此答案为 FALSE。
答案	FALSE

Question 4

题干定位词 / 关键词	a long time; cognition; animals
原文定位	C 段第二句 Bit by bit, in ingenious experiments, researchers have documented these talents in other species, gradually chipping away at what we thought made human beings distinctive while offering a glimpse of where our own abilities came from.
题目解析	题干：人们认识到动物有认知经历了很长的时间。 原文详细地描述了科学家们经过精心设计的实验步骤才渐渐发现其他物种的天赋，逐渐削弱了我们认为人类与众不同的认知，同时让我们得以一窥我们自己的能力从何而来。可见，科学家们认识到动物有认知经历了漫长的过程，这与题干的说法不谋而合，因此答案为 TRUE。
答案	TRUE

Question 5

题干定位词 / 关键词	Alex; approximately imitate; English words; answering; Irene; world
原文定位	G 段第一句 In other words, because Alex was able to produce a close approximation of the sounds of some English words, Pepperberg could ask him questions about a bird's basic understanding of the world.
题目解析	题干：因为亚历克斯能够比较接近地模仿一些英语单词的发音，所以它基本上可以回答一些艾琳的关于世界的问题。 根据关键词定位到 G 段第一句：换句话说，由于亚历克斯能够发出一些与英语单词发音非常接近的声音，佩珀伯格就可以问他一些关于鸟类对世界的基本认识的问题。这与题干表述一致，因此本题的答案为 TRUE。
答案	TRUE

Question 6

题干定位词 / 关键词	breaking in; other parrots; incorrect answers
原文定位	H 段倒数第二句 He knows all this, and he gets bored, so he interrupts the others, or he gives the wrong answer just to be obstinate.
题目解析	题干：亚力克斯试图通过打断其他鹦鹉以及给出错误的答案获得关注。 原文提及亚力克斯知道所有的事，他也会感到无聊，所以他打断别人，或者固执地给出错误的答案。题干中说亚力克斯打断其他鹦鹉和给出错误答案是为了得到关注，这与原文说法相悖，因此答案为 FALSE。
答案	FALSE

Questions 7-10

题型：摘要填空题

Question 7

题干定位词 / 关键词	Alex; vocal tract; more than
原文定位	E 段倒数第二句 Under Pepperberg's patient tutelage, Alex learned how to use his vocal tract to imitate almost one hundred English words, including the sounds for various foods, although he calls an apple a "banerry".
题目解析	题干：经过艾琳的训练，鹦鹉亚历克斯可以用它的声道发出大于 _____。 根据关键词定位到 E 段倒数第二句：在佩珀伯格的耐心指导下，亚历克斯学会了如何用他的声道模仿近 100 个英语单词，包括各种食物的声音，尽管他把苹果说成"banerry"。more than 和 almost 为同义替换，pronounce 和 imitate 为同义替换，可知空格处应填 one hundred English words。由于字数限制，空格处需要缩减答案字数。
答案	100 English words/one hundred words

Question 8

题干定位词 / 关键词	scientists; rather teach
原文定位	E 段第二句 "Scientists thought that chimpanzees were better subjects, although, of course, chimps can't speak."
题目解析	题干：虽然其他科学家认为动物没有这种先进的思维能力，但他们宁愿教 _______。 E 段第二句：科学家们认为黑猩猩是更好的实验对象，当然，黑猩猩不会说话。由此可知，chimpanzees 为正确答案。
答案	chimpanzees

Question 9

题干定位词 / 关键词	Pepperberg; not to teach him to talk
原文定位	F 段倒数第二句和最后一句 "I'm not trying to see if Alex can learn a human language," she added. "That's never been the point. My plan always was to use his imitative skills to get a better understanding of avian cognition."
题目解析	题干：佩珀伯格澄清说，她想进行一项关于 _____ 的研究，但不是教亚历克斯说话。 F 段倒数第二句和最后一句表明佩珀伯格的研究目的，即她并不是想知道亚历克斯能否学会一门人类语言，这从来都不是重点。她的计划一直是利用他的模仿能力来更好地了解鸟类的认知。she wanted to 对应原文中的 My plan，所以答案应该在 F 段最后一句。通过句意可以判断出 avian cognition 为正确答案。
答案	avian cognition

Question 10

题干定位词 / 关键词	store's assistant; picked; other scientists
原文定位	D 段倒数第二句 Pepperberg bought Alex in a Chicago pet store where she let the store's assistant pick him out because she didn't want other scientists saying later that she'd particularly chosen an especially smart bird for her work.
题目解析	题干：为了避免其他科学家事后说这只鸟是 _______，商店的店员随便给她挑了一只鸟。 D 段倒数第二句：佩珀伯格在芝加哥的一家宠物店买的亚历克斯，她让宠物店的助理挑的他，因为她不想让其他科学家事后说她为她的工作专门挑选了一只特别聪明的鸟。saying 后面的内容即答案所在，根据句意可得出 particularly chosen 为正确答案。
答案	particularly chosen

Questions 11-13

题型：简答题

Questions 11

题干定位词 / 关键词	Alex; reply; similarity
原文定位	G 段第六、七句 “What’s same?” she asked. Without hesitation, Alex’s beak opened: “Co-lor.”
题目解析	题干：亚力克斯对他所看到的物体的相似性做了什么回答？ 通过关键词精准定位到 G 段第六、七句。佩珀伯格问这二者有什么相同的地方，亚历克斯回答说“颜色”。same 和 similarity 为同义替换，原文中亚力克斯对物体相似性的回答为 color。
答案	color/colour

Questions 12

题干定位词 / 关键词	problem; young parrots
原文定位	H 段第四句 “Talk clearly!” he commanded, when one of the younger birds Pepperberg was also teaching talked with wrong pronunciation.
题目解析	题干：除了亚力克斯，其他的小鹦鹉还有什么问题？ H 段第四句提到佩珀伯格正在教授的一只小鸟发音出错时，亚力克斯会让它说得清楚些，由此可知，小鹦鹉的问题是 wrong pronunciation。
答案	wrong pronunciation

Questions 13

题干定位词 / 关键词	behaved; call him
原文定位	H 段最后一句 At this stage, he’s like a teenager; he’s moody, and I’m never sure what he’ll do.
题目解析	题干：在某种程度上，通过亚力克斯的行为我们该怎么称呼他呢？ H 段提到了亚力克斯的行为，最后一句指出，在这个阶段，他就像一个青少年，喜怒无常，佩珀伯格不知道他会做什么。因此，teenager 为正确答案。
答案	teenager

长难句分析

C 段：Bit by bit, in ingenious experiments, researchers have documented these talents in other species, gradually chipping away at what we thought made human beings distinctive while offering a glimpse of where our own abilities came from.

思路分析：这个句子的主体可以简化为 researchers have documented these talents in other species，该句子为主谓宾结构，其中主语为 researchers，谓语为 have documented，宾语为 talents。chipping away... 为现在分词作伴随状语，强调前面主句导致的结果；while 为并列连词，chipping away... 与 offering... 形成并列结构。

参考翻译：在巧妙的实验中，研究人员一点一点地记录了其他物种的这些天赋，逐渐削弱了我们认为人类与众不同的认知，同时让我们得以一窥我们自己的能力从何而来。

D 段：Pepperberg bought Alex in a Chicago pet store where she let the store's assistant pick him out because she didn't want other scientists saying later that she'd particularly chosen an especially smart bird for her work.

思路分析：这个句子的主体可以简化为 Pepperberg bought Alex in a Chicago pet store，该句为主谓宾结构，主语为 Pepperberg，谓语为 bought，宾语为 Alex，in a Chicago pet store 为地点状语。where 引导的定语从句修饰 pet store；because 引导原因状语从句，强调 Pepperberg 选择 Alex 的原因；that 引导宾语从句，在该原因状语从句中充当宾语。

参考翻译：佩珀伯格在芝加哥的一家宠物店买的亚历克斯，她让宠物店的助理挑的他，因为她不想让其他科学家事后说她为她的工作专门挑选了一只特别聪明的鸟。

D 段：Alex dominated his fellow parrots, acted huffy at times around Peeperberg, tolerated the other female humans, and fell to pieces over a male assistant who dropped by for a visit.

思路分析：这个句子为并列结构，主语为 Alex，谓语是由逗号和 and 连接的四个并列的动词，分别为 dominated, acted, tolerated 和 fell。who 引导定语从句，用来强调男性助理是来拜访的。

参考翻译：亚历克斯统领着他的鹦鹉同伴，有时在佩珀伯格身边表现得怒气冲冲，他可以容忍其他女性人类，但会因为一个来访的男性助理而崩溃。

参考译文

动物思维：鹦鹉亚历克斯

A 1977 年，刚从哈佛大学毕业的艾琳 · 佩珀伯格做了一件非常大胆的事。在那个动物还被认为是机器的年代，她开始通过与生物交谈来了解它的想法。她把一只一岁大的非洲灰鹦鹉带到她的实验室，给他取名为亚历克斯，教他模仿英语的发音。“我想，如果他学会了交流，我就可以问他如何看待世界的问题。”

B 亚历克斯于去年 9 月去世，享年 31 岁。当佩珀伯格开始与亚历克斯对话时，许多科学家认为动物没有任何思考的能力。它们只是机器，是按照程序对刺激做出反应的机器人，缺乏思考或感知的能力。任何养宠物的人都不会同意这种说法。我们从狗狗的眼睛里看到爱，当然也知道它们有思想和情感。但这种说法仍存在很大争议。直觉不是科学，把人类的思想和感情投射到另一种生物身上太容易了。那么，科学家如何证明动物具有思考的能力，或者说能够获得关于世界的信息并对此采取行动呢？佩珀伯格说：“这就是我要开始和亚历克斯一起研究的原因。”他们坐在佩珀伯格位于布兰迪斯大学的实验室里，这是一个没有窗户的房间，大约有一辆货车那么大。佩珀伯格坐在她的办公桌前，亚历克斯坐在他的笼子上。一排排的报纸铺在地板上，一筐筐亮晶晶的玩具堆在架子上。他们显然是一个团队，而且因为他们的工作，动物能思考的概念不再显得那么异想天开。

C 某些技能被认为是具有较高心智能力的关键标志，如良好的记忆力、对语法和符号的掌握、自我意识、理解他人动机、模仿他人以及富有创造力。在巧妙的实验中，研究人员一点一点地记录了其他物种的这些天赋，逐渐削弱了我们认为人类与众不同的认知，同时让我们得以一窥我们自己的能力从何而来。灌木丛松鸦知道其他松鸦都是小偷，藏起来的食物会变质；绵羊能识别人脸；黑猩猩会用各种工具探测白蚁丘，甚至会用武器猎杀小型哺乳动物；海豚可以模仿人类的姿势；射水鱼用突然的水波击晕昆虫，它们只需观察有经验的鱼执行这项任务，就能学会如何瞄准喷水。而鹦鹉亚历克斯后来被证明是一只出奇健谈的鹦鹉。

D 亚历克斯研究开始三十年后，佩珀伯格和一群不断更换的助手还在给他上英语课。人类和两只年轻的鹦鹉也成为了亚历克斯的同伴，提供了所有鹦鹉都需要的社会输入。像任何鹦鹉群一样，这个鹦鹉群尽管很小，但也有它的戏剧性。亚历克斯统领着他的鹦鹉同伴，有时在佩珀伯格身边表现得怒气冲冲，他可以容忍其他女性人类，但会因为一个来访的男性助理而崩溃。佩珀伯格在芝加哥的一家宠物店买的亚历克斯，她让宠物店的助理挑的他，因为她不想让其他科学家事后说她为她的工作专门挑选了一只特别聪明的鸟。考虑到亚历克斯的大脑只有剥了壳的胡桃那么大，大多数研究人员认为佩珀伯格的跨物种交流研究是徒劳的。

E 她说："实际上有的人因为这个尝试说我疯了。""科学家们认为黑猩猩是更好的实验对象，当然，黑猩猩不会说话。"黑猩猩、倭黑猩猩和大猩猩被教授使用手语和符号与我们交流，经常取得令人印象深刻的效果。例如，倭黑猩猩坎兹随身携带着他的符号交流板，这样他就可以和他的人类研究人员"交谈"了，他还发明了符号组合来表达他的思想。然而，这和让一只动物看着你开口说话是两码事。在佩珀伯格的耐心指导下，亚历克斯学会了如何用他的声道模仿近 100 个英语单词，包括各种食物的声音，尽管他把苹果说成"banerry"。佩珀伯格说："对他来说，苹果尝起来有点像香蕉，而且它们看起来有点像樱桃，所以亚历克斯创造了这个词。"

F 这听起来有点疯狂——让一只鸟去上课练习，而且还是心甘情愿地去。但在观察并听了亚历克斯的表现之后，你很难反驳佩珀伯格对他的行为的解释。她并没有因为重复性的工作而给他吃的，也没有拍打他的爪子让他发出这些声音。在为亚历克斯连续念了十几次"7"之后，佩珀伯格说："他必须一遍又一遍地听这些词，然后才能正确地模仿它们。"她补充说："我并不是想知道亚历克斯是否能学会一门人类语言。那从来都不是重点。我的计划一直是利用他的模仿能力，来更好地了解鸟类的认知。"

G 换句话说，由于亚历克斯能够发出一些与英语单词发音非常接近的声音，佩珀伯格就可以问他一些关于鸟类对世界的基本认识的问题。她不能问他在想什么，但她可以问他关于数字、形状和颜色的知识。为了演示，佩珀伯格把亚历克斯抱在胳膊上，走到房间中央的一个高高的栖木上。然后，她从架子上的篮子里取出一把绿色的钥匙和一个绿色的小杯子。她把那两件东西举到亚历克斯的眼前。"这二者有什么相同的地方吗？"她问。亚历克斯毫不犹豫地张开嘴说"颜色"。"有什么不同？"佩珀伯格问。"形状，"亚历克斯说。他的声音有一种卡通人物的数字化声音。由于鹦鹉没有嘴唇（这也是亚历克斯发不出一些音的另一个原因，如"ba"），这些单词似乎来自他周围的空气，就像一个口技表演者在说话。但这些话语，以及那些只能被称为思想的东西完全是来自于他自己的。

H 在接下来的 20 分钟里，亚历克斯完成了他的测试，区分了颜色、形状、大小和材料（羊毛、木材和金属）。它做了一些简单的算术，比如在一堆颜色混合的积木中数出黄色的玩具积木的数量。然后，亚历克斯似乎在奋力证明自己是有思想的，他开始大声说话。当佩珀伯格正在教授的另一只小鸟发音出错时，亚历克斯命令道："说话要清楚！"。"讲清楚点！""别自作聪明了，"佩珀伯格对他摇着头说。"他知道所有的事，而且他也会觉得无聊，所以他会打断别人，或者固执地给出错误的答案。在这个阶段，他就像一个青少年，喜怒无常，我永远不知道他会做什么。"

READING PASSAGE 2

Brunel: The Practical Prophet

文章结构

体裁	记叙文（人物传记）
题材	工业与建筑
主题	布鲁内尔：一名出色的工程师的生平
段落概括	A段：布鲁内尔作为一名工程师职业生涯的初始。 B段：布鲁内尔参与设计埃文峡谷上的吊桥。 C段：布鲁内尔参与修建大西部铁路。 D段：布鲁内尔修建大气铁路，但失败了。 E段：布鲁内尔建造“大西部号”船，获得巨大成功。 F段：布鲁内尔着手建造一艘更大的船“大不列颠号”。 G段：“大东方号”的挫折和新用途。

重点词汇

A段							
单词	音标	词性	释义	单词	音标	词性	释义
frontispiece	[ˈfrʌntɪspiːs]	*n.*	卷首插图，标题页	quote	[kwəʊt]	*v.*	引用，引述
requisite	[ˈrekwɪzɪt]	*adj.*	必需的，必备的	ingenious	[ɪnˈdʒiːniəs]	*adj.*	精巧的；新颖独特的
tunnel	[ˈtʌnl]	*n.*	地道，隧道	recuperate	[rɪˈkuːpəreɪt]	*v.*	康复，恢复
B段							
单词	音标	词性	释义	单词	音标	词性	释义
span	[spæn]	*n.*	跨度，范围	immense	[ɪˈmens]	*adj.*	极大的，巨大的
thoroughness	[ˈθʌrənis]	*n.*	彻底性	ingenuity	[ˌɪndʒəˈnjuːəti]	*n.*	独创力；聪明才智
technicality	[ˌteknɪˈkæləti]	*n.*	技术性细节				

C段							
单词	音标	词性	释义	单词	音标	词性	释义
civic	[ˈsɪvɪk]	*adj.*	公民的，市民的	controversial	[ˌkɒntrəˈvɜːʃl]	*adj.*	有争议的
gentry	[ˈdʒentri]	*n.*	绅士，贵族，上流社会人士	messy	[ˈmesi]	*adj.*	肮脏的；凌乱的
committee	[kəˈmɪti]	*n.*	委员会	install	[ɪnˈstɔːl]	*v.*	安装，设置

D段							
单词	音标	词性	释义	单词	音标	词性	释义
overpower	[ˌəʊvəˈpaʊə(r)]	*v.*	压制，压倒	advocate	[ˈædvəkeɪt]	*v.*	拥护，支持；提倡
locomotive	[ˌləʊkəˈməʊtɪv]	*n.*	火车头	gradient	[ˈgreɪdiənt]	*n.*	坡度，斜度，梯度
frustration	[frʌˈstreɪʃn]	*n.*	挫败；沮丧				

E段							
单词	音标	词性	释义	单词	音标	词性	释义
steam	[stiːm]	*n.*	蒸汽	appeal to		*phr.*	吸引
engage in		*phr.*	参加，从事于	transatlantic	[ˌtrænzətˈlæntɪk]	*adj.*	跨大西洋的
construction	[kənˈstrʌkʃn]	*n.*	建设，施工	launch	[lɔːntʃ]	*v.*	（船的）下水

F段							
单词	音标	词性	释义	单词	音标	词性	释义
initial	[ɪˈnɪʃl]	*adj.*	最初的，开始的	propeller	[prəˈpelə(r)]	*n.*	螺旋桨
paddle wheel		*phr.*	桨（叶）轮	propulsion	[prəˈpʌlʃn]	*n.*	推动力，推进
rescue	[ˈreskjuː]	*v.*	营救，援救	restoration	[ˌrestəˈreɪʃn]	*n.*	整修；恢复

G段							
单词	音标	词性	释义	单词	音标	词性	释义
conventional	[kənˈvenʃənl]	*adj.*	依照惯例的；遵循习俗的	voyage	[ˈvɔɪɪdʒ]	*n.*	航行；(尤指)航海
displacement	[dɪsˈpleɪsmənt]	*n.*	排水量	standstill	[ˈstændstɪl]	*n.*	停滞，停顿
delayed	[dɪˈleɪd]	*adj.*	延迟的，延误的	explosion	[ɪkˈspləʊʒn]	*n.*	爆炸，爆破
entrepreneur	[ˌɒntrəprəˈnɜː(r)]	*n.*	企业家，创业者	vessel	[ˈvesl]	*n.*	大船，轮船
financial	[faɪˈnænʃl]	*adj.*	财政的，金融的	fuel	[ˈfjuːəl]	*n.*	燃料

题目精解

Questions 14-19

题型：特殊词配对题

解析：这类题型有两个特点：一是乱序，二是考查细节，答案常在定位句前后一两句话中。因此，考生要先通过特殊词定位到原文，再对比答案句与题干，选择表述一致的句子即可。

Question 14

题干定位词 / 关键词	I.K Brunel; not responsible for
原文定位	A 段倒数第二句和尾句 Sir Marc was then building his famous tunnel under the River Thames. Isambard was recuperating near Bristol from injuries received in a tunnel cave-in when he became involved with his own first major project.
题目解析	题干：布鲁内尔并不负责的一个建设项目。 A 段倒数第二句和尾句提到马克爵士正在泰晤士河下建造他那著名的隧道，伊桑巴德在布里斯托尔附近养伤，因为他在一次隧道塌方中受伤，当时他参与了自己的第一个重大项目。根据句意可知，泰晤士河隧道是布鲁内尔参与的第一个大项目，但并非是他负责的项目，因此正确答案为 A：泰晤士河隧道。
答案	A

Question 15

题干定位词 / 关键词	stopped; inconvenience; high maintaining cost
原文定位	D 段第四、五句 Materials were not up to it, and this arrangement was troublesome and expensive to keep in repair. After a year of frustration, the system was abandoned.
题目解析	题干：由于不方便和维护费用过高，该项目已停止。 通过关键词可定位到 D 段第四、五句，原文在描述大气铁路时提到材料不符合要求，而且这种安排很麻烦，维修起来也很昂贵，经过一年的挫折后，该系统被放弃了。因此，正确答案为 C：大气铁路。
答案	C

Question 16

题干定位词 / 关键词	honored; not completed by Brunel
原文定位	B 段倒数第二句和尾句 Unfortunately, he only got so far as to put up the end piers in his lifetime. The Clifton Suspension Bridge was completed in his honor by his engineering friends in 1864, and is still in use.
题目解析	题干：这个项目是为了纪念布鲁内尔的，但却不是布鲁内尔自己完成的。通过关键词定位到 B 段倒数两句，原文在描述埃文峡谷上的吊桥时，最后两句提到布鲁内尔在有生之年只竖起了桥墩，克里夫顿吊桥于 1864 年由他的工程界朋友为纪念他而建成，且至今仍在使用。由此可知，正确答案为 B：克里夫顿吊桥。
答案	B

Question 17

题干定位词 / 关键词	budget problem; a famous engineer
原文定位	G 段第一小段倒数第二句和尾句 He was a well-established engineer and naval architect, but the contract did not go well. Among other things, Scott Russell was very low in his estimates and money was soon a problem.
题目解析	题干：该工程虽然是由一位著名的工程师建造的，但还是存在预算问题。通过关键词定位到 G 段第一小段倒数两句，原文在描述大东方号时提到，建设者是一位知名的工程师和海军建筑师，但合同进行得并不顺利，因为斯科特·拉塞尔预估不足，资金很快就成了问题。因此，正确答案为 G：大东方号。
答案	G

Question 18

题干定位词 / 关键词	serious problem; delayed repeatedly
原文定位	G 段第二小段第一、二句 Construction came to a standstill in 1856 and Brunel himself had to take over the work. But Brunel was nothing if not determined, and by September, 1859, after a delayed and problem ridden launch, the Great Eastern was ready for the maiden voyage.
题目解析	题干：某工程发生了严重的问题，一再拖延。 通过关键词定位到 G 段第二小段的第一、二句，原文在描述大东方号时提到，该工程于 1856 年陷入停滞，布鲁内尔不得不亲自接手。此后，在 1859 年 9 月，在经历了推迟和问题重重的下水之后，大东方号准备好进行首航。因此，正确答案为 G：大东方号。
答案	G

Question 19

题干定位词 / 关键词	the first one; Atlantic
原文定位	E 段第三句 The Great Western was the first steamship to engage in transatlantic service.
题目解析	题干：该项目是人类历史上第一个跨越大西洋的项目。 通过关键词定位到 E 段第三句，原文提到大西部号是第一艘从事跨大西洋服务的蒸汽船。因此，答案是 E：大西部号。
答案	E

Questions 20-22

题型：段落信息配对题

Question 20

题干定位词 / 关键词	a great ship; setting the criteria
原文定位	F 段倒数第二句 The Great Britain ran aground early in its career, but was repaired, sold, and sailed for years to Australia, and other parts of the world, setting the standard for ocean travel.
题目解析	题干：有一艘大船为远洋航行设定了标准。 根据 setting the criteria 定位到 F 段倒数第二句（与原文 setting the standard 对应）：大不列颠号在其职业生涯的早期四处航行，但经过修理、出售，以及多年来航行到澳大利亚和世界其他地区的经历，为远洋旅行制定了标准。这完全符合题干的意思，因此正确答案为 F。
答案	F

Question 21

题干定位词 / 关键词	an ambitious project; unplanned service later
原文定位	G 段第二小段倒数第三句和尾句 Although Brunel did not have it in mind, the Great Eastern was an excellent vessel for this work. The ship continued this career for several years, used for laying cables in many parts of the world.
题目解析	题干：这是一个雄心勃勃的项目，似乎后来被应用在一个计划外的服务中。 通过 G 段第二小段倒数第三句和尾句可知，布鲁内尔没有想到大东方号是一艘非常适合运输电缆的船，这艘船的职业生涯持续了几年，用于在世界许多地方铺设电缆。因此，正确答案为 G。
答案	G

Question 22

题干定位词 / 关键词	inter-personal skills; landlords; gone through
原文定位	C 段第五、六句 Again Brunel showed great skill in presenting his arguments to the various committees and individuals. Brunel built his railway with a broad gauge (7ft) instead of the standard 4ft $8\frac{1}{2}$ in, which had been used for lines already installed.
题目解析	题干：布鲁内尔展示了他与地主沟通的交往能力，最终使项目得以通过。C 段前半部分提到地主阶级和公爵都不同意修建铁路，但第五、六句表明布鲁内尔陈述他的论点时表现出高超的技巧，并且成功修建了新标准的铁路。因此，C 为正确答案。
答案	C

Questions 23-26

题型：摘要填空题

Question 23

题干定位词 / 关键词	the Great Eastern, designed
原文定位	G 段第一小段第三句 He set out to design the biggest ship ever, five times larger than any ship built up to that time.
题目解析	题干：大东方号被特别设计为 _____，以携带更多的燃料。 根据关键词定位到 G 段第一小段第三句，该句提到布鲁内尔开始设计有史以来最大的船（大东方号），比当时建造的任何船都要大五倍。此外，第四句提到这艘船可以携带能够到达澳大利亚的燃料。designed as 对应原文中的 design，正确答案为 biggest ship。
答案	biggest ship

Question 24

题干定位词 / 关键词	the Great Eastern; fuels; long voyage to
原文定位	G 段第一小段第四句 Big enough to carry fuel to get to Australia without refueling, in addition it would carry 4,000 passengers.
题目解析	题干：大东方号将长途航行到 _____。 根据题干可知，该空格处需填写地名。根据关键词定位到 G 段第一小段第四句，该句提到大东方号足够大，可以在不加油的情况下携带燃料到达澳大利亚，此外还可以搭载 4000 名乘客。take long voyage to 对应原文中的 get to，因此 Australia 为正确答案。
答案	Australia

Question 25

题干定位词 / 关键词	physical condition; Brunel, the Great Eastern; unprofitable
原文定位	G 段第二小段第四、五句 Brunel died within a week or so of the accident. The great ship never carried 4,000 passengers (among other things, the Suez Canal came along) and although it made several transatlantic crossings, it was not a financial success.
题目解析	题干：但由于身体原因，布鲁内尔未能完成首航。事实上，大东方号是无利可图的，因为建造了 ____。 根据关键词定位到 G 段第二小段第四、五句，原文提到布鲁内尔在事故发生后一周左右就去世了。这艘巨轮从来没有搭载过 4000 名乘客（除此之外，苏伊士运河的开通也对其造成了影响），尽管它多次横渡大西洋，但在经济上并不成功。这里提到它的不成功（没搭载过那么多乘客，也没有盈利），还提到苏伊士运河的出现对它造成了影响，所以 Suez Canal 为正确答案。
答案	Suez Canal

Question 26

题干定位词 / 关键词	soon after; the Great Eastern; to carry and to lay; Atlantic Ocean floor
原文定位	G 段第二小段第六句 Shortly after the Great Eastern began working life, the American entrepreneur Cyrus Field and his backers were looking for a ship big enough to carry 5,000 tons of telegraphic cables, which was to be laid on the ocean floor from Ireland to Newfoundland.
题目解析	题干：但不久之后，一个具有讽刺意味的机会出现了，大东方号被用来装载和铺设巨大的 ____ 在大西洋海底。 根据关键词定位到 G 段第二小段第六句，原文提到在大东方号开始投入使用后不久，美国企业家赛勒斯 · 菲尔德和他的支持者们正在寻找一艘大到足以装载 5000 吨通信电缆的船，这些电缆将被铺设在从爱尔兰到纽芬兰的海底。lay 对应原文中的 was to be laid，原文被动语态的主语是 which，而 which 指代 telegraphic cables，Atlantic Ocean floor 对应 floor from Ireland to Newfoundland，因此正确答案是 telegraphic cables。
答案	telegraphic cables

长难句分析

G 段：The great ship never carried 4,000 passengers (among other things, the Suez Canal came along) and although it made several transatlantic crossings, it was not a financial success.

思路分析：括号里的内容往往是补充说明，容易被考生忽略，但在这篇文章中，恰恰在这里出了题目，需要引起考生的重视，并正确理解句意。and 连接前后两个并列的句子，although 引导让步状语从句，强调这艘船在经济上并不成功。

参考翻译：这艘巨轮从来没有搭载过 4000 名乘客（除此之外，苏伊士运河也出现了），虽然它曾多次横渡大西洋，但在经济上并不成功。

G 段：Shortly after the Great Eastern began working life, the American entrepreneur Cyrus Field and his backers were looking for a ship big enough to carry 5,000 tons of telegraphic cables, which was to be laid on the ocean floor from Ireland to Newfoundland.

思路分析：这个句子可以简化为 The American entrepreneur Cyrus Field and his backers were looking for a ship，after 引导时间状语从句，该从句为主谓宾结构，the Great Eastern 为主语，began 为谓语，working life 为宾语；big enough to carry 5,000 tons of telegraphic cables 为形容词作后置定语，用来修饰船；which 引导非限定性定语从句，用来解释说明 telegraphic cables 的用途。

参考翻译：在大东方号开始投入使用后不久，美国企业家赛勒斯·菲尔德和他的支持者们正在寻找一艘大到足以装载 5000 吨通信电缆的船，这些电缆将被铺设在从爱尔兰到纽芬兰的海底。

参考译文

布鲁内尔——实用的先知

A 在他关于布鲁内尔的书的卷首插图中，彼得·海引用了尼克尔森 1909 年的《英国百科全书》的内容："工程师出于这些原因是极其必要的；除有独创性之外，他们还必须有相应的胆识"。他的父亲，马克·伊桑巴德·布鲁内尔爵士（1769—1849），是一位著名的工程师，父母都是法国人。他 14 岁时被送到法国学习数学和科学，16 岁时回到英国跟随父亲工作。当时马克爵士正在泰晤士河下建造他那著名的隧道。伊桑巴德在布里斯托尔附近养伤，因为他在一次隧道塌方中受伤，当时他参与了自己的第一个重大项目。

埃文峡谷上的吊桥

B 布鲁内尔的桥跨度超过 700 英尺，设计时比任何当时存在的桥都长，离水面的高度约为 245 英尺。这个工程项目的技术挑战是巨大的，而布鲁内尔以其一贯的彻底性和独创性解决了这些问题。当时举行了两场设计竞赛，伟大的桥梁设计师托马斯·特尔福德是委员会的专家。布鲁内尔提出了四项设计，远不限于技术问题，还讨论了塔楼设计的优雅性等方面。不幸的是，他在有生之年只竖起了桥墩。克里夫顿吊桥于 1864 年由他的工程界朋友为纪念他而建成，至今仍在使用。

大西部铁路

C 当布鲁内尔还在布里斯托尔的时候，随着埃文桥项目的停止或进展缓慢，他意识到市政当局认为有必要修建一条连接伦敦的铁路。铁路的选址是有争议的，因为必须与私人土地所有者和城镇打交道。主要是，地主阶级不希望在他们附近有一条混乱、嘈杂的铁路。威灵顿公爵（因滑铁卢而闻名）当然也反对。布鲁内尔在向各委员会和个人陈述他的论点时再次表现出高超的技巧。布鲁内尔用宽轨（7 英尺）建造了他的铁路，而不是已安装的线路所采用的标准的 4 英尺 8.5 英寸。毫无疑问，宽轨距提供了优越的行驶和稳定性，但它挑战了标准。

大气铁路

D 当布鲁内尔主张在南德文郡安装一条“大气铁路”时，他对新想法的包容战胜了良好的工程判断力（至少在事后看来是这样的）。取消火车头，应对更陡峭的坡度，这是非常有吸引力的。由于这个连接臂必须沿着狭缝运行，当火车前进时，它必须通过一个挡板打开，但在通过后则是密闭的。当时的材料不符合要求，而且这种安排很麻烦，维修起来也很昂贵。经过一年的挫折，这个系统被放弃了。布鲁内尔承认了他的失败并承担了责任。他也没有为自己的工作收取任何费用，树立了一个良好的职业榜样。

布鲁内尔的船舶

E 利用蒸汽驱动船只横跨海洋的想法吸引了布鲁内尔。当大西部铁路线公司的董事们抱怨他们的铁路太长（只有大约 100 英里）时，伊桑巴德开玩笑地建议说，他们甚至可以把它修得更长。为什么不一路直通纽约，并把这条路称为“大西部路”呢？“大西部号”是第一艘从事跨大西洋服务的蒸汽船。布鲁内尔成立了大西部轮船公司，并于 1836 年在布里斯托尔开始建造大西部号。该船只由木材制成，长 236 英尺，于 1837 年下水，由风帆和桨轮驱动。首航前往纽约只用了 15 天，返回时用了 14 天。这是一个巨大的成功，风帆驱动的单程旅行需要超过一个月的时间。大西部号是第一艘从事跨大西洋服务的蒸汽船，共航行 74 次横渡到纽约。

F 由于大西部号的出色表现，布鲁内尔立即开始着手建造一艘更大的船。大不列颠号是铁制的，也是在布里斯托尔建造的，全长 322 英尺。最初的设计是用桨轮驱动船舶，但布鲁内尔看到了第一批抵达英国的其中一只螺旋桨驱动的船舶，于是他放弃了桨轮驱动的计划。大不列颠号于 1843 年下水，是第一艘横跨大西洋的螺旋桨驱动的铁船。大不列颠号在其职业生涯的早期搁浅了，但经过修理、出售，以及多年来航行到澳大利亚和世界其他地区的经历，为远洋旅行制定了标准。20 世纪 70 年代初，这艘老船被从福克兰群岛救起，现在正在布里斯托尔进行修复。

G 在布鲁内尔的时代，传统的观点是蒸汽船不能携带足够量的煤炭进行远洋航行。但他正确地认识到，设计船舶时尺寸很重要。他开始设计有史以来最大的船，比当时建造的任何船都要大五倍。它大到足以携带能够到达澳大利亚的燃料而不需要中途补给，而且它还将搭载 4000 名乘客。大东方号长 692 英尺，排水量约为 32,000 吨。1854 年开始在泰晤士河畔的米尔沃尔建造。布鲁内尔选择了约翰 · 斯科特 · 拉塞尔来建造这艘船。他是一位知名的工程师和海军建筑师，但合同进行得并不顺利。在其他方面，斯科特 · 拉塞尔预估不足，资金很快就成了问题。

1856 年，工程停滞不前，布鲁内尔不得不自己接手这项工作。但是，布鲁内尔是一个非常有决断力的人。到了 1859 年 9 月，在经历了拖延和问题重重的下水之后，大东方号已经准备好进行首航。当时布鲁内尔病重不能去，但幸好如此，因为就在首航几个小时前，引擎室发生了爆炸，这足以摧毁一艘小船。布鲁内尔在事故发生后一周左右就去世了。这艘巨轮从来没有搭载过 4000 名乘客（除此之外，苏伊士运河的开通也对其造成了影响），虽然它曾多次横渡大西洋，但在经济上并不成功。在大东方号开始投入使用后不久，美国企业家赛勒斯 · 菲尔德和他的支持者们正在寻找一艘大到足以装载 5000 吨通信电缆的船，这些电缆将被铺设在从爱尔兰到纽芬兰的海底。虽然布鲁内尔没有考虑到这一点，但大东方号确实是适合这项工作的优秀船只。1866 年 7 月 27 日，它成功完成了连接，百年的跨大西洋电缆通信从此开始。这艘船的职业生涯持续了几年，用于在世界许多地方铺设电缆。

READING PASSAGE 3

Memory Decoding

文章结构

体裁	说明文
题材	常识与科普
主题	对人类记忆力的研究
段落概括	A 段：记忆测试的流程和一些结论。 B 段：通过核磁共振研究参赛者与对照组大脑的使用情况。 C 段：记忆比赛者使用视觉图像和空间导航来记忆数字，以库克为例展开介绍。 D 段：库克是如何把视觉图像和空间导航结合来记忆的。 E 段：位置记忆法的历史起源。 F 段：舍利什维斯基的惊人记忆力与通感。 G 段：埃里克森相信天生的超强记忆力根本不存在，通过大量的练习任何人都可以做到。

重点词汇

A 段							
单词	音标	词性	释义	单词	音标	词性	释义
contestant	[kənˈtestənt]	*n.*	比赛者，竞争者	shuffle	[ˈʃʌfl]	*v.*	洗牌
extraordinary	[ɪkˈstrɔːdnri]	*adj.*	异乎寻常的，非凡的	retention	[rɪˈtenʃn]	*n.*	记忆力
benchmark	[ˈbentʃmɑːk]	*n.*	基准	encode	[ɪnˈkəʊd]	*v.*	编码
B 段							
单词	音标	词性	释义	单词	音标	词性	释义
monograph	[ˈmɒnəgrɑːf]	*n.*	专著，专题文章	neuroscientist	[ˈnjʊroʊˌsaɪəntɪst]	*n.*	神经系统科学家
control subject		*phr.*	对照目标	sequence	[ˈsiːkwəns]	*n.*	序列，顺序
immense	[ɪˈmens]	*adj.*	极大的，巨大的	spatial navigation		*phr.*	空间导航

C 段							
单词	音标	词性	释义	单词	音标	词性	释义
odd	[ɒd]	*adj.*	古怪的，奇怪的	visual	[ˈvɪʒuəl]	*adj.*	视力的，视觉的
deck	[dek]	*n.*	一副牌	spade	[speɪd]	*n.*	黑桃
reveal	[rɪˈviːl]	*v.*	揭示，显示				
D 段							
单词	音标	词性	释义	单词	音标	词性	释义
survive	[səˈvaɪv]	*v.*	幸存，生存	activation	[ˌæktɪˈveɪʃən]	*n.*	开启，激活
whack	[wæk]	*v.*	猛打，重击	wardrobe	[ˈwɔːdrəʊb]	*n.*	衣柜，衣橱
triplet	[ˈtrɪplət]	*n.*	三个一组	downhill	[ˌdaʊnˈhɪl]	*adj.*	下坡的，容易的
E 段							
单词	音标	词性	释义	单词	音标	词性	释义
resonant	[ˈrezənənt]	*adj.*	引起联想的，产生共鸣的	originate	[əˈrɪdʒɪneɪt]	*v.*	起源，发源
collapse	[kəˈlæps]	*n.*	倒塌	reconstruct	[ˌriːkənˈstrʌkt]	*v.*	重建；重现
ancestor	[ˈænsestə(r)]	*n.*	祖先，祖宗	treatise	[ˈtriːtɪs]	*n.*	论文，专著
staple	[ˈsteɪpl]	*n.*	主要部分	rhetoric	[ˈretərɪk]	*n.*	修辞
F 段							
单词	音标	词性	释义	单词	音标	词性	释义
decade	[ˈdekeɪd]	*n.*	十年	syllable	[ˈsɪləbl]	*n.*	音节
distinct	[dɪˈstɪŋkt]	*adj.*	明显的，确切的	synesthesia	[ˌsinəsˈθiːʒiə]	*n.*	联觉，通感
rare	[reə(r)]	*adj.*	稀少的，罕见的	intertwined	[ˌɪntəˈtwaɪnd]	*adj.*	相互缠绕的
evoke	[ɪˈvəʊk]	*v.*	唤起，引起				
G 段							
单词	音标	词性	释义	单词	音标	词性	释义
stretch	[stretʃ]	*v.*	拉长	digit span		*phr.*	数字广度
innately	[ɪˈneitli]	*adv.*	天赋地	superior	[suːˈpɪəriə(r)]	*adj.*	更好的，优越的
compelling	[kəmˈpelɪŋ]	*adj.*	令人信服的	evidence	[ˈevɪdəns]	*n.*	证据

题目精解

Questions 27-31

题型：段落信息配对题

Question 27

题干定位词 / 关键词	reason; super memory; significant; academic
原文定位	E 段倒数三句 After Simonides' discovery, the loci method became popular across ancient Greece as a trick for memorizing speeches and texts. Aristotle wrote about it, and later a number of treatises on the art of memory were published in Rome. Before printed books, the art of memory was considered a staple of classical education, on a par with grammar, logic, and rhetoric.
题目解析	题干：为什么超级记忆能力在学术环境中是重要的。 E 段倒数三句提到"位置记忆法"作为一种记忆演讲稿和文本的技巧在古希腊流行起来。亚里士多德对此撰写过文章，后来在罗马出版了一些关于记忆的艺术的论文。在有纸质书籍之前，记忆的艺术被认为是古典教育的主要内容，与语法、逻辑和修辞同等重要。原文体现了记忆能力在学术环境中是很重要的能力，其原因是记忆的艺术当时正流行，受到了很多学者的重视，因此 E 为正确答案。
答案	E

Question 28

题干定位词 / 关键词	contest; extraordinary memory; consecutive years
原文定位	A 段第三句 In the 14 years since the World Memory Championships was founded, no one has memorized the order of a shuffled deck of playing cards in less than 30 seconds.
题目解析	题干：提及连续几年举办的非凡记忆力比赛。 A 段整体都在描述记忆力比赛的一些项目和参赛成绩。其中第三句最为明显地提到世界记忆锦标赛成立 14 年来，还没有人能在 30 秒内记住一副洗好的扑克牌的顺序。这里体现了记忆力比赛是连续举办的，因此正确答案为 A。
答案	A

Question 29

题干定位词 / 关键词	example; extraordinary person; unusual recalling game
原文定位	C 段
题目解析	题干：一个非凡人物完成了一个非凡的记忆游戏的例子。 C 段的大部分内容都在讲库克是一名记忆大师，他做了哪些事情。C 段后半部分具体提到在一个名叫“羔羊与旗帜”的酒吧，库克手里拿着三张牌——黑桃 7、梅花 Q 和黑桃 10，他指着壁炉说：“真命天女正在用手提包捶打弗朗茨·舒伯特。”接下来的三张牌是红桃 K、黑桃 K 和梅花 J。因此，正确答案为 C。
答案	C

Question 30

题干定位词 / 关键词	extraordinary memory, enough practice
原文定位	G 段第七、九句 When he reviewed original case studies of naturals, he found that exceptionally memorizers were using techniques—sometimes without realizing it—and lots of practice. “If we look at some of these memory tasks, they’re the kind of thing most people don’t even waste one hour practicing, but if they wasted 50 hours, they’d be exceptional at it,” Ericsson say.
题目解析	题干：一种信念，认为通过足够的练习可以获得非凡的记忆力。 G 段第七句提到安德斯 · 埃里克森发现那些特别擅长记忆的人都在使用技巧并进行大量的练习，第九句提到如果花费 50 个小时来练习，大多数人也可以在这方面出类拔萃。由此可知，正确答案为 G。
答案	G

Question 31

题干定位词 / 关键词	rare ability; assist; extraordinary memory reactions
原文定位	F 段第三、四句 Shereshevski also had synesthesia, a rare condition in which the senses become intertwined. For example, every number may be associated with a color or every word with a taste.
题目解析	题干：描述了一种罕见的能力，这种能力能帮助非凡的记忆反应。 F 段第三、四句提到舍利什维斯基也有“通感”，这是一种感官交织在一起的罕见情况。例如，每个数字都可能与一种颜色有关，每个单词都可能与一种味道有关。由此可知，“通感”作为一种罕见的能力能帮助记忆，因此正确答案为 F。
答案	F

Questions 32-36

题型：摘要填空题

Question 32

题干定位词 / 关键词	Ed Cooke; 7 of the spades; encoded
原文定位	D 段第二、三句 Cooke has already memorized a specific person, verb, and object that he associates with each card in the deck. For example, for the 7 of spades, the person (or, in this case, persons) is always the singing group Destiny's Child, the action is surviving a storm, and the image is dinghy.
题目解析	题干：一个叫 Ed Cooke 的人在酒吧里，当他拿着黑桃 7（任意牌组中记忆的第一张，因为他把它编码为 ____）时，说了一串奇怪的词。 根据关键词定位到 D 段第二、三句，这里提到库克已经记住了一个具体的人名、动作和动作的对象，并将其与牌组中的每张牌联系起来。例如，对于黑桃 7，人名是歌唱组合"真命天女"，动作是在风暴中生存，图像是小艇。由此可见，specific person 为正确答案。
答案	specific person

Question 33

题干定位词 / 关键词	card deck; memory; order
原文定位	D 段第五句 When Cooke commits a deck to memory, he does three cards at a time.
题目解析	题干：一个叫 Ed Cooke 的人在酒吧里，当他拿着黑桃 7（任意牌组中记忆的第一张，因为他把它编码为一个具体的人）时，说了一串奇怪的词，并且当记忆牌组时，设置为一次记 ____ 的顺序。 通过关键词定位到 D 段第五句，该句提到当库克记忆一副牌时，他一次记三张牌。
答案	three cards/3 cards

Question 34

题干定位词 / 关键词	recall, Cooke, imaginary scene, cards
原文定位	D 段倒数第二句 When it comes time to recall, Cooke takes a mental walk along his route and translates the images into cards.
题目解析	题干：当需要回忆时，库克一路使用了 _____，并把想象中的场景解释成卡片。 通过关键词定位到 D 段倒数第二句，该句提到当需要回忆时，库克会在头脑中沿着他的路线走一遍，并将图像转译为卡片。along his way 对应原文中的 along his route，所以 mental walk 为正确答案。
答案	mental walk

Question 35

题干定位词 / 关键词	Ancient Greece; strategy; called
原文定位	E 段第四句 That technique, known as the loci method, reportedly originated in 477 B.C. with the Greek poet Simonides of Ceos.
题目解析	题干：这种高超的记忆技巧可以追溯到古希腊，当时的策略被称为 _____。 E 段第四句指出，这种被称为“位置记忆法”的技术据报道起源于公元前 477 年，由希腊诗人西蒙尼德斯发明。strategy 对应 technique，was called 对应 known as，因此 loci method 为正确答案。
答案	loci method

Question 36

题干定位词 / 关键词	major subject; ancient
原文定位	E 段最后一句 Before printed books, the art of memory was considered a staple of classical education, on a par with grammar, logic, and rhetoric.
题目解析	题干：这种高超的记忆技巧在古代 ____ 中曾经是一项主要内容。 E 段最后一句指出，在有纸质书籍之前，记忆的艺术被认为是古典教育的主要内容，与语法、逻辑和修辞同等重要。the art of memory 对应第 35 题填入的 loci method，staple 对应 major，classical 对应 ancient，因此，education 为正确答案。
答案	education

Questions 37-40

题型：多选题

Questions 37-38

题干定位词 / 关键词	World Memory Championships; good memory
原文定位	A 段首句 In timed trials, contestants were challenged to look at and then recite a two-page poem, memorize rows of 40 digit numbers, recall the names of 110 people after looking at their photographs, and perform seven other feats of extraordinary retention.

TEST 5 解析

题目解析	题干：根据世界记忆锦标赛，哪些活动需要良好的记忆力？ A：一组数字中每个数字的顺序 B：忆起人脸 C：背诵一首古希腊长诗 D：将人名与图片和特征对应 E：忆起昨天人们吃了什么和做了什么 根据关键词定位到 A 段，第一句就描述了世界记忆锦标赛的一些项目，包括记住几排 40 位的数字、在看完 110 个人的照片后回忆他们的名字，这些正好对应选项 A 和选项 D。 选项 C、选项 E 均未提及。选项 B 与原文不符，比赛要求记住名字，而不是人脸。
答案	A D

Questions 39-40

题干定位词 / 关键词	Psychologists Elizabeth Valentine; John Wilding, MRI Scan
原文定位	B 段第四句和最后两句 When it came to memorizing sequences of three-digit numbers, the difference between the memory contestants and the control subjects was, as expected, immense. When the researchers analyzed the brain scans, they found that the memory champions were activating some brain regions that were different from those the control subjects were using. These regions, which included the right posterior hippocampus, are known to be involved in visual memory and spatial navigation.
题目解析	题干：心理学家伊丽莎白 · 瓦伦丁和约翰 · 威尔丁的核磁共振扫描实验的结果是什么？ A：冠军的大脑在某些方面与常人不同 B：当记忆三位数序列时，冠军的大脑扫描图片与对照组不同 C：被要求记忆图片时，冠军们表现更差 D：记忆冠军比对照组激活了更多的大脑区域 E：记忆冠军大脑中一些处理视觉和空间记忆的部分被激活了 根据关键词定位到 B 段。B 段第四句指出，当涉及记忆三位数序列时，记忆比赛的参赛者和对照对象之间的差异是巨大的。因此，选项 B 为正确答案。 B 段最后两句指出，当研究人员分析大脑扫描结果时，他们发现记忆冠军激活了一些与对照对象不同的大脑区域。这些区域包括右后海马体，被认为是参与视觉记忆和空间导航的大脑区域。由此可见，E 为正确答案。 选项 A 在原文中未提及。 选项 C 为概念混淆，原文说的是当看到放大的雪花照片时，冠军们的表现并不比对照组好，不比对照组好不代表比他们差。 选项 D 也不对，原文只说激活的区域不同，并没有说激活了更多的大脑区域。
答案	B E

长难句分析

B 段：When the researchers analyzed the brain scans, they found that the memory champions were activating some brain regions that were different from those the control subjects were using.

思路分析：这个句子的主体可以简化为 They found that the memory champions were activating some brain regions，该句子为主谓宾结构，其中主语为 they，谓语为 found，宾语为 that 引导的从句；后面的 that 引导定语从句，用来修饰宾语从句中的 some brain regions；句子开头的 when 引导时间状语从句，强调当研究人员分析大脑扫描结果时怎么样。

参考翻译：当研究人员分析大脑扫描结果时，他们发现记忆冠军激活了一些与对照对象不同的大脑区域。

G 段：When he reviewed original case studies of naturals, he found that exceptionally memorizers were using techniques—sometimes without realizing it—and lots of practice.

思路分析：这个句子的主体可以简化为 He found that exceptionally memorizers were using techniques and lots of practice，该句子为主谓宾结构，主语为 he，谓语为 found, 宾语为 that 引导的从句；破折号中间的内容 sometimes without realizing it 为插入语，用来补充说明；句子开头的 when 引导时间状语从句，强调当他重新审视那些研究天赋型选手的原始案例时怎么样。

参考翻译：当他重新审视那些研究天赋型选手的原始案例时，他发现卓越的记忆者都在使用技巧（有时是在不知不觉中）并进行了大量的练习。

A 段：In timed trials, contestants were challenged to look at and then recite a two-page poem, memorize rows of 40 digit numbers, recall the names of 110 people after looking at their photographs, and perform seven other feats of extraordinary retention.

思路分析：这个句子的主体可以简化为 In timed trials, contestants were challenged to...，五个并列的动词 look at, recite, memorize, recall 和 perform 为主语 contestants 的补足语，表示参赛者被要求做的事情。

参考翻译：在计时比赛中，参赛者被要求阅读然后背诵一首两页的诗，记住几排 40 位的数字，在看完 110 个人的照片后回忆他们的名字，并进行其他 7 项非凡的记忆力表演。

参考译文

记忆解码

试试这个记忆测试：研究每一张脸，为这个人的名字和姓氏构造一个生动的形象。例如，罗斯 · 利奥，可以是一朵玫瑰花蕾和一只狮子。牛津大学的考试学院是一座朴素的建筑，有镶着橡木板的房间、大型哥特式窗户和隐约可见的知名公爵和伯爵的画像。它是几代牛津大学学生在期末考试时测试记忆力的地方，也是去年 8 月世界记忆锦标赛上 34 名选手以一种完全不同的方式接受考试的地方。

A 在计时比赛中，参赛者被要求阅读然后背诵一首两页的诗，记住几排 40 位的数字，在看完 110 个人的照片后回忆他们的名字，并进行其他 7 项非凡的记忆力表演。有些测试只花了几分钟，有些则持续了几个小时。在世界记忆锦标赛成立以来的 14 年里，没有人能在 30 秒内记住一副洗好的扑克牌的顺序。这个漂亮的整数已经成为竞争性记忆比赛的里程碑，这是世界上最优秀的“脑力运动员”（他们中的一些人喜欢这样称呼）正在接近的基准。大多数参赛者声称自己的记忆力一般，科学测试也证实了他们并不是在谦虚。他们的壮举是建立在利用人脑编译信息的技巧之上的。任何人都可以学会这些。

B 心理学家伊丽莎白 · 瓦伦丁和约翰 · 威尔丁，专著《论超常记忆》的作者，最近与伦敦大学学院的神经科学家埃莉诺 · 马奎尔合作，研究包括卡斯滕在内的八个人，他们在世界记忆锦标赛中获得了接近最高的成绩。他们想知道这些参赛者的大脑是否在某些方面有所不同。研究人员将参赛者和一组对照对象放入一台核磁共振仪，要求他们进行几种不同的记忆测试，同时扫描他们的大脑。当涉及记忆三位数序列时，正如预期的那样，记忆比赛的参赛者和对照对象之间的差异是巨大的。然而，当他们看到放大的雪花照片时（参赛者之前从未尝试记忆过的图像），冠军们的表现并不比对照组好。当研究人员分析大脑扫描结果时，他们发现记忆冠军激活了一些与对照对象不同的大脑区域。这些区域包括右后海马体，被认为是参与视觉记忆和空间导航的大脑区域。

C 记忆比赛者会利用视觉图像和空间导航来记忆数字，这似乎很奇怪，但当他们的技术被揭示时，这种利用就有意义了。库克，一个 23 岁的认知科学研究生，留着一头齐肩的卷发，是一个大脑记忆的高手。他可以在不到一个小时内记住 10 副扑克牌的顺序，或者在不到一分钟内记住一副扑克牌的顺序。他正在向 30 秒内记住一副牌靠近。在一个名叫“羔羊与旗帜”的酒吧，库克拿出一副扑克牌并洗了起来。他举起三张牌——黑桃 7、梅花 Q 和黑桃 10。他指着一个壁炉说：“真命天女（R&B 组合）正在用手提包捶打弗朗茨·舒伯特（奥地利作曲家）。”接下来的三张牌是红桃 K、黑桃 K 和梅花 J。

D 他是如何做到的？库克已经记住了一个具体的人名、动作和动作的对象，他将它们与牌组中的每张牌联系起来。例如，对于黑桃 7，人名（或者，在这种情况下，多个人名）就是歌唱组合“真命天女”，动作是在风暴中生存，图像是小艇。梅花 Q 的人名就是他的朋友汉丽埃塔，动作是用手提包捶打，图像是装满名牌衣服的衣柜。当库克记忆一副牌时，他一次记忆三张牌。每组的三张牌构成了某个人对某个物体做某事的单一图像。三张牌中的第一张是人，第二张是动作，第三张是动作的对象。然后，他将这些图像沿着特定的熟悉路线放置，如他在羔羊与旗帜使用的路线。在比赛中，他使用一条自己构想的路线，这条路线被设计得尽可能平滑和容易。当需要回忆的时候，库克会在头脑中沿着他的路线走一遍，并将图像转译为卡片。这就是记忆比赛者们的核磁共振成像显示与视觉图像和空间导航有关的大脑区域被激活的原因。

E 图像越有共鸣，就越难忘记。但是，即使是有意义的信息，当它的数量很多时，也很难记住。这就是有竞争力的记忆者会将他们的图像放在一条自己构想的路线上的原因。据报道，这种被称为“位置记忆法”的技术起源于公元前 477 年的希腊诗人西蒙尼德斯。西蒙尼德斯是一次屋顶坍塌事故中唯一的幸存者，这次坍塌使参加皇家宴会的其他客人全部丧生。尸体被砸得面目全非，但西蒙尼德斯能够闭上眼睛回忆起餐桌上的每个人，重建宾客名单。他发现，我们的大脑特别擅长记忆图像和空间信息。进化心理学家提供了一个解释：据推测，我们的祖先发现，在回山洞的路途中回忆上一顿食物是在哪里找到的十分重要。在西蒙尼德斯的发现之后，“位置记忆法”作为一种记忆演讲稿和文本的技巧在古希腊流行起来。亚里士多德对此撰写过文章，后来在罗马出版了一些关于记忆的艺术的论文。在有纸质书籍之前，记忆的艺术被认为是古典教育的主要内容，与语法、逻辑和修辞同等重要。

F 最著名的天赋型选手是俄罗斯记者 S.V. 舍利什维斯基，他可以回忆起几十年前记忆的一长串数字，以及诗歌、一串无意义的音节和几乎所有被要求回忆的东西。“他的记忆能力没有明显的限制，”从 20 世纪 20 年代到 50 年代研究舍利什维斯基的俄罗斯心理学家亚历山大·卢里亚写道。舍利什维斯基也有“通感”，即一种感官交织在一起的罕见情况。例如，每个数字都可能与一种颜色有关，每个单词都可能与一种味道有关。协同反应会唤起大脑中更多区域的反应，使记忆更容易。

G 佛罗里达州立大学的瑞典裔心理学家 K·安德斯·埃里克森认为，任何人都可以获得舍利什维斯基的技能。他引用了 S.F. 的一个实验，S.F. 是一名本科生，被雇来参加一个被称为“数字跨度”的标准记忆测试，每天一小时，每周两到三天。开始的时候，他和大多数人一样，在任何时候都只能在大脑里记忆大约 7 个数字（就是一个电话号码的长度）。两年来，S.F. 完成了 250 小时的测试。到那时，他的“数字跨度”已经从 7 位扩展到了 80 多位。对 S.F. 的研究使埃里克森相信，天生的超强记忆力根本就不存在。当他重新审视那些研究天赋型选手的原始案例时，他发现卓越的记忆者都在使用技巧（有时是在不知不觉中）并进行了大量的练习。通常情况下，卓越的记忆力只针对某一类型的材料，如数字。“如果我们看一下其中的一些记忆任务，它们是大多数人甚至不会花费一小时来练习的东西，但如果他们花费了 50 个小时来练习，他们就会在这方面出类拔萃，”埃里克森说。他补充说，“要找到一个在多项任务中都很出色的人是非常不容易的。我不认为有任何有力的证据表明有这样的人。”

TEST 6 解析

READING PASSAGE 1

Foot Pedal Irrigation

文章结构

体裁	说明文
题材	常识与科普
主题	绿色革命的局限性及一种适合小规模战略的灌溉方式
段落概括	A 段：农业灌溉现状及对廉价的灌溉系统的需求。 B 段：绿色革命增加了总体粮食供应，但没有根除贫困和饥饿。 C 段：自给自足的农业不能复制发达国家的成功，要另辟蹊径。 D 段：小规模战略的必要性，农业用水问题急需解决。 E 段：脚蹬式抽水机的原理及应用。 F 段：脚蹬式抽水机给一个农民带来的翻天覆地的变化。 G 段：因为便宜好用，脚蹬式抽水机特别适合孟加拉国。

重点词汇

A 段							
单词	音标	词性	释义	单词	音标	词性	释义
dam	[dæm]	*n.*	水坝	irrigation	[ˌɪrɪˈgeɪʃən]	*n.*	灌溉；水利
revolution	[ˌrevəˈluːʃn]	*n.*	革命；变革	reservoir	[ˈrezəvwɑː(r)]	*n.*	水库，蓄水池
sediment	[ˈsedɪmənt]	*n.*	沉积物	productivity	[ˌprɒdʌkˈtɪvəti]	*n.*	生产率，生产力
poverty	[ˈpɒvəti]	*n.*	贫穷，贫困	canal	[kəˈnæl]	*n.*	运河

B 段							
单词	音标	词性	释义	单词	音标	词性	释义
income	[ˈɪnkʌm]	*n.*	收入	rural	[ˈrʊərəl]	*adj.*	乡村的，农村的
eradicate	[ɪˈrædɪkeɪt]	*v.*	根除，消灭	granary	[ˈgrænəri]	*n.*	谷仓，粮仓
malnourished	[ˌmælˈnʌrɪʃt]	*adj.*	营养不良的	deficient	[dɪˈfɪʃnt]	*adj.*	缺少的，不足的

C 段							
单词	音标	词性	释义	单词	音标	词性	释义
subsistence	[səbˈsɪstəns]	*n.*	勉强生存	strategy	[ˈstrætədʒi]	*n.*	策略，计策
surplus	[ˈsɜːpləs]	*n.*	剩余，盈余	subsidize	[ˈsʌbsɪdaɪz]	*v.*	资助，补贴
exploit	[ɪkˈsplɔɪt]	*v.*	利用，运用	intensely	[ɪnˈtɛnsli]	*adv.*	专注地

D 段							
单词	音标	词性	释义	单词	音标	词性	释义
harvest	[ˈhɑːvɪst]	*n.*	收获	survive	[səˈvaɪv]	*v.*	生存，幸存
scattered	[ˈskætəd]	*adj.*	分散的	inherit	[ɪnˈherɪt]	*v.*	继承
afford	[əˈfɔːd]	*v.*	买得起，负担得起				

E 段							
单词	音标	词性	释义	单词	音标	词性	释义
device	[dɪˈvaɪs]	*n.*	设备，仪器	treadle pump		*phr.*	脚蹬式抽水机
cylinder	[ˈsɪlɪndə(r)]	*n.*	气缸	preserve	[prɪˈzɜːv]	*v.*	保留，维持
integrity	[ɪnˈtegrəti]	*n.*	完整	component	[kəmˈpəʊnənt]	*n.*	组成部分，部件
piston	[ˈpɪstən]	*n.*	活塞	pulse	[pʌls]	*n.*	脉冲

F 段							
单词	音标	词性	释义	单词	音标	词性	释义
drill	[drɪl]	*v.*	钻	loan	[ləʊn]	*n.*	贷款
dowry	[ˈdaʊri]	*n.*	嫁妆	replace	[rɪˈpleɪs]	*v.*	代替，取代
tin	[tɪn]	*n.*	镀锡铁皮				

G 段							
单词	音标	词性	释义	单词	音标	词性	释义
initiate	[ɪˈnɪʃieɪt]	*v.*	发起	manufacture	[ˌmænjuˈfæktʃə(r)]	*v.*	制造
install	[ɪnˈstɔːl]	*v.*	安装	purchase	[ˈpɜːtʃəs]	*v.*	购买
leverage	[ˈliːvərɪdʒ]	*v.*	充分利用	investment	[ɪnˈvestmənt]	*n.*	投资
equivalent	[ɪˈkwɪvələnt]	*adj.*	相等的，等同的				

题目精解

Questions 1-6

题型：判断题

Question 1

题干定位词 / 关键词	more effective; poverty or food problem; large scale; small scale
原文定位	A 段最后一句 Continued improvements in the productivity of large farms may play the main role in boosting food supply, but local efforts to provide cheap, individual irrigation systems to small farms may offer a better way to lift people out of poverty.
题目解析	题干：大规模解决贫困或粮食问题比小规模解决更有效。 A 段最后一句提到，大型农场生产力的持续提高可能会在促进粮食供应方面发挥主要作用，但一些为小型农场提供廉价的个人灌溉系统的当地做法可能是帮助人们摆脱贫困的更好方法。由此可知，小规模比大规模解决贫困或粮食问题更有效，因此本题的答案为 FALSE。
答案	FALSE

Question 2

题干定位词 / 关键词	gigantic dams; more time; developing countries
原文定位	原文无相关内容
题目解析	题干：在发展中国家，建造巨型水坝需要花费更多的时间。 原文 A 段第一句虽然提到了发展中国家，但说的是绿色革命是一场著名的运动，旨在提高发展中国家的粮食产量，与题干描述毫不相关，因此本题的答案为 NOT GIVEN。
答案	NOT GIVEN

Question 3

题干定位词 / 关键词	Green revolution; mid of 20th century
原文定位	A 段倒数第二句 Furthermore, although the Green Revolution has greatly expanded worldwide farm production since 1950, poverty stubbornly persists in Africa, Asia and Latin America.
题目解析	题干：自 20 世纪中期起，绿色革命未能提高全球作物产量。 A 段倒数第二句提到，自 1950 年以来，尽管绿色革命极大地扩大了世界范围内的农业生产，但贫困问题始终存在于非洲、亚洲和拉丁美洲。原文说的是绿色革命已经极大地提高了全球作物的产量，这与题干描述相反，因此本题的答案为 FALSE。
答案	FALSE

Question 4

题干定位词 / 关键词	Bangladesh; declined; last decade
原文定位	原文无相关内容
题目解析	题干：孟加拉国的农业生产在过去十年中有所下降。 原文 C 段第二句虽然提到了孟加拉国，但说的是其家庭农场的平均面积；G 段也提到了孟加拉国，但说的是脚蹬式抽水机在该国的应用推广及给农民带来的好处。上述内容都没提及该国农业生产在过去十年中是上升的还是下降的，因此，本题的答案为 NOT GIVEN。
答案	NOT GIVEN

Question 5

题干定位词 / 关键词	Abdul Rahman; increase production
原文定位	D 段最后两句 As Polak walked with him through the scattered fields he had inherited from his father, Polak asked what he needed to move out of poverty. "Control of water for my crops," he said, "at a price I can afford."
题目解析	题干：农民阿卜杜勒 · 拉赫曼自己知道如何提高产量。 D 段最后两句提到，当波拉克和阿卜杜勒 · 拉赫曼一起走过他从父亲那里继承来的零散田地时，波拉克问他需要什么才能摆脱贫困，他的回答是以他能承受的价格灌溉他的农作物。由此可知，阿卜杜勒 · 拉赫曼知道如何增产，只是负担不起。因此，本题的答案为 TRUE。
答案	TRUE

Question 6

题干定位词 / 关键词	small pump; Bangladesh; in the past decade
原文定位	G 段第二、三句 In the early 1980s IDE initiated a campaign to market the pump, encouraging 75 small private-sector companies to manufacture the devices and several thousand village dealers and tube-well drillers to sell and install them. Over the next 12 years one and a half million farm families purchased treadle pumps, which increased the farmers, net income by a total of $150 million a year.
题目解析	题干：在过去的十年里，小型抽水机逐渐发展成为孟加拉国的大型项目。 原文 G 段第二、三句提到，在 20 世纪 80 年代早期，IDE 发起了一场推广这种抽水机的运动，鼓励 75 家小型私营企业生产这种设备，并鼓励数千名乡村经销商和管井钻井工人销售和安装这种抽水机。在接下来的 12 年里，150 万农民家庭购买了脚蹬式抽水机，这使农民每年的净收入增加了 1.5 亿美元。12 年里 150 万农民家庭购买脚蹬式抽水机，这与题干描述相符，因此答案为 TRUE。
答案	TRUE

Questions 7-10

题型：图表填空题

Question 7

题干定位词 / 关键词	handles; pump; materials
原文定位	E 段第二句 Developed in the late 1970s by Norwegian engineer Gunnar Barnes, the pump is operated by a person walking in place on a pair of treadles and two handle arms made of bamboo.
题目解析	题干：抽水机的手柄的材料是 ____。 E 段第二句提到，这种抽水机由一个人在一对踏板上原地行走，用两个竹制手柄来操作。题干问 handle 的材料，因此，bamboo（竹子）为正确答案。
答案	bamboo

Question 8

题干定位词 / 关键词	two; plastics
原文定位	E 段第四句 Each treadle pump has two cylinders which are made of engineering plastic.
题目解析	题干：两个 ______ 是由塑料制成的。 E 段第四句提到，每台脚蹬式抽水机有两个气缸，这两个气缸由工程塑料制成。定语从句 which are made of engineering plastic 用来修饰 cylinders，所以 cylinders（气缸）为正确答案。
答案	cylinders

Question 9

题干定位词 / 关键词	foot valves, pump mechanism, water pulse
原文定位	E 段倒数第一、二句 The pump mechanism has piston and foot valve assemblies. The treadle action creates alternate strokes in the two pistons that lift the water in pulses.
题目解析	题干：连接泵装置的脚踏阀和 _____ 可以产生水脉冲。 E 段最后两句提到，该抽水机的工作机制是活塞和脚踏阀的配合。脚踏动作在两个活塞中产生交替的冲程，以脉冲的方式将水抽上来。foot valve 和 pump mechanism 原词重现，因此，piston/pistons（活塞）为正确答案。
答案	piston/pistons

Question 10

题干定位词 / 关键词	treadle pump; up to; metres
原文定位	E 段第六句 The pump is capable of working up to a maximum depth of 7 meters.
题目解析	题干：脚蹬式抽水机可以抽取水下 ______ 米深的水。 E 段第六句提到，这种抽水机的最大工作深度为 7 米。up to 对应 maximum，因此 7 为正确答案。
答案	7

Questions 11-13

题型：简答题

Question 11

题干定位词 / 关键词	large area; treadle pump; irrigate; low level of expense
原文定位	F 段第一句 The human-powered pump can irrigate half an acre of vegetables and costs only $25 (including the expense of drilling a tube well down to the groundwater).
题目解析	题干：脚蹬式抽水机能以较低的费用灌溉多大面积的农田？ F 段第一句提到，这种人力抽水机可以灌溉半英亩的蔬菜，成本仅为 25 美元（包括钻一个管井直通地下水的费用）。因此，half an acre（半英亩）为正确答案。
答案	half an acre

Question 12

题干定位词 / 关键词	Abdul; new roof
原文定位	F 段倒数第三句 When Polak visited him again in 1984, he had doubled the size of his vegetable plot and replaced the thatched roof on his house with corrugated tin.
题目解析	题干：阿卜杜勒的新屋顶是用什么做的？ F 段倒数第三句提到，1984 年，波拉克再次拜访阿卜杜勒时，他已经把自己的菜地面积扩大了一倍，并把房子的茅草屋顶换成了波纹铁皮。因此，corrugated tin（波纹铁皮）为正确答案。
答案	corrugated tin

Question 13

题干定位词 / 关键词	Bangladesh farmers; invest; IDE
原文定位	G 段倒数第二句 The cost of IDE's market-creation activities was only $12 million, leveraged by the investment of $37.5 million from the farmers themselves.
题目解析	题干：孟加拉国农民在 IDE 的倡议下投资了多少？ G 段倒数第二句提到，IDE 的市场创造活动的成本只有 1200 万美元，农民自己投资了 3750 万美元。因此，$37.5 million/37.5 million dollars 为正确答案。
答案	$37.5 million/37.5 million dollars

长难句分析

A 段：Until now, governments and development agencies have tried to tackle the problem through large-scale projects: gigantic dams, sprawling irrigation canals and vast new fields of high-yield crops introduced during the Green Revolution, the famous campaign to increase grain harvests in developing nations.

思路分析：这个句子的主体可以简化为 Governments and development agencies have tried to tackle the problem，该句为主谓宾结构，Governments and development agencies 为主语，have tried 为谓语，不定式 to tackle the problem 为宾语。through large-scale projects 为方式状语；冒号后的内容用来具体解释说明 large-scale projects，其中 introduced during the Green Revolution 为分词作后置定语，修饰 vast new fields of high-yield crops；the famous campaign to increase grain harvests in developing nations 与 the Green Revolution 为同位语，用来进一步解释说明绿色革命。

参考翻译：到目前为止，各国政府和发展机构一直在试图通过大型项目来解决问题：巨大的大坝、绵延的灌溉渠，以及绿色革命期间引入的大片高产作物新田地。绿色革命是一场著名的运动，旨在提高发展中国家的粮食产量。

G 段：In the early 1980s IDE initiated a campaign to market the pump, encouraging 75 small private-sector companies to manufacture the devices and several thousand village dealers and tube-well drillers to sell and install them.

思路分析：这个句子的主体可以简化为 IDE initiated a campaign to market the pump，该句

为主谓宾结构，主语为 IDE，谓语为 initiated，不定式 to market the pump 作宾语。encouraging... 为现在分词作状语，用来说明主句的目的，其中 encourage sb. to do sth. 为固定搭配，这个固定搭配在这里为两个并列的结构，即 encourage 75 small private-sector companies to manufacture the devices 和 (encourage) several thousand village dealers and tube-well drillers to sell and install them。

参考翻译： 在 20 世纪 80 年代早期，IDE 发起了一场推广这种抽水机的运动，鼓励 75 家小型私营企业生产这种设备，并鼓励数千名乡村经销商和管井钻井工人销售和安装这种抽水机。

参考译文

脚蹬灌溉

A 到目前为止，各国政府和发展机构一直在试图通过大型项目来解决问题：巨大的大坝、绵延的灌溉渠，以及绿色革命期间引入的大片高产作物新田地。绿色革命是一场著名的运动，旨在提高发展中国家的粮食产量。然而，传统的灌溉已经使许多地区的土壤退化，大坝后面的水库很快就会被淤泥填满，降低了水库的蓄水能力，使下游的农民失去了肥沃的沉积物。此外，自 1950 年以来，尽管绿色革命极大地扩大了世界范围内的农业生产，但贫困问题始终存在于非洲、亚洲和拉丁美洲。大型农场生产力的持续提高可能会在促进粮食供应方面发挥主要作用，但一些为小型农场提供廉价的个人灌溉系统的当地做法可能是帮助人们摆脱贫困的更好方法。

B 绿色革命旨在增加总体食品供应，而不是提高农村穷人的收入，所以它没有消除贫困和饥饿也就不足为奇了。以印度为例，印度已经在粮食上自给自足了 15 年，粮仓也很充足，但超过 2 亿印度人（占该国人口的五分之一）营养不良，原因是他们买不起所需的食物，也因为国家的安全保障不足。2000 年，189 个国家致力于实现千年发展目标，呼吁到 2015 年将世界贫困人口减少一半。然而，按照正常情况计算，无论富裕国家向贫穷国家提供多少资金，我们实现大部分千年发展目标的希望都微乎其微。

C 然而，绿色革命的供应驱动战略可能对自给自足的农民没有什么帮助，他们必须发挥自己的优势，在全球市场上竞争。在印度，家庭农场的平均面积不到 4 英亩，孟加拉国为 1.8 英亩。联合收割机和其他现代农耕用具太贵，无法在这么小的面积上使用。一个印度农民在出售自己那一英亩土地上种植的剩余小麦时，不可能与加拿大那些通常占地数千英亩的高效并且有补贴的小麦农场竞争。相反，自给自足的农民应该利用他们的劳动力成本是世界上最低的这一事实，这会使他们在种植和销售需要深耕细作的高价值作物方面具有相对的优势。

D 1981 年，当保罗 · 波拉克遇到孟加拉国诺阿卡利地区的农民阿卜杜勒 · 拉赫曼时，他直接看到了小规模战略的必要性。在他四分之三英亩的雨水灌溉田里，阿卜杜勒每年只能收获 700 公斤大米，比养活家人所需数量少 300 公斤。在 10 月水稻收获之前的三个月里，阿卜杜勒和他的妻子不得不默默地看着他们的三个孩子每天只吃一顿或更少的饭。当波拉克和他一起走过他从父亲那里继承来的零散田地时，波拉克问他需要什么才能摆脱贫困。他说："以我能承受的价格灌溉我的农作物。"

E 很快，波拉克了解到一种简单的装置可以帮助阿卜杜勒实现他的目标：脚蹬式抽水机。这种抽水机是挪威工程师贡纳尔 · 巴恩斯在 20 世纪 70 年代末开发的，由一个人在一对踏板上原地行走，用两个竹制手柄来操作。经过适当的调整和保养，它可以每天运行几个小时，而不会让使用者感到疲劳。每台脚蹬式抽水机有两个由工程塑料制成的气缸。气缸的直径为 10.05 厘米，高度为 28 厘米。该抽水机的最大工作深度为 7 米。为了保持橡胶部件的完整性，不建议在 7 米以下作业。该抽水机的机件包括活塞和脚踏阀。脚踏动作在两个活塞中产生交替的冲程，以脉冲的方式将水抽上来。

F 这种人力抽水机可以灌溉半英亩的蔬菜，成本仅为 25 美元（包括钻一个管井直通地下水的费用）。阿卜杜勒从一个表亲那里听说了脚蹬式抽水机，他是孟加拉国第一批购买这一工具的农民之一。他向一位叔叔借了 25 美元，4 个月后就轻松还清了借款。在 5 个月的旱季，孟加拉国人通常很少耕种，阿卜杜勒用脚蹬式抽水机种植了四分之一英亩的辣椒、西红柿、卷心菜和茄子。他还通过灌溉提高了其中一块稻田的产量。他的家人吃掉了一些蔬菜，其余的在村里的市场上出售，净赚了 100 美元。有了新收入，阿卜杜勒能够买大米给家人吃，让他的两个儿子上学上到 16 岁，并为女儿留了一点钱作为嫁妆。1984 年，波拉克再次拜访他时，他已经把自己的菜地面积扩大了一倍，房子的茅草屋顶也换成了波纹铁皮。他家养了一头小牛和几只鸡。他告诉我，脚蹬式抽水机是上帝赐予的礼物。

G 孟加拉国特别适合使用脚蹬式抽水机，因为在农民脚下几米深的地方就有一个巨大的地下水蓄水池。在 20 世纪 80 年代早期，IDE 发起了一场推广这种抽水机的运动，鼓励 75 家小型私营企业生产这种设备，并鼓励数千名乡村经销商和管井钻井工人销售和安装这种抽水机。在接下来的 12 年里，150 万农民家庭购买了脚蹬式抽水机，这使农民每年的净收入增加了 1.5 亿美元。IDE 的市场创造活动的成本只有 1200 万美元，利用了农民自己投资的 3750 万美元。相比之下，建造一个常规水坝和运河系统来灌溉同等面积的农田，其费用将在每英亩 2000 美元左右，也就是 15 亿美元。

READING PASSAGE 2

The Secret of The Yawn

文章结构

体裁	说明文
题材	常识与科普
主题	对打哈欠进行的科学实验及相关研究
段落概括	A 段：打哈欠科学很难让人相信，但确实合乎发育神经科学的逻辑。 B 段：打哈欠是一种人类和动物的古老而原始的行为。 C 段：在第一个实验中，同情心项目得分不高的参与者不会回以哈欠。 D 段：在第二个实验中，大脑的某个区域控制着同理心。 E 段：第三个实验主要研究患有脑部疾病的人打哈欠以及打哈欠的规律。 F 段：打哈欠和伸懒腰的联系。 G 段：打哈欠和伸懒腰之间的关联的特殊表现。 H 段：临床神经病学提供的惊喜。

重点词汇

A 段							
单词	音标	词性	释义	单词	音标	词性	释义
yawn	[jɔːn]	v.	打哈欠	convince	[kənˈvɪns]	v.	使确信，使信服
merit	[ˈmerɪt]	n.	优点，长处	quirky	[ˈkwɜːki]	adj.	奇特的，离奇的
neuroscience	[ˈnjʊərəʊsaɪəns]	n.	神经科学	flap	[flæp]	v.	拍打
B 段							
单词	音标	词性	释义	单词	音标	词性	释义
primitive	[ˈprɪmətɪv]	adj.	原始的，本能的	womb	[wuːm]	n.	子宫
unhinge	[ʌnˈhɪndʒ]	v.	使分开	mating	[ˈmeɪtɪŋ]	n.	交配
cognitive	[ˈkɒgnətɪv]	adj.	认知的	contagious	[kənˈteɪdʒəs]	adj.	传染性的
primate	[ˈpraɪmeɪt]	n.	灵长类动物				

C 段							
单词	音标	词性	释义	单词	音标	词性	释义
psychological	[ˌsaɪkəˈlɒdʒɪkl]	*adj.*	心理上的	empathic	[emˈpæθik]	*adj.*	感情移入的
participant	[pɑːˈtɪsɪpənt]	*n.*	参与者	compassion	[kəmˈpæʃn]	*n.*	同情，怜悯
literally	[ˈlɪtərəli]	*adv.*	字面上；确实地				

D 段							
单词	音标	词性	释义	单词	音标	词性	释义
magnetic resonance		*phr.*	磁共振	indicator	[ˈɪndɪkeɪtə(r)]	*n.*	标志，迹象
posterior cingulate		*phr.*	后扣带回（大脑区域）	rear	[rɪə(r)]	*n.*	后面，后部

E 段							
单词	音标	词性	释义	单词	音标	词性	释义
disorder	[dɪsˈɔːdə(r)]	*n.*	紊乱，杂乱	autism	[ˈɔːtɪzəm]	*n.*	自闭症，孤独症
schizophrenia	[ˌskizəuˈfriːniə]	*n.*	精神分裂症	victim	[ˈvɪktɪm]	*n.*	患病者；受害者
interval	[ˈɪntəvl]	*n.*	间隔	mystery	[ˈmɪstri]	*n.*	神秘的事物
hypothalamu	[ˌhaɪpəˈθæləməs]	*n.*	下丘脑	gender	[ˈdʒendə(r)]	*n.*	性别

F 段							
单词	音标	词性	释义	单词	音标	词性	释义
stretch	[stretʃ]	*v.*	伸展	property	[ˈprɒpəti]	*n.*	性质，特性
co-occur	[ˌkəʊ əˈkɜː(r)]	*v.*	共现	chart	[ˈtʃɑːt]	*v.*	记录；绘制
fetus	[ˈfiːtəs]	*n.*	胎儿	ultrasound	[ˈʌltrəsaʊnd]	*n.*	超声波

G 段							
单词	音标	词性	释义	单词	音标	词性	释义
paralyze	[ˈpærəlaiz]	*v.*	使麻痹；使瘫痪	stroke	[strəʊk]	*n.*	中风
prominent	[ˈprɒmɪnənt]	*adj.*	杰出的，著名的	hemiplegic	[heˈmɪpliːdʒɪk]	*adj.*	偏瘫的
therapeutic	[ˌθerəˈpjuːtɪk]	*adj.*	有疗效的	reinnervation	[riːɪnəˈveɪʃn]	*n.*	再生
unconsciously	[ʌnˈkɒnʃəsli]	*adv.*	无意识地	limb	[lɪm]	*n.*	四肢
prognosis	[prɒgˈnəʊsɪs]	*n.*	预后	recovery	[rɪˈkʌvəri]	*n.*	恢复，痊愈

H 段							
单词	音标	词性	释义	单词	音标	词性	释义
clinical	[ˈklɪnɪkl]	*adj.*	临床的	syndrome	[ˈsɪndrəʊm]	*n.*	综合征
deprive	[dɪˈpraɪv]	*v.*	剥夺，使丧失	voluntarily	[ˈvɒləntrəli]	*adv.*	自动地，自愿地
spontaneous	[spɒnˈteɪniəs]	*adj.*	自发的，自然的	stimuli	[ˈstɪmjʊlaɪ]	*n.*	刺激（物），促进因素
respiratory	[rəˈspɪrətri]	*adj.*	呼吸的				

题目精解

Questions 14-18

题型：摘要填空题

Question 14

题干定位词 / 关键词	psychology professor; six seconds
原文定位	E 段第三句 He found the basic yawn lasts about six seconds and they come in bouts with an interval of about 68 seconds.
题目解析	题干：一位心理学教授观察到，打一个哈欠平均需要 6 秒，在下一个哈欠到来之前，需要 _____。 原文提到打哈欠的时间是在 E 段第三句，该句提到一般的哈欠会持续大约 6 秒，而且是阵发性的，隔 68 秒就会打一次。before a following yawning comes 即两个哈欠的时间间隔（interval），所以下一个哈欠来临需要 68 秒。
答案	68 seconds

Question 15

题干定位词 / 关键词	same frequency; male and female; genders
原文定位	E 段第四句 Men and women yawn or half-yawn equally often, but men are significantly less likely to cover their mouths which may indicate complex distinction in genders.
题目解析	题干：男性和女性打哈欠或者半打哈欠的频率几乎相同，但伴随着打哈欠的行为表现出性别上的 ______。 E 段第四句提到男性和女性打哈欠或半打哈欠的频率相同，但男性明显不太可能捂住他们的嘴，这可能是性别方面的一个复杂区别。indicate 对应 showing，in genders 原词重现，所以 (complex) distinction 为正确答案。
答案	(complex) distinction

Question 16

题干定位词 / 关键词	cause; uncertain; coordinated in; brain; also manage
原文定位	E 段最后两句 However, the physical root of yawning remains a mystery. Some researchers say it's coordinated within the hypothalamus of the brain, the area that also controls breathing.
题目解析	题干：虽然打哈欠的原因尚不清楚，一些研究者认为它是由大脑中的某一区域协调的，这一区域也管理着______。 E 段最后两句提到，打哈欠的物理根源仍然是个谜，一些研究人员说，它是在大脑的下丘脑内调控的，这个区域也控制着呼吸。the area of brain 对应 hypothalamus of the brain，also 原词重现，manages 对应 controls，因此，breathing 为正确答案。
答案	breathing

Question 17

题干定位词 / 关键词	baby; link between; yawning
原文定位	F 段最后一句 Studies by J. I. P, G. H. A. Visser and H. F. Prechtl in the early 1980s, charting movement in the developing fetus using ultrasound, observed not just yawning but a link between yawning and stretching as early as the end of the first prenatal trimester.
题目解析	题干：另一项成果是，在婴儿出生之前，打哈欠和 ____ 之间就有联系。 F 段最后一句提到在 20 世纪 80 年代初，H. F. Prechtl 等人利用超声波记录了发育中的胎儿的运动，他们不仅观察到了打哈欠，而且早在孕早期结束时就观察到了打哈欠和伸懒腰之间的联系。a link 原词重现，yawning 也原词重现，所以 stretch/stretching 为正确答案。
答案	stretch/stretching

Question 18

题干定位词 / 关键词	connection; damaged
原文定位	G 段第一句 The most extraordinary demonstration of the yawn-stretch linkage occurs in many people paralyzed on one side of their body because of brain damage caused by a stroke.
题目解析	题干：这种联系也存在于即使是 _____ 有损伤的人中。 G 段第一句讲述了发生在因中风造成脑损伤而导致身体一侧瘫痪的人身上的关于打哈欠和伸懒腰之间的联系的例子。connection 对应原文中的 linkage，is damaged 对应原文中的 damage，所以 brain 为正确答案。
答案	brain

Questions 19-23

题型：段落信息配对题

Question 19

题干定位词 / 关键词	rate; regular pattern
原文定位	E 段第三句 He found the basic yawn lasts about six seconds and they come in bouts with an interval of about 68 seconds.
题目解析	题干：打哈欠的频率有一定的规律。 E 段第三句：他发现一般的哈欠会持续大约 6 秒，而且它们是阵发性的，间隔时间大约为 68 秒。这里的 6 秒和 68 秒就是打哈欠的规律，因此正确答案为 E。
答案	E

Question 20

题干定位词 / 关键词	inherent ability; animals; humans
原文定位	B 段前四句 Yawning is an ancient, primitive act. Humans do it even before they are born, opening wide in the womb. Some snakes unhinge their jaws to do it. One species of penguins yawns as part of mating.
题目解析	题干：打哈欠是动物和人类与生俱来的能力。 B 段前四句提到打哈欠是一种古老、原始的行为，人类甚至在子宫里就会张大嘴巴（打哈欠）；有些蛇会张开它们的下颚来打哈欠；有一种企鹅交配时会打哈欠。这里提到了人、蛇和企鹅都会打哈欠，并且是一种原始的、不需要教的行为，因此正确答案为 B。
答案	B

Question 21

题干定位词 / 关键词	stretching and yawning; not always going together
原文定位	F 段第二句 But they do not always co-occur—people usually yawn when we stretch, but we don't always stretch when we yawn, especially before bedtime.
题目解析	题干：伸懒腰和打哈欠并不总是同时发生的。 F 段主要说明伸懒腰和打哈欠的联系，其中第二句提到伸懒腰和打哈欠并不总是同时发生的，伸懒腰时通常会打哈欠，但打哈欠时并不总是伸懒腰，尤其是在睡觉前。not always going together 对应原文中的 not always co-occur，因此 F 段内容与题干表述相符。
答案	F

Question 22

题干定位词 / 关键词	positive notice or response; communicating
原文定位	D 段最后两句 "I don't know if it's necessarily that nice people yawn more, but I think it's a good indicator of a state of mind," said Professor Platek. "It's also a good indicator if you're empathizing with me and paying attention."
题目解析	题干：打哈欠可能表明人们在交流中有积极的注意或回应。 根据关键词定位到 D 段最后两句，这里普拉特克教授说道"我不知道是不是友善的人打哈欠更多，但我认为这是精神状态的一个很好的指标。如果你对我感同身受并给予关注，这也是一个很好的指标。"这里的 a good indicator of a state of mind，a good indicator if...paying attention 对应题干中的 positive notice or response，所以 D 段提及了题干描述的内容。
答案	D

Question 23

题干定位词 / 关键词	superior areas; brain; infectious
原文定位	H 段最后一句 The multiplicity of stimuli of contagious yawning, by contrast, implicates many higher brain regions.
题目解析	题干：大脑中的某些高级区域可能与打哈欠的传染特征有关。 根据关键词定位到 H 段最后一句，该句提到哈欠传染的多重刺激牵涉到许多高级脑区。superior areas 对应原文中的 higher brain regions，infectious feature of yawning 对应 contagious yawning，所以正确答案为 H。
答案	H

Questions 24-26

题型：判断题

Question 24

题干定位词 / 关键词	several students; Platek; not comprehend; yawn back
原文定位	无相关内容
题目解析	题干：在普拉特克的实验中，有些学生不明白为什么他们的导师要他们也打哈欠。 原文 C 段提到在普拉特克的第一个实验中，他用一个心理测试对人们的共情感受进行排名，他发现那些同情心项目得分不高的参与者不会回以哈欠。然后有人问"为什么我要看着别人打哈欠？"。这里的信息非常容易让考生误选 FALSE，但题干是在偷换概念，有疑问的是参加测试的人，且文中并未对他们的身份进行说明，没有提及他们是否是学生，也没有提及人数，更没有提及是否是老师让他们打哈欠的。因此，本题的正确答案为 NOT GIVEN。
答案	NOT GIVEN

Question 25

题干定位词 / 关键词	certain experiment, link, yawning and compassion
原文定位	C 段第二句 He found that participants who did not score high on compassion did not yawn back.
题目解析	题干：某些实验的结果表明了打哈欠和同情心之间的联系。 C 段第二句提及普拉特克通过实验发现那些同情心项目得分不高的参与者不会回以哈欠，这说明了打哈欠和同情心之间的联系。原文与题干描述一致，因此正确答案为 TRUE。
答案	TRUE

Question 26

题干定位词 / 关键词	affirmative impact; recovery; brain damage; stroke
原文定位	G 段最后一句 It is not known whether the associated response is a positive prognosis for recovery, nor whether yawning is therapeutic for reinnervation or prevention of muscular atrophy.
题目解析	题干：打哈欠对因中风造成的脑损伤的恢复有积极的影响。 G 段最后一句：目前还不知道这种相关反应是否对康复有积极的预示作用，也不知道打哈欠是否对神经再生或预防肌肉萎缩有治疗作用。原文说的是尚不明确，题干说的是有积极影响，题干表述与原文说法不符，因此正确答案为 FALSE。
答案	FALSE

长难句分析

G 段：The prominent British neurologist Sir Francis Walshe noted in 1923 that when these hemiplegics yawn, they are startled and mystified to observe that their otherwise paralyzed arm rises and flexes automatically in what neurologists term an “associated response”.

思路分析：这个句子的主体可以简化为 The prominent British neurologist Sir Francis Walshe noted in 1923 that...，其中主语为人名 Sir Francis Walshe，谓语为 noted，that 引导的宾语从句充当宾语成分。在该宾语从句中，还包含一个 when 引导的时间

状语从句和 that 引导的另一个宾语从句。

参考翻译：英国著名的神经学家弗朗西斯·沃尔什爵士在 1923 年指出，当这些偏瘫患者打哈欠时，他们惊讶而困惑地发现，患者原本瘫痪的手臂不由自主地抬起和弯曲，这就是神经学家所说的“相关反应”。

F 段：Studies by J.I.P, G.H.A.Visser and H.F. Prechtl in the early 1980s, charting movement in the developing fetus using ultrasound, observed not just yawning but a link between yawning and stretching as early as the end of the first prenatal trimester.

思路分析：这个句子的主体可以简化为 Studies observed not just yawning but a link between yawning and stretching，该句为主谓宾结构，主语为 Studies，谓语为 observed，宾语部分为 not just...but... 连接的两个并列成分，突出 but 后面的内容。介词 by 引导的一系列人名作定语；charting movement in the developing fetus using ultrasound 为现在分词作方式状语，说明通过超声波记录胎儿的运动；as early as the end of the first prenatal trimester 为时间状语。

参考翻译：J.I.P、G.H.A. 维瑟和 H.F. 普瑞其特在 20 世纪 80 年代初进行的研究，利用超声波对发育中的胎儿的运动进行了记录，他们不仅观察到了打哈欠，还最早在妊娠早期（前三个月）结束时观察到了打哈欠和伸懒腰之间的联系。

参考译文

打哈欠的秘密

A 20 世纪 80 年代，当一位科学家开始研究打哈欠时，很难说服他的一些研究学生相信“打哈欠科学”的优点。虽然看起来很古怪，但他研究打哈欠的决定是他在发育神经科学方面的研究在人类身上的逻辑延伸，这些研究在“发育和进化过程中的扑翼”等论文中都有报道。作为一个神经行为问题，鸟类的扑翼和人类打哈欠时的面部和身体摆动并没有什么区别。

B 打哈欠是一种古老、原始的行为。人类甚至在出生前就会打哈欠，在子宫里就张大了嘴。有些蛇会把它们的下颚打开来打哈欠。在某种企鹅中，打哈欠是交配的一部分。直到现在，研究人员才开始理解我们为什么打哈欠，什么时候打哈欠，以及为什么看到别人打哈欠时自己也会打哈欠。费城德雷克塞尔大学的认知神经科学教授史蒂文·普拉特克研究了打哈欠的传染性行为，这种行为只有人类和其他灵长类动物才有。

C 在他的第一个实验中，他对参与者进行了一场心理测试，以对他们的共情感受进行排名。他发现，在同情心项目得分不高的参与者不会回以哈欠。“真的会有人问‘为什么我要看着别人打哈欠’，”普拉特克教授说，“它就是没有效果。”

D 在他的第二个实验中，他让 10 名学生在观看人们打哈欠的录像时接受磁共振成像扫描。当学生们观看视频时，大脑中做出反应的部分是科学家们认为控制同理心的部分——位于大脑中后部的后扣带回。“我不知道是不是友善的人打哈欠更多，但我认为这是精神状态的一个很好的指标，”普拉特克教授说。“如果你对我感同身受并给予关注，这也是一个很好的指标。”

E 他的第三个实验是研究那些患有脑部疾病的人打哈欠，如自闭症和精神分裂症患者，在这些疾病中，受害者很难与他人进行情感交流。马里兰大学的一位心理学教授罗伯特·普罗文是其他少数研究打哈欠的人之一。他发现一般的哈欠会持续大约 6 秒，而且它们是阵发性的，间隔时间大约为 68 秒。男性和女性打哈欠或半打哈欠的频率相同，但男性明显不太可能捂住他们的嘴，这可能是性别方面的一个复杂区别。普罗文教授说：“一个被监视的打哈欠者从不打哈欠。”然而，打哈欠的物理根源仍然是个谜。一些研究人员说，它是在大脑的下丘脑内调控的，这个区域也控制着呼吸。

F 打哈欠和伸懒腰也有共同的特性，可以作为一个运动综合整体的一部分一起进行。但它们并不总是同时出现的，人们通常在伸懒腰时打哈欠，但我们并不总是在打哈欠时伸懒腰，特别是在睡前。J.I.P、G.H.A. 维瑟和 H.F. 普瑞其特在 20 世纪 80 年代初进行的研究，利用超声波对发育中的胎儿的运动进行了记录，他们不仅观察到了打哈欠，还最早在妊娠早期（前三个月）结束时观察到了打哈欠和伸懒腰之间的联系。

G 打哈欠与伸懒腰之间的关联的最特殊表现发生在许多因中风造成脑损伤而导致身体一侧瘫痪的人身上。英国著名的神经学家弗朗西斯·沃尔什爵士在 1923 年指出，当这些偏瘫患者打哈欠时，他们惊讶而困惑地发现，患者原本瘫痪的手臂不由自主地抬起和弯曲，这就是神经学家所说的“相关反应”。打哈欠显然激活了大脑和支配瘫痪肢体的脊髓运动系统之间未受损伤、无意识控制的联系。目前还不知道这种相关反应是否对康复有积极的预示作用，也不知道打哈欠是否对神经再生或预防肌肉萎缩有治疗作用。

H 临床神经病学提供了其他的惊喜。一些患有“闭锁”综合征的病人，他们几乎完全被剥夺了自主运动的能力，但却能正常打哈欠。自发打哈欠的神经回路必定存在于脑干中，靠近其他呼吸和血管舒缩中心，因为打哈欠是由只拥有延髓的无脑症患者进行的。相比之下，哈欠传染的多重刺激牵涉到许多高级脑区。

READING PASSAGE 3

Thomas Harriot—The Discovery of Refraction

文章结构

体裁	记叙文（人物传记）
题材	历史与发展
主题	哈里奥特的生平及其对折射研究的贡献
段落概括	A 段：折射定律的广泛应用，托马斯 · 哈里奥特首次发现正弦定律。 B 段：哈里奥特的兴趣和研究遍布各个领域。 C 段：哈里奥特远征新大陆。 D 段：哈里奥特与其他科学家和数学家（尤其是开普勒）保持定期通信。 E 段：哈里奥特的笔记揭示了他关于折射的研究，但他未发表作品的原因不明。 F 段：哈里奥特在其他领域的发现未发表的原因猜测。 G 段：对哈里奥特贡献迟来的赞赏。

重点词汇

A 段							
单词	音标	词性	释义	单词	音标	词性	释义
medium	[ˈmiːdiəm]	*n.*	媒介	refraction	[rɪˈfrækʃn]	*n.*	折射
lens	[lenz]	*n.*	透镜，镜片	magnification	[ˌmæɡnɪfɪˈkeɪʃn]	*n.*	放大
prism	[ˈprɪzəm]	*n.*	棱柱	spectrum	[ˈspektrəm]	*n.*	光谱
beam	[biːm]	*n.*	光线，光束	overlook	[ˌəʊvəˈlʊk]	*v.*	忽视，忽略

B 段							
单词	音标	词性	释义	单词	音标	词性	释义
contemporary	[kənˈtemprəri]	*n.*	同代人	mathematician	[ˌmæθəməˈtɪʃn]	*n.*	数学家
biographer	[baɪˈɒɡrəfə(r)]	*n.*	传记作家	profound	[prəˈfaʊnd]	*adj.*	影响深远的
navigation	[ˌnævɪˈɡeɪʃn]	*n.*	航行，航海术	comet	[ˈkɒmɪt]	*n.*	彗星
orbit	[ˈɔːbɪt]	*n.*	轨道	rotation	[rəʊˈteɪʃn]	*n.*	转动

C段							
单词	音标	词性	释义	单词	音标	词性	释义
explorer	[ɪkˈsplɔːrə(r)]	*n.*	探索者，探险者	expedition	[ˌekspəˈdɪʃn]	*n.*	远征，探险
topography	[təˈpɒgrəfi]	*n.*	地形，地貌	flora	[ˈflɔːrə]	*n.*	植物群
fauna	[ˈfɔːnə]	*n.*	动物群	transcription	[trænˈskrɪpʃn]	*n.*	抄写，转录
estate	[ɪˈsteɪt]	*n.*	个人财产，私有土地，庄园	ballistics	[bəˈlɪstɪks]	*n.*	弹道学；发射学

D段							
单词	音标	词性	释义	单词	音标	词性	释义
correspondence	[ˌkɒrəˈspɒndəns]	*n.*	通信	approximation	[əˌprɒksɪˈmeɪʃn]	*n.*	近似值
forthcoming	[ˌfɔːθˈkʌmɪŋ]	*adj.*	乐于提供信息的，乐于帮助的	reluctance	[rɪ'lʌktəns]	*n.*	不情愿
constant	[ˈkɒnstənt]	*adj.*	恒定的，不变的	data	[ˈdeɪtə]	*n.*	数据

E段							
单词	音标	词性	释义	单词	音标	词性	释义
extensive	[ɪkˈstensɪv]	*adj.*	广泛的	predate	[ˌpriːˈdeɪt]	*v.*	早于，先于
sine	[saɪn]	*n.*	正弦	dispersion	[dɪˈspɜːʃn]	*n.*	色散
indice	[ˈɪndɪs]	*n.*	指数	liquid	[ˈlɪkwɪd]	*n.*	液体

F段							
单词	音标	词性	释义	单词	音标	词性	释义
treatise	[ˈtriːtɪs]	*n.*	论文，专著	religious	[rɪˈlɪdʒəs]	*adj.*	宗教的
suspicious	[səˈspɪʃəs]	*adj.*	怀疑的，可疑的	algebra	[ˈældʒɪbrə]	*n.*	代数
posthumously	[ˈpɒstjʊməslɪ]	*adv.*	死后				

G段							
单词	音标	词性	释义	单词	音标	词性	释义
dwindle	[ˈdwɪndl]	*v.*	减少	diminished	[dɪˈmɪnɪʃt]	*adj.*	减少的
genuinely	[ˈdʒenjuɪnli]	*adv.*	真正地	descendant	[dɪˈsendənt]	*n.*	后代
tutor	[ˈtjuːtə(r)]	*n.*	家庭教师，导师	appreciation	[əˌpriːʃiˈeɪʃn]	*n.*	欣赏，赞赏
overlap	[ˌəuvəˈlæp]	*v.*	重叠	acknowledge	[əkˈnɒlɪdʒ]	*v.*	承认

题目精解

Questions 27-31

题型：标题题

小标题	译文
i. A misunderstanding in the history of science	关于科学历史的一个误解
ii. Thomas Harriot's biography	托马斯·哈里奥特的传记
iii. Unknown reasons for his unpublished works	他未发表作品的未知原因
iv. Harriot's 1588 publication on North America studies	哈里奥特于 1588 年发表的关于北美的研究
v. Expedition to the New World	远征新大陆
vi. Reluctant cooperation with Kepler	不愿意与开普勒合作
vii. Belated appreciation of Harriots contribution	对哈里奥特贡献的迟来的赞赏
viii. Religious pressures keeping him from publishing	宗教压力使他没有发表
ix. Correspondence with Kepler	与开普勒通信
x. Interests and researches into multiple fields of study	对多个研究领域有兴趣和研究

Question 27

题干定位词 / 关键词	interests; researches; multiple fields
原文定位	B 段第一、二句 A contemporary of Shakespeare, Elizabeth I, Johannes Kepler and Galilei Galileo, Thomas Harriot (1560-1621) was an English scientist and mathematician. His principal biographer, J. W. Shirley, was quoted saying that in his time he was "England's most profound mathematician, most imaginative and methodical experimental scientist".
题目解析	B 段第一、二句概括了本段的主旨，指出托马斯·哈里奥特是英国最渊博的数学家、最富有想象力和最有条理的实验科学家。后面的内容都在具体介绍托马斯·哈里奥特在各个领域的成就。因此，选项 x 符合本段主旨。
答案	x

Question 28

题干定位词 / 关键词	expedition; the New World
原文定位	C 段
题目解析	C 段首句提到托马斯 · 哈里奥特是早期到达北美的英国探险家。本段主要描述了他在罗阿诺克岛上观察地形、植物群和动物群，学习当地语言，写了一篇报告，并且还为罗利进行了弹道学和船舶设计的研究。选项 v 符合本段主旨。选项 iv 很容易被考生误选，但它只是本段中的一个细节，只在一句话中出现过，并不是本段的主旨。
答案	v

Question 29

题干定位词 / 关键词	correspondence; Kepler
原文定位	D 段首句 Harriot kept regular correspondence with other scientists and mathematicians, especially in England but also in mainland Europe, notably with Johannes Kepler.
题目解析	D 段首句直接表明本段主旨：哈里奥特与其他科学家和数学家保持定期通信，特别是在英格兰的科学家和数学家，也有欧洲大陆的，尤其是约翰内斯 · 开普勒。本段主要讲述了哈里奥特与开普勒的通信往来。因此选项 ix 符合本段主旨。本题容易被考生误选 vi，应注意本段大部分内容强调的是通信本身，而非哈里奥特不愿与开普勒合作，这只是本段结尾处的一个细节，并非整段的主旨，考生应注意区分细节和主旨。
答案	ix

Question 30

题干定位词 / 关键词	unknown reasons; unpublished works
原文定位	F 段第一、二句 As his studies of refraction, Harriot's discoveries in other fields were largely unpublished during his lifetime, and until this century, Harriot was known only for an account of his travels in Virginia published in 1588, and for a treatise on algebra published posthumously in 1631. The reason why Harriot kept his results unpublished is unclear.
题目解析	F 段第一句指出，正如他关于折射的研究一样，哈里奥特在其他领域的发现在他有生之年基本上没有发表过。第二句紧接着说他不发表研究结果的原因尚不清楚。这些内容正好对应选项 iii。
答案	iii

Question 31

题干定位词 / 关键词	belated appreciation; Harriots contribution
原文定位	G 段
题目解析	G 段主要讲述了哈利奥特未发表过的研究被人发现，学者们开始研究它们，对他的贡献的赞赏在 20 世纪下半叶开始增长，此时哈利奥特已经去世了几百年。由此可知，选项 vii 符合本段主旨。
答案	vii

Questions 32-36

题型：摘要填空题

Question 32

题干定位词 / 关键词	applications; image; lens; refraction; such as
原文定位	A 段第三、四句 Refraction has many applications in optics and technology. A lens uses refraction to form an image of an object for many different purposes, such as magnification.
题目解析	题干：各种现代应用，例如 ______，基于透镜使用折射产生的图像。 A 段第三、四句提到折射在光学和技术领域有很多应用，透镜利用折射形成物体的图像，有许多不同的用途，比如放大。various modern applications 对应 many different purposes，an image 原词重现，produced by lens uses refraction 对应 a lens uses refraction to form，空格处要填入一个关于折射应用的例子，such as 后面的 magnification 为正确答案。
答案	magnification

Question 33

题干定位词 / 关键词	spectrum of colors; a beam of light
原文定位	A 段第五句 A prism uses refraction to form a spectrum of colors from an incident beam of light.
题目解析	题干：一束光的光谱可以用 ______ 产生。 A 段第五句提到棱镜利用入射光束的折射形成不同颜色的光谱，a beam of light 对应原文中的 an incident beam of light，a spectrum of colors 原词重现，因此 a prism/prisms 为正确答案。
答案	a prism/prisms

Question 34

题干定位词 / 关键词	Harriot; Virginia; American
原文定位	C 段第四至六句 On shore, Harriot observed the topography, flora and fauna, made many drawings and maps, and met the native people who spoke a language the English called Algonquian. Harriot worked out a phonetic transcription of the native people's speech sounds and began to learn the language, which enabled him to converse to some extent with other natives the English encountered. Harriot wrote his report for Raleigh and published it as *A Briefe and True Report of the New Found Land of Virginia* in 1588.
题目解析	题干：哈里奥特前往弗吉尼亚，主要研究关于美洲 _____ 的两个课题。 原文 C 段讲述了哈里奥特前往新大陆的经历。第四至六句详细介绍了他在那里做的事情：观察了地形、植物群和动物群，绘制了许多图画和地图，学会了一种叫阿尔冈琴语的语言，还出版了《关于弗吉尼亚新发现地的简要而真实的报告》。 题干要求填入关于美洲什么的两个课题，本题难度较大，需要考生有较强的概括能力。哈利奥特主要研究了美洲的地形、语言、植物群和动物群，因为题干要求填写两个课题，且有字数限制，因此考生选择任意两个满足字数要求的答案都算正确。
答案	(land and) language/(topography and) language/topography/flora and fauna

Question 35

题干定位词 / 关键词	study; flight dynamics; one of his friends; major European competitor
原文定位	C 段最后一句 He also undertook a study of ballistics and ship design for Raleigh in advance of the Spanish Armada's arrival.
题目解析	题干：之后，他又为了一个朋友进行飞行动力学和 ____ 的研究，远远领先于主要的欧洲竞争对手。 根据关键词定位到 C 段最后一句：他还在西班牙无敌舰队抵达之前，为罗利进行了弹道学和船舶设计的研究。flight dynamics 对应 ballistics，因此 ship design 即为正确答案。
答案	ship design

Question 36

题干定位词 / 关键词	extensive other studies; predated; corrected the misconception
原文定位	E 段最后一句 Around 1606, he had studied dispersion in prisms (predating Newton by around 60 years), measured the refractive indices of different liquids placed in a hollow glass prism, studied refraction in crystal spheres, and correctly understood refraction in the rainbow before Descartes.
题目解析	题干：他进行了其他的广泛研究，这些研究只有他自己记录了下来，但比许多其他伟大的科学家都早。例如，其中一个结果纠正了人们对_____的误解。 根据关键词定位到 E 段最后一句：1606 年左右，他研究了棱镜中的色散（比牛顿早了大约 60 年），测量了放置在中空玻璃棱镜中的不同液体的折射率，研究了水晶球中的折射，并在笛卡尔之前正确地理解了彩虹中的折射。corrected the misconception 对应原文中的 correctly understood，纠正误解即正确理解，根据文意以及题目字数限制，(the) rainbow refraction/refraction in rainbow 为正确答案。
答案	(the) rainbow refraction/refraction in rainbow

Questions 37-40

题型：人名观点配对题

解析：人名观点配对题属于乱序题，较为简单，先根据人名去文中寻找表达其观点的句子，再与题干中的句子对比，选择意思接近的即可。

Question 37

题干定位词 / 关键词	discovered; Jupiter
原文定位	B 段倒数第三句 Between October 17, 1610 and February 26, 1612, he observed the moons of Jupiter, which had already discovered by Galileo.
题目解析	题干：发现木星的卫星的人。 根据关键词定位到原文 B 段倒数第三句：从 1610 年 10 月 17 日到 1612 年 2 月 26 日，他（哈利奥特）观测到了伽利略已经发现的木星的卫星。注意，题干问的是谁发现了木星的卫星，而非谁观测到了木星的卫星，由原文可知，先发现木星的卫星的是伽利略，因此选项 D Galileo 为正确答案。
答案	D

Question 38

题干定位词 / 关键词	distracted; calculation on refraction
原文定位	D 段第二、三句 About twenty years before Snell's discovery, Johannes Kepler (1571-1630) had also looked for the law of refraction, but used the early data of Ptolemy. Unfortunately, Ptolemy's data was in error, so Kepler could obtain only an approximation which he published in 1604.
题目解析	题干：被关于折射的实验计算搞的心烦意乱。 D 段第二、三句提到，在斯奈尔的发现之前约 20 年，约翰内斯 · 开普勒（1571—1630）也曾探寻过折射定律，但他使用的是托勒密的早期数据。不幸的是，托勒密的数据有误，所以开普勒只能得到一个近似值，他在 1604 年发表了这个近似值。 根据文意，开普勒尝试探寻折射定律，但是并未成功，因为他采用的数据有误。后文提到开普勒试图获取更多的实验结果，但未能成功。整个过程让他感到心烦意乱，因此选项 B Johannes Kepler 为正确答案。
答案	B

Question 39

题干定位词 / 关键词	discovery; sunspots
原文定位	B 段倒数第二句 While observing Jupiter's moons, he made a discovery of his own: sunspots, which he viewed 199 times between December 8, 1610 and January 18, 1613.
题目解析	题干：太阳黑子的发现。 根据关键词可以定位到 B 段倒数第二句，该句提到哈利奥特在观测木星的卫星时，发现了太阳黑子，并且在 1610 年 12 月 8 日至 1613 年 1 月 18 日期间观测到了 199 次。由此可知，选项 E Harriot 为正确答案。
答案	E

Question 40

题干定位词 / 关键词	name; Snell's Law; attributed to
原文定位	A 段倒数第三句 The law of refraction is also known as Snell's Law, named after Willbrord Snell, who discovered the law in 1621.

题目解析	题干：斯奈尔定律的名字源自谁。 A段倒数第三句提到折射定律也被称为斯奈尔定律，以威尔布罗德·斯奈尔的名字命名，他在1621年发现了这一定律。由此可知，斯奈尔定律是以Willobrord Snell的名字命名的，选项A Willobrord Snell为正确答案。
答案	A

长难句分析

E段：Around 1606, he had studied dispersion in prisms (predating Newton by around 60 years), measured the refractive indices of different liquids placed in a hollow glass prism, studied refraction in crystal spheres, and correctly understood refraction in the rainbow before Descartes.

思路分析：虽然这个句子比较长，但结构相对简单，是常见的主谓宾结构。主语为he；谓语动词有四个，分别为studied, measured, studied和understood，由逗号和and连接成并列结构；placed in a hollow glass prism为分词定语后置，用来修饰liquids。

参考翻译：1606年左右，他研究了棱镜中的色散（比牛顿早了大约60年），测量了放置在中空玻璃棱镜中的不同液体的折射率，研究了水晶球中的折射，并在笛卡尔之前正确地理解了彩虹中的折射。

A段：Perhaps the most interesting thing is that the first discovery of the sine law, made by the sixteenth-century English scientist Thomas Harriot (1560-1621), has been almost completely overlooked by physicists, despite much published material describing his contribution.

思路分析：这个句子的主体可以简化为Perhaps the most interesting thing is that...，其中the most interesting thing为主语，is为系动词，that引导表语从句，充当表语成分；made by the sixteenth-century English scientist Thomas Harriot (1560-1621)为插入语，从结构上可以看作过去分词短语作sine law的后置定语；despite表示转折、让步。

参考翻译：也许最有趣的事情是，16世纪英国科学家托马斯·哈里奥特（1560—1621）首次发现正弦定律这一事实几乎被物理学家完全忽视了，尽管有许多的出版材料描述了他的贡献。

参考译文

托马斯 · 哈里奥特——折射的发现

A 当光从一种介质进入到另一种介质时，通常会发生弯曲或折射。折射定律给我们提供了一种预测弯曲量的方法。折射在光学和技术领域有很多应用。透镜利用折射形成物体的图像，有许多不同的用途，比如放大。棱镜利用入射光束的折射形成不同颜色的光谱。折射在海市蜃楼和其他光学错觉的形成中也起着重要的作用。折射定律也被称为斯奈尔定律，以 1621 年发现该定律的威尔布罗德 · 斯奈尔的名字命名。虽然斯奈尔的正弦折射定律现在是本科课程的常规课程，但对它的探索跨越了许多世纪，有许多著名的科学家参与其中。也许最有趣的事情是，16 世纪英国科学家托马斯 · 哈里奥特（1560—1621）首次发现正弦定律这一事实几乎被物理学家完全忽视了，尽管有许多的出版材料描述了他的贡献。

B 托马斯 · 哈里奥特 (1560—1621) 是与莎士比亚、伊丽莎白一世、约翰内斯 · 开普勒和伽利略 · 伽利雷同时代的英国科学家和数学家。他的主要传记作者 J.W. 雪利曾说，在他的时代，他是“英格兰最渊博的数学家，最富有想象力和最有条理的实验科学家”。作为一名数学家，他为代数的发展做出了贡献，并引入了“>”和“<”的符号来表示“大于”和“小于”。他还研究了航海学和天文学。1607 年 9 月 17 日，哈里奥特观测到一颗彗星，后来被确定为海莉 -s。在他的辛苦观测下，后来的工作人员能够计算出这颗彗星的轨道。哈里奥特也是第一个在英格兰使用望远镜观察天空的人。他在 1609 年绘制了月球的草图，然后研制出了放大倍率不断增加的透镜。到 1611 年 4 月，他研制出了放大倍率为 32 的透镜。从 1610 年 10 月 17 日到 1612 年 2 月 26 日，他观测到了伽利略已经发现的木星的卫星。在观测木星的卫星时，他也有了自己的发现：太阳黑子，在 1610 年 12 月 8 日至 1613 年 1 月 18 日期间，他观测到了 199 次太阳黑子。通过这些观测，他计算出了太阳的自转周期。

C 他也是早期到达北美的英国探险家。他是英国宫廷和探险家沃尔特 · 罗利爵士的朋友，并在 1585 年的一次殖民探险中以科学观察员的身份前往弗吉尼亚。1585 年 6 月 30 日，他的船在弗吉尼亚附近的罗阿诺克岛抛锚。在岸上，哈里奥特观察了那里的地形、植物群和动物群，绘制了许多图画和地图，并遇到了说英国人称之为阿尔冈琴语的土著居民。哈里奥特对当地人的语音进行了语音转录，并开始学习这种语言，这在某种程度上使他能够与遇到的其他英国当地人交谈。哈里奥特为罗利写了报告，并在 1588 年以《关于弗吉尼亚新发现地的简要而真实的报告》出版。罗利把他自己在爱尔兰的庄园给了哈里奥特，哈里奥特开始对罗利在爱尔兰的财产进行调查。他还在西班牙无敌舰队抵达之前，为罗利进行了弹道学和船舶设计的研究。

D 哈里奥特与其他科学家和数学家保持定期通信，特别是在英格兰的科学家和数学家，也有欧洲大陆的，尤其是约翰内斯·开普勒。在斯奈尔的发现之前约 20 年，约翰内斯·开普勒（1571—1630）也曾探寻过折射定律，但他使用的是托勒密的早期数据。不幸的是，托勒密的数据有误，所以开普勒只能得到一个近似值，他在 1604 年发表了这个近似值。后来，开普勒试图获得更多关于折射的实验结果，并在 1606 年至 1609 年期间与托马斯·哈里奥特通信，因为开普勒听说哈里奥特进行了一些详细的实验。1606 年，哈里奥特给开普勒寄来了一些不同材料在恒定入射角下的折射数据表格，但没有提供足够的细节，因此这些数据用处不大。开普勒要求提供进一步的信息，但哈里奥特并不乐意提供，似乎开普勒最终放弃了通信，对哈里奥特的不情愿感到沮丧。

E 除了与开普勒的通信，没有证据表明哈里奥特曾发表过他关于折射的详细研究结果。然而，他的个人笔记揭示了他的广泛研究远远早于开普勒、斯奈尔和笛卡尔的研究。16 世纪 90 年代，哈里奥特进行了许多关于折射的实验，从他的笔记中可以清楚地看出，他至少早在 1602 年就发现了正弦定律。1606 年左右，他研究了棱镜中的色散（比牛顿早了大约 60 年），测量了放置在中空玻璃棱镜中的不同液体的折射率，研究了水晶球中的折射，并在笛卡尔之前正确地理解了彩虹中的折射。

F 正如他关于折射的研究一样，哈里奥特在其他领域的发现在他有生之年基本上没有发表过。直到本世纪，哈里奥特也只是因为 1588 年在弗吉尼亚旅行的一篇报道和 1631 年他去世后发表的一篇关于代数的论文而为人所知。目前尚不清楚哈里奥特为什么不公布他的研究结果。哈里奥特写信给开普勒说，他的健康状况不佳，无法提供更多的信息，但也有可能是他害怕 17 世纪的英国宗教机构，因为他们对数学家和科学家的工作持怀疑态度。

G 在发现太阳黑子之后，哈里奥特的科学工作减少了。他的生产力下降的原因可能是在他鼻子上发现的癌症。哈里奥特于 1621 年 7 月 2 日在伦敦去世，但他的故事并没有随着他的死亡而结束。最近的研究揭示了他的广泛兴趣和真正的原创发现。一些作家所描述的他的“成千上万张纸的数学和科学观察”似乎丢失了，直到 1784 年，珀西的一个后裔在亨利珀西的乡间庄园发现了它们。她把它们送给了弗朗茨·泽维尔·扎克，她丈夫的儿子的家庭教师。扎克最终把一些论文交给了牛津大学出版社，但要出版它们还需要很多准备工作，而且从来没有人去做过。学者们已经开始研究它们，对哈里奥特贡献的赞赏在 20 世纪下半叶开始增长。哈里奥特对折射的研究只是他的工作与欧洲其他人进行的独立研究重叠的一个例子，但在任何关于光学的历史研究中，他的贡献都应该得到肯定。

READING

03

Section 3

参考答案

READING

Test 1

Reading Passage 1		21	TRUE
1	G	22	NOT GIVEN
2	H	23	NOT GIVEN
3	E	24	TRUE
4	C	25	NOT GIVEN
5	B	26	C
6	D	Reading Passage 3	
7	forward thrust	27	i
8	rolling and yawing	28	v
9	pectoral and pelvic/paired	29	x
10	slows and stops	30	vii
11	white muscle	31	ix
12	fat and glycogen	32	ii
13	a predator/ danger	33	vi
Reading Passage 2		34	iv
14	A	35	B
15	C	36	C
16	C	37	B
17	D	38	G
18	E	39	H
19	D	40	D
20	TRUE		

Test 2

Reading Passage 1		21	TRUE
1	FALSE	22	NOT GIVEN
2	NOT GIVEN	23	FALSE
3	NOT GIVEN	24	fighting
4	TRUE	25	commerce
5	FALSE	26	flower lovers
6	tram	Reading Passage 3	
7	(in) 1954	27	iii
8	beach volleyball	28	vii
9	environment	29	iv
10	wealthy people	30	ix
11	Manly	31	ii
12	Bondi	32	i
13	(tiled) roofs	33	vi
Reading Passage 2		34	tunnels
14	I	35	air
15	D	36	moisture
16	B	37	evaporation
17	G	38	YES
18	F	39	NO
19	TRUE	40	NOT GIVEN
20	FALSE		

Test 3

Reading Passage 1		22-23	B D
1	C	24	social history
2	C	25	tags
3	A	26	protective equipment
4	B	27	low-pressure water
5	A	Reading Passage 3	
6	YES	28	iv
7	NO	29	vii
8	NO	30	iii
9	NOT GIVEN	31	ii
10	YES	32	ix
11	NOT GIVEN	33	F
12	YES	34	B
13	A	35	D
Reading Passage 2		36	A
14	D	37	FALSE
15	G	38	NOT GIVEN
16	B	39	TRUE
17	E	40	TRUE
18	C		
19	B		
20-21	B D		

Test 4

Reading Passage 1		21	NOT GIVEN
1	F	22	TRUE
2	I	23	TRUE
3	C	24	covering
4	B	25	chocolate liquor
5	G	26	cocoa fat
6	C	27	mold (form)
7	B	Reading Passage 3	
8	A	28	F
9	YES	29	E
10	YES	30	A
11	NO	31	E
12	NOT GIVEN	32	B
13	NO	33-34	A C
Reading Passage 2		35-36	A D
14	D	37	YES
15	E	38	NOT GIVEN
16	D	39	NOT GIVEN
17	C	40	NO
18	B		
19	FALSE		
20	NOT GIVEN		

Test 5

Reading Passage 1		21	G
1	NOT GIVEN	22	C
2	NOT GIVEN	23	biggest ship
3	FALSE	24	Australia
4	TRUE	25	Suez Canal
5	TRUE	26	telegraphic cables
6	FALSE	Reading Passage 3	
7	100 English words/one hundred words	27	E
8	chimpanzees	28	A
9	avian cognition	29	C
10	particularly chosen	30	G
11	color/colour	31	F
12	wrong pronunciation	32	specific person
13	teenager	33	three cards/3 cards
Reading Passage 2		34	mental walk
14	A	35	loci method
15	C	36	education
16	B	37-38	A D
17	G	39-40	B E
18	G		
19	E		
20	F		

Test 6

Reading Passage 1		21	F
1	FALSE	22	D
2	NOT GIVEN	23	H
3	FALSE	24	NOT GIVEN
4	NOT GIVEN	25	TRUE
5	TRUE	26	FALSE
6	TRUE	Reading Passage 3	
7	bamboo	27	x
8	cylinders	28	v
9	piston/pistons	29	ix
10	7	30	iii
11	half an acre	31	vii
12	corrugated tin	32	magnification
13	$ 37.5million/37.5million dollars	33	a prism/prisms
Reading Passage 2		34	(land and) language/(topography and) language/topography/flora and fauna (任意一个答案都算对)
14	68 seconds	35	ship design
15	(complex) distinction	36	(the) rainbow refraction/refraction in rainbow
16	breathing	37	D
17	stretch/stretching	38	B
18	brain	39	E
19	E	40	A
20	B		